SCRAPPY STARTUPS

HOW 15 ORDINARY WOMEN TURNED THEIR UNIQUE IDEAS INTO PROFITABLE BUSINESSES

MELANIE R. KEVELES

PRAEGER

An Imprint of ABC-CLIO, LLC

A B C CLIO

Santa Barbara, California • Denver, Colorado • Oxford, England

Library of Congress Cataloging-in-Publication Data

Keveles, Melanie R.
Scrappy startups : how 15 ordinary women turned their unique ideas into profitable businesses/Melanie R. Keveles.
    p. cm.
Includes bibliographical references and index.
ISBN 978-0-313-36511-9 (hbk : alk. paper) — ISBN 978-0-313-36512-6 (e-book)
1. Women-owned business enterprises.   2. New business enterprises.
3. Entrepreneurship.   4. Businesswomen—Case studies.
I. Title.

HD2358.K22 2009
658.1'1–dc22

                                                                        2009027519

14 13 12 11 10   1 2 3 4 5

This book is also available on the World Wide Web as an eBook.
Visit www.abc-clio.com for details.

ABC-CLIO, LLC
130 Cremona Drive, P.O. Box 1911
Santa Barbara, California 93116-1911

This book is printed on acid-free paper ∞
Manufactured in the United States of America

To the ones I love:
Dad, Gary, and Ross

CONTENTS

ACKNOWLEDGMENTS

Scrappy Startups has many mid-wives who have enabled her to be born and gifted to the world. I am forever grateful to my dear friend, Martha Finney, who introduced me to my editor, Jeff Olson. Jeff has been a dream to work with every step of the way as a coach, cheerleader, and respectful collaborator. No words can properly thank Martha, who has been a champion, friend, and sister, as well as a significant role model, with so many successful books under her belt now that I've lost count. I would like to gift her with your checking her out on Amazon and ordering her great reads!

Also significant was the Coaches Training Institute's Quest program and all the many participants I shared my passion with during that workshop in Washington, D.C., who cheered me on to my life's work. That program enabled me to see the connection between this work and my life mission and so had me go at my proposal to Jeff with gusto. Special thanks to Jennifer Lee for leading me to several wonderful women through her Ladies Who Launch connections. Thanks to fearless leaders Karen Kimsey-House and Art Shirk for their inspiration.

I also want to shout out to my two coaches, Patricia Kennedy and Spruce Krause, for the important roles they played in egging me on and keeping my creative juices flowing at critical points along the way. Spruce, especially, was instrumental in my finishing my manuscript on deadline. Patricia had me walk my talk. Also significant is my coach friend Karen Carr, who shared her enthusiasm for what I was doing whenever we spoke.

My Co-Active leadership buddies, Meade Dickerson, Jeannie Campanelli, Marcia Dorfman, and Kathy Curry have been my weekly foundation as well as sounding boards, not to mention sharing a bit of editing advice and a few wacky ideas for endorsements. Thanks also to Tammy Gooler-Loeb, who was my partner in gathering early success stories, and to Jean Feraca, host of Here on Earth on Wisconsin Public Radio who led me to Sarah Chayes.

Important also have been my certification students from the Co-Active Coach training program who shared their excitement for my project and coached me well at junctures in our calls when I was the guinea pig client.

Thanks go to Bill Dueeasse of the Coach Connection for sending a request for entrepreneurs to his contacts at Make Mine A Million. I also appreciate Cenmar Fuertes of CoachLink for reading early chapters and giving me helpful feedback as well as encouragement. Fellow CTI certification leader Bonnie Hill was generous also with ideas for interviewees.

How many of my wonderful clients shared their excitement with me for *Scrappy Startups!* Thank you one and all for your curiosity, willingness to read excerpts, and faith in my dreams. You are an inspiration to me, and I am glad for the role I play in helping you make your dreams come true.

Thank you coach Jeff Staggs for allowing me to use *The Belief Transformation Matrix* in the context of this book. May we spur many women on to their greatness with this simple tool.

My father, Abraham Shenkman, 98 years young in 2009, has been a coach in his own way, forever asking me in his endearing style whether I was going to make my deadline. Thanks Dad—I made it—and I'm so glad you're here to celebrate another book I've birthed. I hope you're proud, even if you have trouble defining just what kind of work it is that I do.

To my dearest husband Gary, who is the love of my life and my life-long companion, this book would not be here without your enduring belief in me. I knew I had something going when you had positive words about my writing because you don't give such praise lightly—professor, you're a hard marker!

Thanks also to son Ross who cheered me on along the way and believed in me. I appreciated your helpful suggestions. And thanks to my daily companion poodle dog Grace, who allowed me to work in between games of fetch with her favorite green ball.

I am truly grateful to the wonderful women entrepreneurs who gave me their time and energy, allowing me to probe and question their processes of becoming successful business women. I appreciate what it took for you to return your release forms to me and I apologize for all my nagging. You are all muses and pioneer mothers for the scrappy startups soon to be born.

INTRODUCTION

I have allowed myself to lead this little life when inside me there was so much more. And it's all gone unused . . . Why do we get all this life if we don't ever use it? Why do we get all these feelings and dreams and hopes if we don't ever use them?

Shirley Valentine, character in the movie,
—*Shirley Valentine, 1989*

When you find a great purpose in life, you've got to pursue it.
—*Shai Agassi,* Silicon Valley millionaire,
Founder of Better Place, an electric grid and car solution

I'm stealing a few minutes away from my coaching practice to write. I feel like a juggler, keeping many balls in the air, but that's much like any entrepreneur worth her salt. It's all about keeping a perspective and making the best use of precious moments.

I'm a career and life coach. For those unaware or unclear about what this is, I am a member of a relatively new profession. Coaches like me collaborate with people to help them get what they want. As with the definition of a stage coach, a career and life coach can act as a vehicle that gets you from where you are to where you want to be. People hire me to be their collaborator in helping them set a direction, gain the courage to do what they must to get where they are going, and get into action. For example, I work with people changing career direction, people wanting to become published, and entrepreneurs. You'll hear more about this later when I describe my specific process.

Scrappy Startups has been calling to me for days now, wanting to spill out onto these pages. My enthusiasm for getting down to business actually started with a session with one of my own coaches. (A coach can hire a coach to walk her own talk and achieve her own aspirations.) I brought my anxiety about getting this book to deadline to our coaching session, and I emerged with renewed energy and some great ideas. That's the power of coaching.

Before I set the stage for this book, I want to provide insight into my excitement about writing it. You see, I have ALWAYS been intrigued with how things start—so scrappy startup stories are a perfect way to express that interest.

I grew up impressed by the story of how my parents met. Their meeting and my existence were not only unlikely but nearly didn't occur!

It was right after World War II, and my father had recently returned to Brooklyn from the Pacific, where he had been assigned on a navy ship. He was looking for something to do on a Saturday night and phoned his old friend Oscar to see what he was up to. Oscar had been invited to an engagement party in Greenpoint, Brooklyn, and asked my father to tag along. Dad was delighted to join him, an uninvited guest.

At the other end of the world, in Yonkers, New York, my mother was preparing to use public transportation—several buses and a long subway ride—to reach this same party. A friend from her neighborhood was the bride-to-be. Yonkers, located in Westchester, New York, only 23 miles from Brooklyn as the crow flies, is maybe 40 minutes by car today, but with public transportation in the mid-1940s the trip took Mom several hours. Upon reaching the bus stop, she discovered she had forgotten the engagement gift. As she told me often when I begged to hear the story, she flirted with turning back and forgetting about going to the party. But something egged her on, and she retraced her steps, retrieved the gift, and made it to the party.

There she met my father. They courted and married, and I appeared a year later. The family story of that meeting that started everything put me on a course to revel in all sorts of startup stories. I'm forever asking, "How did that start?"

I'm equally enamored of success stories. Years ago when I worked for a boutique outplacement company that served companies who were downsizing their employees, I prevailed on the founders to allow me to write and produce a company newsletter, sharing success stories of people who had triumphed and landed their best-suited jobs and careers. What a joy it was to collect those stories and share them in our monthly newsletter. I found in turn that as the members of our staff and our clients read the entries, they were inspired to continue their good work.

My job with that company later morphed into a position as the editor of Alta Vista Careers, a Web site that included content on issues related to career and job change, entrepreneurism, and recruiting. With no budget to secure content, I took to approaching publishers and asking to excerpt content from their newly published manuscripts and interview their authors on topics related to our site.

I also had a stint as a radio interviewer on a Wisconsin Public Radio show that I hosted for several years. There it was great fun to hear success stories as well, and I went out of my way to find subjects for my programs who would share their success stories with my audience.

According to Dan Pink, author of *A Whole New Mind*, the ability to tell good stories is becoming increasingly important in the twenty-first century. He counts "story" among six senses we need to nurture in this conceptual age. He makes a strong case that stories are the way we remember.

Facts and data become less valued in an age when we can source information on the Internet more quickly and easily than can the head librarian at Cambridge University. Pink reminds us:

What begins to matter more is the ability to place these facts in *context* and to deliver them with *emotional impact*.[1]

Pink relates how Joseph Campbell, the American comparative mythology professor best known for his landmark book, *Hero with a Thousand Faces*, uncovered a universal story told in every culture in every age. He called this "the hero's journey," and proposed that it has three main parts:

1. The hero hears a call.
2. During "initiation" the hero faces stiff challenges and stares into the abyss.
3. Along the way the hero (with the help of mentors) transforms and returns as a new self.

---

[1]Pink, *A Whole New Mind*, Berkley Publishing Group, 2005, p. 103.

Truly, I saw this pattern among those I interviewed for Alta Vista Careers and on the radio, and most recently, in the women you'll meet in this book—the brave, trailblazing entrepreneurs whose stories I relate to you here. We're all on a hero's journey—whether we know it or not. As you meet these wonderful women I had the privilege to interview for *Scrappy Startups*, you'll acquire an understanding of what is to be gained, not only monetarily but also in personal growth, by setting aside a more conventional life for one in which you carve out your own destiny.

Pink also reminds us that businesses are realizing today that telling a story can mean big money for them. Witness the way companies tell stories to sell their products. Would you remember Travelocity as vividly if the company had not brought us a talking elflike statue that gets kicked around as it tries to save the day for a traveler in distress? How many PC users were taken in by the Apple ads that told a story with two characters—a casual Apple guy and a more formal corporate-looking PC guy?

Subconsciously, I may have chosen to tell you the stories of these 15 women in part because their businesses tell such good tales! After all, there are many sites on the Internet where you can find software for creating a great business plan. Why would I want to inspire you with ordinary stories? My job is to share these tales of triumph so you reinvigorate yourself and dust off those ideas you've been teasing yourself with and get out there and make hay in the marketplace!

Aside from being enamored of how things start and stories of success, in my life as a career and life coach, I am dedicated to helping people become fully self-expressed. When I shared that mission with Susan Bratton, founder of Personal Life Media, she pinned me down and asked, "What does being self-expressed mean?" Good question!

It means that I would love everyone to be fully themselves in the marketplace. No more "I can't do this art that I love because I can't make a living at it." No more people going to their graves with much of their music still inside them. I'm selfish. I want us all to benefit from everyone doing what they'd love to be doing with their lives. My part is giving the green light to people to do what makes them happy and lets the whole of them shine in the world.

Now that I've set the stage for why I've got my skin in this game, let me give you more about why I'm writing this book.

More than ever before, women want to be their own bosses. With the fast-paced demands of twenty-first–century life, the need for flexibility in caring for children and elderly parents, the uncertainty in the workplace, and the technological support available, they have the opportunity to control their destiny as never before.

However, most women don't have enough good role models for entrepreneurial success, and they often stall out before they even begin. They end up spinning their wheels or reverting to ineffective patterns that keep them small. They shy away from the ideas that pop into their heads, telling themselves they are unrealistic, their ideas are too corny, they just won't succeed!

This I know from my role as a professional coach who works with these women (and men as well) day in and day out. Aside from being their cheerleader, confidante, and accountability partner, I offer my clients a formula I created that works for bringing nebulous ideas to fruition. They love this approach and find it useful for staying focused on their entrepreneurial ideas, but additionally, they need inspiration to fuel their ambitions.

Artists, when they want to be inspired, go to art museums and look at the masters' creations. Likewise, would-be entrepreneurs need inspiration from women just like themselves—without silver spoons in their mouths—who took a seed of an idea and grew it to full flower and profitability. I have chosen to write this book to offer such inspiration to my clients and others like them.

Although there are many books out there and many places to be inspired by others' entrepreneurial success, just as a woman can't have enough shoes or handbags or clothes, she needs an ever-ready supply of female entrepreneurial success stories. Additionally, many success stories gloss over the nitty-gritty steps it took for the women to get started and get over the bumps that stall most people out. Rather than inspiring, they become discouraging.

This book sets out to tell the stories of 15 ordinary women who created fun, meaningful, unique and profitable businesses from scratch—no franchises, MLM schemes, or buyouts of existing businesses. I benchmark my formula against their success and see how my coaching strategies match what these women experienced in launching and steering their businesses to success. I'm retrofitting my model to the actual experience these women entrepreneurs found in building their business, and thus we will learn together how these elements fit. I will also leave you with a structure for remembering the significance of these examples and a way for you to approach the evolution of your own business ideas.

I interviewed these women using my background and experience as a professional coach and radio interviewer to elicit actionable information that you can use to identify what works and doesn't work in entrepreneurial success. I have asked the questions as a surrogate, mindful that we all want to know specifically, "How the heck did you pull this off?" "How did you handle the circumstances in your life such as the need for health insurance?" "How did you manage your doubts and your fears?" "What made you think you could actually succeed?"

As I shared my book idea with others, I heard many questions:

- What does *scrappy* mean?
- How did you choose the subjects for your book?
- What's significant about your coaching model?

I'm assuming these questions are on your mind too.

As far as scrappy, that term was suggested to me by my editor, Jeff Olson. I took an immediate liking to it—it resonated with me intuitively. I also liked the alliteration of scrappy startups. When I dug deeper, I found the following dictionary definitions.

From AudioEnglish.net (http://www.audioenglish.net/dictionary/scrappy.htm): "full of fighting spirit"

I like that. When I think of the women I profile in this book, I see every one of them having a fighting spirit. They have it on behalf of their businesses and they have it within themselves. They stand by their businesses as they would by one of their children, much like a mama bear defending her cub.

From Wiktionary (http:// en.wiktionary.org/wiki/scrappy): "consisting of scraps; fragmentary; lacking unity or consistency"

Many other definitions were variations on these themes. To me *scrappy* means making something out of nothing—essentially starting from scratch or from scraps. These are feisty women all, and everyone is a genius in her own right. I so admire them for the birth of their business progeny, and as any woman who has given birth knows, there's much scrappiness that goes into the birthing process. This is not a neat, antiseptic process, and no matter how much people try to clean up around you, giving birth can be quite a mess—very chaotic. It's the same with the process of giving birth to a business—unpredictability abounds.

How did I choose the subjects for my book? Well, much of it was serendipity, and a lot was how excited I was to hear about these businesses. My own enthusiasm about the stories was a barometer by which I judged entry. I guess you might say I used my heart more than my head in choosing the selections—if I was moved, I assumed you would be as well.

When my project came along, I asked my friends and colleagues for ideas of people to interview. Sarah Chayes, who heads up a soap collective in war-torn Afghanistan, came through my dear friend Jean Feraca, host of Wisconsin Public Radio's *Here on Earth*. When you read Sarah's story in section two of my book, Courage, you'll most likely be amazed at what she and her cooperative were able to accomplish with little or no electricity, much skepticism, and great risk to their lives.

Other subjects, such as Nancy Gruver of New Moon Media, were on my radar screen for years. I first interviewed Nancy in the early 1990s as a guest on my radio show and have watched the progress and impact her media business for young girls has had over many years, especially when she took her adolescent and younger girls to China to report on an international women's conference. Her magazine has earned many outstanding awards, and she has played an important role in taking a stand for preserving girls' self esteem. You'll read her story in section one, Dream.

Marissa McTasney, who you'll meet in the last section, Action, was a woman I found while scouring the Internet. Her business, which focuses on providing feminine clothing for women in the building trades, caught my attention and imagination. We had some difficulty connecting for our interview, but I doggedly pursued her. To her credit, she allowed me to continue to pursue her, and on one occasion when we missed our meeting, she generously gave me my own set of pink work boots, which I proudly wear. My husband hopes they'll inspire me to get more hands on in fixing up the house and the yard.

My criteria for choosing these women to profile also came from my interest in finding pioneers who were involved in fun businesses that were also meaningful, unique, and profitable. Fun comes into the picture when you see the irony with which these entrepreneurs approach their work. Meaningful shows up in relation to engagement with work that makes a difference to clients and customers. Unique appears in the specific stamp that each places on the contribution they are making. As far as profitable goes, well, I must admit, I've taken some license here.

I don't think of profitable in monetary terms only. Some of the people I've profiled are still in the early stages of their businesses—the full bloom of their work has not taken hold yet—but they are certainly on the path to monetary profit. Judging by the ones who have been in business for seven or more years and have created businesses earning a million dollars or more, the early ones are in good shape. All of the women have seen profit in terms of fulfillment, expression of who they are in the world, and certainly in making an impact on others by what they are providing.

I chose these women ultimately because they inspired me—and I wanted to share their stories for the same effect. I want you to find yourself in these people and see that, although they faced seemingly insurmountable odds, they used their creativity and inventiveness—and, yes, their scrappiness—to find a way to succeed. I want you to see that you too can make your business dreams come true, just as these women have.

And now I'd like to introduce you to the approach I take with my clients and share with you how I will be benchmarking this approach as I share the scrappy startup stories with you.

THE MAGIC APPROACH

To help people manifest their dreams, whether it's finding a job with an organization, becoming an entrepreneur, or getting published—whatever the dream may be—I have developed a simple approach to move people forward in realizing their heart's desires. I want to give special credit to my friend and colleague, Meade Dickerson, who worked diligently with me throughout Co-Active Space Leadership to create this model, which I have further refined.

To explain this approach, I use a Venn diagram. The Venn diagram is made up of two or more overlapping circles. In this case, picture three overlapping circles, much like one of those three-ringed pretzels.

One circle represents the **Dream** a person has, which can be a career contribution, a business, a book, or something they want to birth into existence that is truly worth striving for, such as a business to be created from scratch. **Dream** simply stands for whatever it is you want to achieve.

Overlapping this first circle is another circle that represents the **Courage** it takes to make this dream a reality. It is what you have to

THE MAGIC APPROACH

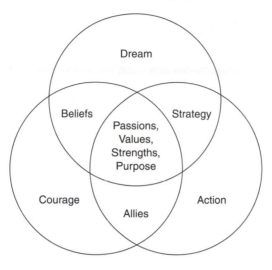

risk. After all, anything that is worth striving for takes energy and other resources to accomplish. Often when we set out to realize the fruition of a dream, we have no idea how it will come into existence. We just know that we are enamored of the dream, and we have passion for making it a reality.

Courage comes from the French word "coeur," which means heart. To realize our dreams, we must open our hearts—and this is no small feat, especially if we are feeling fear, which has the tendency to close our hearts. This circle represents the feelings that encourage us to take the risks we need to take to bring our **Dream** into reality.

The third overlapping circle in this model is represented by the word **Action**. These are the steps you must take to realize any dream. After all, if I didn't sit down at the keyboard of my computer and start pounding these letters out on it, this book you are reading would not have come into form.

In the center where all the circles meet, a space is formed that represents a unit that all three circles share. Here we write the words that underpin the importance of the person in this project. The words are **Passions, Values, Strengths,** and **Purpose.** This is the juice behind this endeavor—it's what gives it life. If the project or activity is not aligned with the passions, values, strengths, and purpose of the person behind it, the activity is just not worth pursuing. It peters out.

When we look at the intersection of **Dream** and **Courage**, the word **Belief** needs to be inserted. A dream can stall like nobody's business when negative beliefs get in our way—the disempowering beliefs of the gremlin or saboteur voice that keep us from realizing our dream, or the part of us that wants to keep the status quo intact no matter how uncomfortable it may be.

Debbie Ford, in her book *The Secret of the Shadow,* writes that there are three universal beliefs that impede us: "I'm not good enough," "I don't matter," or "There's something wrong with me."[2] Some of us have all three, others may have one that is especially crippling. If you have any or all of these beliefs or any variations on the themes, they could stall you out. Here's where the need for courage comes into play. We'll be especially attentive to how the women we profile handled the beliefs that might otherwise have gotten in their way.

The word in the space between **Courage** and **Action** is **Allies**. No one ever accomplishes anything alone. In order to be successful in this world, we need to be willing to accept help. We must be willing to reach out to others and ask for the help we need. Actually, it's the people who have more allies who succeed in the big stuff. When you think of successful people in every area—business, sports, media, and politics—the successful people have many allies—people supporting them, pulling for them, and helping them accomplish what they set out to accomplish. We'll learn from our women who the people were in their camp and how those allies helped them achieve their dreams.

Finally, to complete the Venn diagram, the word between **Dream** and **Action** is **Strategy**. There may be many ways to get from point A to point B, but without some sort of strategy for getting there, you won't arrive. We'll see what strategies our profiled women used, and we'll hear about what worked and didn't work.

I have singled out the women in my book because the businesses they have birthed have made a unique difference to their immediate communities or the world at large. I have found these women and their projects unique, meaningful, fun, and profitable, and I hope you will be as delighted to meet them and be mentored by them through the pages of this book as I was in getting to know them.

---

[2]Ford, *The Secret of the Shadow*. Harper San Francisco, 2002, p. 47.

Before we begin to read their stories in the coming sections and chapters, I invite you to draw your own Venn diagram and begin filling it out. These questions and activities will help you get started.

Dream

- How clear are you about your dream?
- What would you like to manifest in the world?
- How much do you know about yourself—your talents, skills, interests, passions?
- What are your strengths?
- What do you value most?

Courage

- What beliefs do you have that get in your way?
- What thoughts do you have about yourself that keep you small and prevent you from taking action on an entrepreneurial endeavor?
- What do you fear you have to risk?
- Who are your allies?
- What are your strategies?

Action

- Begin by starting a journal or notebook, either on paper or on your computer, to jot down the ideas that occur to you as you read this book. A small, portable spiral notebook that you carry with you can also be a boon for capturing insights and ideas that occur at various moments.
- Collect inspiring quotes or poems that speak to you and place them prominently in your journal or in the folder on your computer.
- Find images from magazines or from the Internet and place these in your journal or folder to remind you what you are doing.
- Think about what makes you *you*. What are your values? What are your interests? What are your strengths? What are your passions? What's important to you? What are the gaps in the world that you wish someone would tackle? Answers to these questions will contribute to helping you explore what you do next.

Give yourself the gift of beginning to explore your own Dream, Courage, Action map. Don't worry if there are many blank places now. You'll find much as you read ahead to spur you on, and I'll be giving you opportunities through questions and exercises along the way to capture your own nuggets.

Your journal will allow you to reflect on your journey. After all, the purpose of sharing these stories with you is to encourage you to get out there and make your unique contribution. The world is ready for you. We need you to contribute.

SECTION 1

DREAM

It doesn't interest me what you do for a living. I want to know what you ache for, and if you dare to dream of meeting your heart's longing.

The Invitation
—*Oriah Mountain Dreamer*

One of my most satisfying experiences has been giving a presentation to a group of cancer patients who were members of a monthly group led by a number of health professionals, including an oncology nurse and a social worker.

The patients were asked to go around the circle they had formed around me while I was seated in the front of the room and share their name and their cancer. The energy in the room got heavier and heavier as people introduced themselves and their disease. In some cases, people had multiple cancers to announce.

After briefly introducing myself and almost apologetically relating my own positive state of health, I entered the silence and the heaviness with a favorite Langston Hughes poem, *What happens to a dream deferred?*, remembered from high school days when we studied *A Raisin in the Sun*, his famous 1950s play.

The poem is short, so I read it twice. *What happens to a dream deferred?* Already, I could feel the energy in the room shift. I asked people to turn to another person next to them and share a story of a dream left on the back burner. The room buzzed with stories.

Even though this event occurred more than five years ago, I remember distinctly how when asked about their dreams, a woman with advanced lung cancer raised her hand and declared how much she wanted to have her own Web site—that was her dream. Without hesitation, members of the group volunteered to help her. Spontaneously, others expressed their dreams as well. One woman wanted to write a book; others volunteered to edit it for her. Life had returned! It seemed as if all that was needed was an invitation to remember an important dream.

This experience with this group spurred me on to let it be known in my community that I wanted to coach people with life-threatening illnesses. A hospital chaplain got wind of this interest and connected me with a nurse practitioner heading up a heart failure program. Members of this group had heart-related issues. I didn't particularly like the name of their program, but I was ready to lend a hand to help their patients find a reason to live.

My work ultimately led me to address the monthly gathering of about 75 patients in the program. This was a far larger group than the group of cancer patients. I stood in front of them with a slide show I had created about life coaching and walked among them with a microphone, feeling a bit like Oprah.

Once again, I whipped out my trusty Langston Hughes poem and I asked them to share a dream left behind. One man volunteered he had always wanted to learn how to play guitar. I challenged him to teach himself how and play a song for us three months later when the group reconvened. A woman shared her love of creating heart healthy recipes. I challenged her to contact the newspaper to propose writing a column on that subject. Both of these brave people accepted my invitations.

When we returned months later, I learned that the newspaper had done a big spread on the woman and her recipes. Some of the nurses had approached her after the last program and offered to share their network contacts with her at the newspaper. This was all the more bittersweet because in the intervening months she had died. Her family was as proud as she was herself, of the recognition and chance to make a contribution through the newspaper. The article was seen as her legacy.

The man with the guitar-playing dream had not only taught himself how to play, but also wrote a song about the heart program and the medical personnel to the tune of Yankee Doodle Dandy, and he even included me in the lyrics. We all had fun clapping along as he played—and he beamed from ear to ear. His wife thanked me later, saying how much he had engaged in life since he had dedicated himself to the challenge of learning how to play the guitar. He was a new man!

With both these groups of health-challenged people, I saw how life-giving engaging in a dream can be. It's in this context that I prepare you to be engaged with the stories of five women included here who have scrappy startups related to a dream. Although every one of them could also be included in later chapters on courage and action, I see them as more fully representing this part of my model.

As you read their stories, think about your own dreams—those perhaps deferred and those that have yet to be born. My hope is that reading these tales will provide some fertilizer for you. When you see how ordinary these women are and how their dreams are simply an extension of who they are—a need they had, a need they saw, or a talent they were aching to express—I hope you will consider just what you have to offer the world as well in the gift of your dream. You'll find some questions posed at the end of each story. After all, we coaches are a curious lot—and we are steeped in questions, in order to evoke answers from our clients—in this case related to a dream of the heart. After I've shared the five stories in this section, you'll find more activities for you to engage in that will help you gain greater clarity about your own dream.

CHAPTER 1

NEW MOON MEDIA

A Conversation with Nancy Gruver, Founder of New Moon Girl Media (www.newmoon.com)

> The moment one definitely commits oneself, then providence moves in too. All sorts of things occur to help that would never otherwise have occurred. Whatever you can do or dream you can, begin it.
>
> —*Johann Wolfgang von Goethe*

> Making this magazine to support girls' dreams also was the living out of my dreams.
>
> —*Nancy Gruver*, founder of New Moon Magazine

Sometimes providence enters our lives, guiding us to what we were meant to do, not necessarily by the straight, narrow path we would wish, but through a convoluted, circuitous route we would never dream of at all. As Joseph Campbell once told Michael Toms on *New Dimensions Radio,* when quoting the philosopher Schopenhauer, we look back on our lives that read like a Dickens novel. In other words, twists and turns may make sense in retrospect, but certainly not at the time they're happening.

Such was the route Nancy Gruver took to starting *New Moon Magazine* in 1992, now *New Moon Girl Media*. Actually, her business evolved from a giant disappointment. Being a woman of ambition and determination, she had decided to return to school for a master's degree in public administration and had been accepted at Harvard's prestigious Kennedy School. As the mother of twin 11-year-old girls in a family of modest means, she needed a way to fund this education. So she applied for a highly competitive and lucrative award for people seeking leadership roles in their communities in Minnesota, a Bush Fellowship.

That Nancy even was considered for this award is a tribute to her intelligence and capacity. Sad to say at the time, Nancy did not gain the Bush Fellowship, which meant she did not have the financial means to go to Harvard. This was a crushing blow.

Faced with a disappointment like this, many would get angry or bitter or cynical. Many people would beat themselves up and slink away, settling and giving up on going forward, and many would stagnate and tread water.

Not Nancy Gruver. She took this door closing as a signal to take time out to consider her options and find an alternative. Actually, she had previously demonstrated her ability to reinvent herself often. By her own admission, she had followed a checkered and eclectic career path.

Nancy graduated from college with a degree in psychology and a minor in art. In those days her passion was creating ceramics. She worked in a studio and a gallery and then joined three women to open a craft gallery in Minneapolis, Minnesota, in 1981.

This was Nancy's first foray into the world of entrepreneurism. Yet this business lasted only four years because the women could support the business with their sales but not themselves. Nonetheless, Nancy found this a "fabulous learning experience" one that whetted her appetite for being her own boss.

TAKING STOCK AND ENVISIONING THE FUTURE

When the Bush Fellowship became unavailable to her, Nancy didn't know what to do next. Not recovered, but determined, within two weeks, she took a mini, solitary, day-long sabbatical in a friend's vacant apartment, which was three hours from home.

While alone, Nancy considered what truly mattered to her. She explored her passions to see where they would lead her. Coincidentally, she had been reading *Meeting at the Crossroads,* by Carol Gilligan and Mikel Brown, whose premise was that on the way to adulthood young adolescent girls give up their self-esteem and self-confidence. With this concept fresh in her mind, Nancy realized she *was* extremely passionate about women's rights and women's issues. Here was a clue.

Even though Nancy was a strong feminist, having come of age as a young woman at the height of feminist activism in the early 1970s, she had never thought about engaging in a career associated with this interest. She thought of women's rights as an underpinning value, not as a path for her passion in life. Yet her concerns about women in our culture became aroused again from the perspective of her role as mother of twin pre-adolescent girls.

Nothing became defined for Nancy during this retreat day, but she did resolve to actively continue on her hunt:

Ok, I want to look around and explore over the next year or whatever—what could I do? What kinds of careers [related to feminism] are there? What work is there to be done that would provide a paying job?

As the primary bread winner, Nancy wanted and needed a paying job, or so she thought, to do her part in supporting her family.

She returned home and discussed with husband Joe her lingering disappointment about the Kennedy School. She continued to wonder if there *was* another way to go to grad school. Nancy divided her time between conversing and thinking on her own. Yet nothing dawned on either of them.

A month passed and then the couple decided to take a weekend away by themselves. They wanted a mini retreat to create a vision for themselves, separately and together.

Off they went to Copper Harbor, Michigan, a pristine, quiet, semi-desolate place before the summer season, an idyllic setting in a state park. The pair walked the beach and soaked up the nature around them.

Ironically enough, they arrived at no solution during their visit. However, in the car driving home, all of a sudden an idea popped full blown into Nancy's head. It was the core of what *New Moon* is today more than 17 years later!

What about a feminist magazine for girls that girls run?

That was it! Within five minutes Nancy knew she had her idea. A new dream was born, and she affirmed to Joe:

That's what I want to be doing in five years. That's it!

Joe didn't miss a beat. He was on board from the word go. He was completely interested, especially as a journalist himself. What a twist of fate; Nancy was married to a man whose passion was and is journalism and telling stories, and getting them out to other people.

With hindsight, Nancy realized this venture was equally well-suited to her interest in psychology and human development, but at the time, she didn't connect these dots.

It was nine months to the day from when the idea was conceived that the magazine was birthed, an irony not lost on Nancy. Yet the path getting there could not have been predicted.

The idea for *New Moon*, the name Nancy later coined for this concept, magazine and business, related to her concern for her twin 11-year-old daughters, Mavis and Nia. As a mother, she worried about their impending adolescence, not because of their behavior, but because of her own difficulty transitioning during that period in her life.

Nancy fretted about her daughters, wondering whether her fears were founded only on her own experience at that age, on the reality of who her daughters were, or on a universal concern about young girls. Whatever the source, the fear wouldn't rest, which ultimately led to her reading Gilligan and Brown's book, *Meeting at the Crossroads*.

The book recounted an eight-year study conducted by a group of researchers at Harvard who evaluated girls' psychological development between the ages of 8 and 16.

What this ground-breaking research study showed was that Nancy's own loss of confidence and self-worth as she entered adolescence was more common than not. Nancy wondered what she could do to help her daughters. What resources were there? How could she give her daughters support? How could she learn more and be a better mother to help them? All of these questions were on her mind. The more she explored, the more she found nothing addressing this issue. All Nancy found was the book by Gilligan and Brown, and although it resonated, it didn't offer any solutions; it only highlighted the problem.

No wonder the idea for *New Moon* reverberated completely when it dawned on Nancy. It was truly aligned with her concerns for her daughters and offered a solution that not only might help them but also other girls facing the challenges of growing up in a culture that does not entirely support their full blossoming. She had taken a concern that had been brewing under the surface and had allowed it to bubble up into in a practical solution of a business idea.

FRIENDS AND FAMILY JOIN IN ON THE DREAM TO MAKE IT REAL

Nancy started sharing her inspiration for *New Moon* with others. One friend especially caught the excitement. Together they talked about the concept quite a bit. One night they dined out while Nancy's twins babysat the other woman's younger daughters. Extending the dinner conversation afterwards about the magazine to include Nancy's twins Mavis and Nia, the women stayed on fire.

Yet the 11-year-old twins' questions rang out:

What do you mean start a magazine? You don't know how to do that!

Their subtext was that this was another of mom's crazy ideas. Even so, Nancy's response was:

Yeah, it's true, we have no idea how to do this, but right now I don't want to hear about that. What I want to know is would you want to do this? Is this something you would want to do? Do you want a magazine created by girls for girls?

Nancy was determined to redirect her daughters, asking them to be co–decision makers with her, not simply give her their opinion.

As soon as the context of the question changed from how they would do this to whether they wanted to do this, the girls affirmed their interest. Out poured 3 hours worth of ideas of what the magazine could be and what girls would want.

Within a week, *New Moon* had the first meeting of its girls' editorial board, including Gruver's twins and several of their friends who had gotten wind of the process.

Not long afterward, Nancy collected the girls into a conference room at the offices of her current job on a Saturday morning to have a "real" meeting, brainstorming more ideas on flip charts. From the very start, the girls ran the show, with Nancy acting as orchestra leader, allowing the talents of the girls to shine through. Her role was not to direct the process but to create the environment in which the girls could be brilliant.

A clue that Nancy had seized upon a hit idea came the day afterward, when a girl showed up at 8:30 a.m. Sunday morning at the Gruver house, demanding to know when the next meeting would be held. She wanted in on the editorial board.

Nancy thought to herself:

Here's a nine year old asking when we were going to have another meeting. There's something good here.

Consequently, Nancy and Joe threw themselves into doing work on the project in the evenings and on weekends.

TEACHING HERSELF WHAT SHE NEEDED TO KNOW ABOUT STARTING A MAGAZINE

Nancy realized she needed to learn how to start a magazine.

I knew nothing about publishing; I never wanted to be a publisher or a journalist. My professional background and interests were not in that field at all.

Yet her lack of knowledge about publishing did not deter her. Off she went to the Duluth Public Library where she found a book entitled, *How to Start a Magazine*, written by an authority on magazine startups, Semir Husni. In reading his book, Nancy discovered several absolute necessities for starting a magazine, including a million dollars (in 1992 dollars) and a location in New York City, center of the universe for the magazine industry.

Nancy found these musts intimidating and liberating at the same time because she knew:

I don't have a million dollars to do this, and I'm not going to get a million dollars to do this; and number two, I'm not moving to New York City. That's what's happening in my life right now!

End of story! Although Nancy knew people who loved New York, and she herself had even lived there several years after graduating from college, she knew for sure she was not willing to relocate herself and her family to start this magazine. She realized:

Obviously I can't do it according to this book.

Although many aspects of the book on magazine publishing were useful to her, Nancy found she didn't measure up in the assessment within it, which was designed to inform her whether she was truly a candidate for starting a magazine. Rather than give up her dream, she thought:

Ok, I'm going to have to find out some other way. So maybe the best way to find that out is to find some other magazine that has started up without being in New York and without a million dollars and that also has kind of an alternative mission the same way we were going to have with New Moon. We were not looking to start a magazine that would be a direct competitor with Seventeen or YM. I came upon a magazine that had been started a couple of years earlier in the Twin Cities—The Utne Reader.

With that idea, Nancy phoned *The Utne Reader*, asking to talk with its founder, Erik Utne. The receptionist declared he was on sabbatical for six weeks and wondered if someone else could help. So Nancy asserted her desire to start an alternative magazine for girls and confided her need to discover how the *Utne Reader* had started, to learn from their experience.

Nancy was connected with then managing editor, Lynette Lamb. After a brief exchange, the woman agreed to have lunch with her the next time Nancy planned a trip to the Twin Cities.

When they met, Lynette demonstrated enthusiasm for Nancy's magazine idea. However, as *Utne's* editor she could not provide business startup help. Lynette *did* offer to connect Nancy with two consultants who had worked closely and been helpful to *Utne*. Nancy set up a meeting with one situated in the Twin Cities.

After yet another 3-hour drive to meet the consultant, Nancy and Joe were stood up at the appointed location. Since these were the days before cell phones, Gruver rang up the woman's home office, in an effort to connect. The consultant's husband apologetically responded that his wife was at the county fair with the kids. Not thinking she'd be long, he invited Nancy and Joe to the house. The man, himself an entrepreneur, couldn't conceive of letting the pair drive home disappointed.

When she returned, realizing she had forgotten the appointment, the consultant was mortified. Apologetically, she offered the couple five free hours of consulting. This serendipitous event may have played a part in the positive course of events in the conception of *New Moon*; Nancy honestly believes she and Joe would not have felt they could have otherwise afforded the woman's consulting fees at the time.

Those first 5 hours as well as the subsequent ones Nancy paid for were worth way more than their cost. In essence, the consultant taught Nancy the publishing business, offering practical solutions whenever the fledgling entrepreneur posed questions.

The stroke of luck in the missed appointment felt like "the force was with them" as Nancy looked back on those early events. Yet this didn't diminish the difficulties she encountered along the way. "You've got to do the slog," Nancy insists, addressing the grit it took to launch her endeavor, in spite of her good fortune.

DECIDING TO MOVE FORWARD

Much had been accomplished at this early point. Nancy had put systems in place, established an editorial board process, and developed a method for girls and adults to share decision-making power, a rare occurrence in our culture. Content had been created, a graphic designer was engaged, a logo was formed, and the name, *New Moon Magazine,* had been chosen. Everything was ready to go for the first issue of the publication.

Now Nancy and Joe came to a monumental yes or no point. They faced the question of whether or not they were going to pay a designer to establish the layout and pay the printer for the first issue. The cost estimate was $10,000 for 2,000 copies. As Nancy remembers:

This is another thing that just makes me laugh when I think about it. Right at the time we were in the midst of needing to make this decision one day we open the mail. There's a telephone company bill there and inside the bill is this little scrap of paper that says on it, "You can't steal second with your foot on first," which is a baseball metaphor, meaning that you'll never get to where your vision is if you are not willing to step into that unknown between where you are now and where you want to get.

She actually read the message, showed it to Joe, and said:

This seems totally ridiculous, but I think this is the force. I didn't say it in those words. I said if we're getting messages in our phone bill, we'd have to have some pretty darn good reasons not to. At this point it was a passion for our whole family.

And yet $10,000 was a huge sum to the couple, literally their entire life savings. Even so, she and Joe discussed the ramifications of spending their money in this way and arrived at a feasible conclusion:

Well you know if we spend the $10,000 and it doesn't work out, doesn't go anywhere, we will have spent the $10,000 for something that really means a lot to all of us, which is really important to us and is putting our actions where our mouth is. It's walking the talk of this journey we have been on already for eight months and all these other people who've gotten involved in it.

In the end the logical side of this whole decision was well, yes this is a lot of money, but we are still young, we've got long work lives ahead of us and even if this $10,000 doesn't go anywhere, financially we'll be ok—we can recover from that—it's not going to be a crippling blow to our family.

So they went ahead and printed 2,000 copies of the magazine.

RUNNING A SMALL BUSINESS AND SETTING GOALS FOR THE MAGAZINE

Nancy readily admits her naiveté about what she'd be facing starting a publication.

You can learn a lot of things in your head, when you're doing them, it's different. I learn more by doing than by thinking about something, even though I'm a devoted reader and researcher.

She knew that she didn't know anything about starting and running a publication. She *did* know how 24/7 consuming a business could be because of her previous experience, but she didn't take into consideration how much this new enterprise would invade her personal space. For the first year or more, her home number doubled as the *New Moon* phone number.

Nancy was under no illusions about how hard it would be to start a business, or for that matter to start anything of any kind. It requires much persistence and drive.

A goal-driven person, Nancy liked having goals and meeting them. At the outset, she set simple goals such as getting the first story, completing the first issue, getting feedback and letters from girls around the country, getting the name decided, and getting a logo designed. Each of these goals she further broke down into a series of smaller steps, all adding up to realizing the publication. Nancy is motivated by the biggest goals, but she is fulfilled along the way by reaching and completing the smaller goals.

Her subscription goals were vague. Her notion was someday to have *New Moon* in the hands of 3,000 subscribers. No timeline accompanied that goal; the number simply seemed significant and attainable. She wanted to stretch beyond a goal that seemed too easy and land on one that would make a significant difference, reaching a sizable number of girls.

As it happened, the goal of having 3,000 subscribers was reached just about a year and a half after Nancy conceived the idea for *New Moon*. At that point the company had published two issues of the magazine, its premiere as well as the first regular issue.

As more people became aware of *New Moon*, Nancy and her girls began hearing about great events that girls were engaged in or that were happening for them. The publication became a magnet for stories generally under the radar screen—hopeful, positive situations. Nancy was pleasantly surprised as she realized that so many other people shared her concerns and goals and were determined to make life better for girls. The more *New Moon* became a magnet for the positive, the more Nancy gained energy and hope.

And not surprisingly, she saw her own daughters maintain their sense of self as they participated on the magazine and grew into adolescents. Their membership on the editorial board as well as their full absorption in the activities of the magazine gave Mavis and Nia the very strength and sure-footedness that Nancy had hoped for them. Consequently, they were able ultimately to enter young adulthood as whole human beings, primarily as a result of being engaged in the family business.

REACHING SUBSCRIBERS THROUGH PERSISTENCE AND SERENDIPITY

Author Esther Hicks suggests aligning with universal forces by offering up the activities you'll handle and putting the rest in the realm of the great spirits. Nancy may not have known about this approach or thought about making room for providence, but she demonstrated her ability to do so clearly and reaped the rewards. She also verified the power of the pull of a goal, knowing someday she wanted 3,000 subscribers.

Starting simply in the fall of 1992, Nancy connected with her personal network and let people know what was happening at the magazine. Her technique was circulating a Xeroxed brochure, designed more to tell the story of the venture than to ask for subscriptions. As word got out, a reporter at the local Duluth newspaper, *The News Tribune*, heard about what the girls were doing and asked if she could sit in on one of the girls' editorial board meetings.

With agreement from all concerned, the reporter viewed the meeting and ultimately wrote a story about *New Moon*, published in February 1993, almost two months before the first issue of the magazine went to press. While fact checking the story, the reporter pressed for subscription and cost details.

These questions motivated Nancy to develop an issue price with advice from her consultant. No market research went into this cost, just a reasonable guesstimate in relation to other high-quality children's magazines. No advertisements would support the publication, only subscriptions.

Checks started arriving shortly after the article appeared in the paper. Caught by surprise, Nancy scrambled to set up a checking account. Then, because at the time Duluth's paper participated in a syndicate of Knight Ridder newspapers, the story about *New Moon* showed up also in Denver, Miami, and southern California, bringing in more subscription orders. By the time the first issue went to print, 500 subscribers existed.

Most magazines then gained new readers by issuing thousands of pieces of direct mail, a practice beyond Nancy's ability to afford. Instead, she continued to rely on word of mouth and returned to the trusty library to research top newspapers and markets around the country, as well as a few specific magazines, such as *Ms. Magazine*, to target.

Nancy also relied on Joe's journalism talents to draft a compelling news release, which they included along with a sample magazine in 400 media kits they sent to the outlets on Nancy's list of newspapers and magazines. Although this was a huge investment, it paid off when they started getting interest from the media.

Nancy doggedly pursued *Ms. Magazine*, even after receiving no response from the kit she had sent the editor-in-chief. The assistant insisted that before any conversation could take place about a possible article, she'd have to locate the *New Moon* magazine sample.

Unfazed, Nancy decided to go all out and send a press kit to every name on the masthead, mailing them all the same day, timed to arrive in unison. Her hope was that at least two people would read the magazines and create some buzz. Even so, she had misgivings because of the great cost of this gamble. With the short press run of 2,000, every issue was precious, but she went ahead with this plan anyway. It worked! Ultimately a great piece about *New Moon* appeared in *Ms. Magazine*, bringing in many subscriptions.

Beyond word of mouth, the other big event to increase subscription numbers was a break from a popular children's television program. Linda Ellerbee, star of *Nick News* on Nickelodeon, called wanting to do a story about *New Moon*.

Her crew came to Duluth to film a feature story, requesting that the girls on the magazine be engaged in activity related to *New Moon*. The crew followed the editorial board around, particularly interested in filming them at the local Walden Bookstore, where *New Moon* was featured on the newsstand. An event was arranged with the girls at the bookstore, and it was captured on video.

Everything was set for the feature program to air in August, right before the regular issue of the magazine would be published in September. Yet prior to release, the Nickelodeon staff needed to ensure that Walden Books had given its permission for the store event.

Nancy had no idea corporations such as Walden were required to sign off on such situations. She had relied on her relationship with the local manager of the store, who was excited about what *New Moon* was up to and had agreed to sell the magazine and host the event. As it turned out, Walden Books had *not* signed off. Its policy was that individual store managers could sell only publications that were on a certain list from the official Walden Books magazine distributor.

With this new understanding, the *New Moon* event request made its way through the proper channels at Walden corporate, with the result that the Nickelodeon piece could be run only if the magazine were carried at *all* Walden Bookstores before the piece aired on television. A distributor had to sign *New Moon* immediately to enable the magazine to be sold so widely.

Ordinarily, it would have been impossible for such a small magazine to gain a national distributor. But Walden Books was making such a substantial order that the company hooked Nancy up with two potential distributors with whom they worked. These happened to be the two largest magazine distributors in the country, and fortunately, one of them took *New Moon* on as a participant.

THE FELLOWSHIP COMES THROUGH AND
NEW MOON SUPPORTS THE FAMILY

Soon after they published the first issue of *New Moon*, Nancy reapplied for a Bush Fellowship for the following year. This time she was awarded the grant! She pursued a master's degree at Harvard when the magazine was in its infancy, dividing her attention between both. At the time, she took a leave from her job, ultimately departing entirely not quite a year after having published the premiere issue.

The degree actually helped Nancy with the business. The mid-career program offered an opportunity to attend courses at any of Harvard's graduate schools. Conveniently, Harvard happened to be the place where research had been done on girls in Carol Gilligan's book. Nancy gained access to the researchers, learning firsthand about their studies.

Eighteen months after publishing the premiere issue, Nancy and Joe started taking a salary from *New Moon*—quite an accomplishment considering that originally Nancy had thought the magazine may amount to no more than a hobby. What helped their being able to live from the earnings of the fledgling business was their location in Duluth, Minnesota, a reasonably affordable spot. Staying put, as Nancy had desired, eliminated the high cost of living associated with the East Coast, home to most magazines.

The family was able to live frugally. A second mortgage on their house provided additional money to live on. They purchased health insurance for catastrophic care and paid out of pocket for primary care needs. Finally, two years after starting *New Moon*, the business fully supported them. Being typical entrepreneurs, they thought in terms of tapping into multiple streams of income. Never turning away a means to earn money, Joe accepted free-lance public relations work as it came along.

A generous grant, the Bush fellowship paid Nancy a monthly stipend in addition to helping to cover a majority of the costs of tuition. So Nancy kicked in these monies as well to contribute to the support of the family.

THE ROLE OF GENDER AND ADVICE
TO OTHER WOMEN

Although Nancy believes it would have been unusual for a man to conceive of a business such as *New Moon*, she has continued to see the value of having her husband standing by her side in it from the very beginning. Sometimes others have had difficulty understanding how a man could be so involved with this business, yet Joe's role was never in question to Nancy. To her it seemed perfectly appropriate. After all, they had always been co-parents. His journalistic talents were helpful with all aspects of the magazine production, which were not interests or strengths of Nancy's.

Being a woman helped Nancy with the mission and subject matter of the magazine. The whole reason for *New Moon's* existence rested on girls' and women's development and identity. As well, with girls on the editorial board, a woman as spokesperson was only natural.

As she demonstrated, Nancy believes that women with dreams for a business should learn what they can by reading and working with consultants. If people have never started a business of their own before, Nancy believes they should consider working in a small business. It makes no difference what business it is, any such exposure adds know-how.

Entrepreneurs need to acquire a "do-it-yourself" mentality. To start a small business, people have to be willing to stretch into roles they never otherwise imagined for themselves. They may never become expert in certain activities, but the work has to be done nonetheless.

Those concerned about covering their health care needs should explore offerings through professional associations to which they belong. Member benefits may provide some reduction in cost.

Although people need to consider the practical issues, they also need to remember what drives them. Nancy believes almost all business dreams are worth pursuing:

I'm a real believer in that if you have a passion so deep that you are willing to take risks for it, go for it! It doesn't mean you're going to get there, but it might take you to the spot where a different door opens. That is the different dream you're going to achieve.

To women who question their capacity to approach a dream and find themselves asking, "Who am I to do this?" Nancy retorts that women with passion need to ask another question: "Who else will do this?"

Often nobody else is doing something about the issue, as was Nancy's experience with *New Moon*. With a little bit of research, a woman can discover if the opportunity remains open. If nothing does exist, another set of questions arise: "Do you want the world not to have this?" "Do you want to leave this need unmet?"

Nancy doesn't minimize the courage it takes to respond. It takes hubris and ego—believing you can meet the challenge. By focusing on the passion, if that is truly the driving force, women can accomplish what they might not otherwise be willing to tackle. It allows them to take risks and put themselves in difficult situations. Women need a broader perspective than just "How is this related to me?" They have to draw energy and support from the universe and see themselves as part of the larger whole.

THE BUSINESS MATURES AND
NEW OPPORTUNITIES ARISE

A business that has matured 17 years, such as *New Moon,* meets new challenges. As a corporation thrives and grows, it has to change and adapt. Over the years, Nancy has gradually given up day-to-day decision making and control, becoming more strategic and visionary. She has learned how to create an environment where other people can pursue their passions, melding them into the lifeblood of her business. She's gathered the human and financial resources to enable her to accomplish her new goals.

Technology has been a boon to *New Moon.* The Internet has proven to be a giant word-of-mouth vehicle for the organization. This has been embraced in part, too, because direct mail, marketing, and paid advertising have never been favored by this entity, which is known for bucking the mainstream tide.

As the periodical business has changed over to the Internet, *New Moon* has seen opportunity emerge. Rather than resist the transition, it has aligned with it. Even several years ago, it became apparent that the business needed to move primarily onto the Internet and eventually out of print. As of September 2008, *New Moon Girl Media,* the new name for the organization, launched an online community for girls, NewMoonGirls.com, the first entity of its kind to do so.

In a real sense, Nancy believes she is starting a new business again, which is exciting, stimulating, and fulfilling as well as tricky and risky. They have to start at a whole new level, beyond what they did 17 years ago. It's a challenge to launch new elements among the established parts of the business. The Internet membership portion needs to integrate with the ongoing aspects of the business.

For *New Moon,* as with many businesses today, it's a risk to stay static, just as it's a risk to change. Print publications are disappearing.

The costs associated with creating them in physical space and distributing them are increasing. Nancy decided at the beginning not to accept ad revenue, and so she must transfer these higher costs to the end subscriber. That situation has forced her to change and grow with the times.

Yet, with an eye to inviting a second generation of *New Moon* girls into the fold, Nancy finds energy in her mission, and she can't conceive of doing anything but ride the waves of change. It's been a constant companion in the evolution of her dream.

ONE DREAM INSPIRES ANOTHER

Now that you have learned about Nancy Gruver's story and the emergence of *New Moon*, it's time to reflect on how this story can inspire you in your quest for your entrepreneurial dream. Take some time to reflect on what you've just read and allow the following questions to guide you. Use your journal to take notes so that you can ground your understanding and learning for future reference.

1. What doors in your life have closed? What doors opened as a result for you?
2. What is your process? Do you need to spend time alone in reflection when you are trying to sort out your future? Or do you do better in concert with others?
3. What's a passion you've long held?
4. What's a gap that's out there that you just wish someone would do something about?
5. From Nancy's story, what can you learn about the role of serendipity in the unfolding of entrepreneurial dreams that you can apply to your dreams?

WHAT CAN YOU LEARN FROM NANCY GRUVER?

The story of Nancy Gruver taking her passion for feminist issues and turning it into a viable, long-lasting business offers many useful lessons to women considering their own dreams. Like the other women throughout this book, she took her uniqueness and allowed it to direct her to situations in which she could thrive.

She took time alone to sort out what was important, and she acted as her own coach, asking herself questions about what fulfilled her.

She demonstrated patience, recognizing that she needed to steep and brew in her own juices while she waited for something to surface. She didn't push the river; she allowed nature to take its course and had faith that something would occur to her.

Nancy demonstrated her resourcefulness in digging up experts to help her, both in books as well as in the form of consultants. She unabashedly asked for help all along the way. When experts told her she needed to pursue her business in ways that didn't match her vision, she found reasonable alternative avenues, without compromising her values and goals.

Fortune shone on Nancy and she took every advantage that came her way, riding the waves of opportunity. She didn't shrink from risks but calculated them and took action while giving herself alternative options.

Nancy Gruver's *New Moon* adventure epitomizes the successful evolution of a dream, and it also demonstrates every part of the Magic Formula of Dream, Courage, Action. Look for this formula as we continue to explore more scrappy startup stories in the rest of the book.

YOUR TURN NOW—WHAT DID *YOU* LEARN FROM NANCY'S STORY?

CHAPTER 2

DRIVING MISS DAISY

A Conversation with Bev Halisky, Founder and President of the Driving Miss Daisy Franchise (www.drivingmissdaisy.net)

Creative imagination: The ability to create the wheel while observing a man walking.

—*Jacques Lipchitz*

You get up in the morning and you go out and help all these people and you come home at night and you just feel worthwhile. You've made a difference in somebody's day. I just wanted something different in my life.

—*Bev Halisky*, founder and president of Driving Miss Daisy

When opportunity knocks, it helps to be located in a city reputed to be among Canada's top five wealthiest cities, even if it's no more than 50,000 people large. Bev Halisky had been a lifelong resident in St. Albert, Alberta, Canada, now a bedroom community of Edmonton. The wealth of her surrounding area most likely provided the fertile ground for the successful enterprise she dreamed up. An equal asset was her practical intelligence, which she put to work on a visible need in her community.

In her early fifties at the time she started her business, Bev saw herself as a "typical married in the 1960s" woman. Like many of her peers, she had been raised on the notion that your children and your family come first. Her job as an office manager for a health organization had grown more out of the necessity of contributing to the family's financial stability than from any career ambition.

For a number of years Bev had been thinking about slowing down and getting out of the "rat race" of her job routine. Her children were grown and her husband semi-retired. She was naturally talented at organizing, which she put to good use running the office of a retinal specialist, but there was nothing particularly compelling to her about the work she was doing. Frankly, she was a bit bored.

What caught her attention were the seniors who frequented the doctor's office. For three years she had been thinking about a need she saw for a personalized service: driving these elders to their appointments and wherever else they needed to go. The more she thought about it, the more she also saw a way to contribute to her community.

As Bev flirted with her idea, she also considered her own senior parents, who were in their late seventies and early eighties, as well as her sister with Down syndrome. Her mother had become an Alzheimer patient who couldn't go anywhere alone. Bev considered them all to be a potential ideal market for a driving service. As Bev thought about her family's needs, she realized the service could include not only seniors but also people with any kind of mental or physical disability, regardless of their age.

GETTING STARTED

As with just about every scrappy startup woman I've met, Bev was not thinking about the money she would make from this potential business. Her motivation essentially was an urge to put something back into her community. It was her dream. At the time she began her journey, she had little idea where it would lead her, and she didn't think about the potential complications she might encounter along the way. A straightforward, no-nonsense woman, Bev put her attention on offering dignity to the less fortunate, and she didn't look back.

Bev committed herself to her new task and left her full-time job. She launched her business officially in January 2002, enlisting the help of her husband, her hero, a semi-retired baker, in choosing a name for her business:

While I was busy preparing to start my business, I told my husband that I needed a "really good name." While we had never seen the movie Driving Miss Daisy, my husband did see it listed in the movie line-up on our satellite television stations. One morning, while stirring his coffee, he looked at me and said, "How about Driving Miss Daisy?" To which I replied, "I love it!" and thus the name.

Talk about seizing a brand that would capture the essence of what Bev was attempting to accomplish! It's amazing that neither of them had actually seen the movie that bore the name of the business. If so, they would have appreciated the protagonist being treated with dignity by her driver, which epitomized Bev's dream. Regardless, the name rang true to Bev and seemed appropriate, so she chose it. Fortunately, no legal tangles arose with using the name in Canada.

Bev's husband also persuaded her that her adored Saturn would not be suitable for her service. He predicted her passengers would have trouble getting in and out of the car, and he told her if she was really serious, he'd help her find the right car for the task.

After a bit of shopping around, the Chrysler PT Cruiser was chosen because of its big hatch in the back, which could accommodate walkers and wheel chairs, and because of its bench seating feature, which allowed passengers to easily slide in and out of the car. As a bonus, the Cruiser offered a nostalgic look. It was perfect!

To drum up business, Bev ran an ad in her local paper. She also announced her service to the four senior residences in the city, letting the administrators who ran these complexes know what she was doing. Although many of the senior residences had their own buses, the vehicles did not run on Thursdays, stopped running at 3 PM, and would not take passengers into Edmonton, nearly 10 miles away. There were many gaps Driving Miss Daisy could fill.

As a result of these small steps, Bev's phone started ringing and she was busy right away. It was as simple as that. The fact that she was a woman didn't hurt; people felt more comfortable and less intimidated by a female driver. Her age seemed to be an asset too, because the elders felt an affinity for her. She was young enough to accommodate their needs but old enough to be able to relate to them.

Although some of the "powers that be" in charge at the residences initially needed some convincing about the importance of what she was offering to the elders and the disabled, Bev found these gatekeepers to be irrelevant. In the end, the consumers were the ones who made her business viable through their demand.

Bev became visible all over town in her car with its prominent Driving Miss Daisy decal. The daisy itself came to symbolize the founder and her business—both cheery and reliable. She offered complete door-to-door service, helping her clients gather their belongings when leaving home and taking them to all the varied destinations to which they desired to be driven. Bev's mission became giving people their independence, freedom, and dignity.

Upon returning home with her charges, she would even put their groceries and packages away for them if they desired this extra effort. She'd leave only when she was convinced they were settled in. To Bev, these were not her customers so much as her friends. She enjoyed filling a void in these people's lives and found her work rewarding beyond measure:

You get up in the morning and you go out and help all these people and you come home at night and you just feel worthwhile. You've made a difference in somebody's day.

Bev had not set out to develop Miss Daisy into a full-blown business. She actually had no business plan at all. Yet within a short time after she had begun operating, she started to see a need for her service all over the city of Edmonton.

OVERNIGHT FROM SMALL BUSINESS
TO FRANCHISE OWNER

Six months into her business, Bev wanted to expand, but she had no desire to hire employees and become responsible for their welfare. Nor did she want the expense and administration of purchasing and maintaining a fleet of vehicles. So with some thought and a bit of advice from business people, Bev Halisky created a franchise operation. Bev's businessman son-in-law was instrumental in helping her choose a franchise lawyer, who in turn started the ball rolling on a trademark for Driving Miss Daisy in Canada, a two-and-a-half-year process. She had a prospectus drawn up and was ready to sell franchises to people who wanted to provide the driving service in their areas.

Bev had no idea whether a franchise would fly, but people began coming forward almost immediately, wanting to become owners. This supported her belief that if people really wanted to engage in this work they would buy into it. Initially, four people lined up for the final paperwork for the franchise and each paid Bev $10,000 as well as a monthly $300 administration fee per vehicle to be part of the business.

New franchisees were located in Edmonton at first. Nine months after starting Driving Miss Daisy, Bev found herself wanting to focus on expanding the franchise. So she sold the St. Albert franchise, her home base, to someone in whom she felt confident. She's always been particular about to whom she offers her franchises:

I always say I hand pick my Daisies. If they don't seek me, I don't sell to them. I just feel we have to be a certain kind of person. You have to be doing this for the right reasons. If you're doing it to make a lot of money, then you shouldn't do it. This has got to be a heartfelt job. It's something you need to want to help people and that's what it's all about. And if you go out there and you buy a franchise and you actually turn a profit and make some money, then it's a bonus.

Bev gained great satisfaction watching the first person drive away in a vehicle decorated to match the original. She appreciated that someone else believed in what she was doing. She felt like a proud mama and was amazed that everything worked out so well.

To ensure that she finds appropriate people as new franchise owners, "heartfelt people," as she puts it, she meets and interviews the likely candidate. Bev wants to get a general feel for the impetus behind a person's desire to join the franchise.

She wants to know what the person did in the past and asks for the driver's abstract, which is equivalent to a U.S. driver's license. She accepts only those with clean driving records. Bev also conducts security checks to ensure that no one has a criminal record. She finds that people who are in their mid-forties and up in age seem to acclimate best to the work.

Bev sells franchises only in Canada, but she's had a lot of interest from the United States, Ireland, Portugal, and as far away as Australia. For people who want to mimic the Driving Miss Daisy concept outside of Canada, Bev offers a consultation package since she can't sell them a franchise. She provides information to help people in international locations get up and running.

I do up a correspondence letter telling them the dos and don'ts and what they need to do. What they have to look out for. Then I send them copies of my franchise agreement and franchise information kit and all the tools that I have used to grow my business.

She estimates that she's helped more than a dozen people in various places around the world start their own businesses. Some add the services to other business offerings, such as home care services. Most operate their businesses with different names.

GROWING THE FRANCHISE IN CANADA

Over the course of seven years, Bev has grown Driving Miss Daisy in Canada to more than 37 franchises operating in 37 territories with 50 vehicles. The largest cities where the service is offered in Canada presently are Vancouver, Edmonton, and Calgary.

In 2007, Bev brought her daughter into the business as director. Doing so has been good for the business because her daughter has spearheaded franchise sales in British Columbia and has sold more than 18 franchises in less than two years.

Some of the original franchises have resold over time. Once they get up and operational, their value increases. They've sold for as little as $15,000 and as much as $40,000, depending on their profitability and length of operation.

Accordingly, Driving Miss Daisy has become a lucrative business for Bev. She sees this circumstance as being a win-win outcome for everybody. Her only complaint is that she has to work too hard:

I was doing this to get out of work, and I never worked so hard in my life!

Although her previous job as office manager for a retinal specialist had been a fairly high-stress activity with a lot of responsibility, her work as president and founder of the Driving Miss Daisy franchise necessitates almost 24/7 duty. She's never away from it, and she works long hours just staying on top of everything. Bev wakes up Driving Miss Daisy and goes to bed Driving Miss Daisy, even though she gave up actual driving years ago.

As with any business, changes have needed to be instituted along the way. Bev learned sadly that Chrysler's PT Cruiser was being discontinued in 2008. She had heard rumblings about this circumstance and once again put her husband to the task of locating a substitution vehicle. With a bit of research, he found that GM's Chevy HHR was an almost-identical car. Rumor had it that the Chrysler designer for the Cruiser had moved over to GM and had therefore had the capacity to create a similar car. Long before the Cruiser disappeared, Bev saw that the HHR was added to the Daisy fleet and the transition seemed smooth.

LEGACY REWARDS OF THE BUSINESS

Even though she no longer drives, Bev continues to be proud of the achievements of her business. She is quicker to cite the intrinsic rewards than the monetary ones. Driving Miss Daisy is a private business, and revenues come from clients and their families. Often, adult children who don't live in the vicinity of where their parents reside hire the service to transport their parents as they would if they lived nearby. The existence of this service for elderly relatives provides great peace of mind, especially for people living far away, such as Texas, and having loved ones in Edmonton.

Bev truly believes she is doing this work on behalf of all the sisters with Down syndrome and the families with elderly parents. For her this work is a mission as well as a business. Being in business for more than seven years, she has seen untold examples of people, who otherwise couldn't go anywhere, gaining dignity and independence because of the existence of her business.

Bev has been nominated for and won many awards for her work. She was designated a Woman of Vision for Global TV, her local Edmonton television station, in 2005. St. Albert nominated her for the small business award several years ago, and she received a nomination for the Royal Bank of Canada's 2008 Woman Entrepreneur.

On the verge of 60, Bev figures she'll be working with the franchise until she's 65. She laments, "We all have to retire at some point." She's considering turning the business over to her daughter eventually or possibly bringing someone else in and keeping a piece of the action for herself.

Summing up her tenure as an entrepreneur, Bev is philosophical about her achievements:

Success is just a word. I believe that we can be successful not only from a monetary perspective, but by being who you say you are and "feeling" successful irrespective of monetary gain. After working for 30+ years for a paycheck this was somewhat of a gamble, but most definitely something that made me feel that I had made a difference in someone else's life and that alone made my day.

Bev advises women with a dream to do it for the right reasons. Don't set out to make monetary gain, but give back to others, who can benefit from what you have to offer.

ONE DREAM INSPIRES ANOTHER

Now that you have heard Bev Halisky's story and followed the emergence of the Driving Miss Daisy franchise, it's time to reflect on how this story can inspire you in your quest for your entrepreneurial dream. Take some time to reflect on what you've just read, and allow the following questions to guide you. Use your journal to take notes so that you can ground your understanding and learning for future reference.

1. Look around your world. What are the gaps out there that are begging to be filled?
2. What special talents and skills do you bring to the table? If there were a purpose behind your having been the recipient of these talents and skills, what could it be?
3. What activities are you unwilling to do? What structure could you devise that would allow you to do a business easily? (Bev didn't want to hire drivers—she decided to franchise her business from the beginning.)
4. What problems or issues do family members have that could be solved with an appropriate business response?
5. What would you like your legacy to be?

WHAT CAN YOU LEARN FROM BEV HALISKY?

Bev is one of those women who, without much fuss, makes what they do look so easy. Perhaps you're lucky enough to have one in your extended family. She's like that Olympic skater who gets out on the ice and performs so naturally that you wonder if she ever spent any time practicing.

As she was going about her daily routine, she was considering the gap she saw in front of her, which was providing a useful service to those around her. She took her time and considered what she wanted to do for three years before she got into action. But once she made up her mind, she moved quickly.

Bev enlisted the help of her husband, himself a straight-shooting, no-nonsense man, who lovingly performed important tasks for his wife. How fortunate that he happened to catch *Driving Miss Daisy* on the satellite listing! It may not be a stretch to say it was a bit of serendipity. But a key for many of us to observe is the importance of having our antenna up when we are about to move into a new venture. It's a good habit to continually perform a sweep of the environment to see what can be gained.

Here again, as with Nancy Gruver's story, we see how scrappy startup women do themselves a service by drawing a line in the sand about what they will and will not do for the sake of their businesses. Bev was determined not to grow her business with employees and vehicles, choosing instead to create a franchise. This decision proved not only to be lucrative but also made the business capable of greater scalability, allowing it to grow more rapidly and reach more environments than if she had tried to grow in a more traditional way.

This is not a woman who doubts herself. Bev never gave it a thought that she hadn't done anything like this before or didn't know much about franchising. She reached out to those who could help her with the legal aspects of franchising and never looked back. We can learn much from such a confident woman.

One of her secrets may have been not telling anyone in her family other than her husband what she had up her sleeve. The first inkling her friends and family knew of her business was when they saw her driving down the street in her decaled Cruiser. Rather than let anyone else's doubts seep in, she simply showed up in all her glory.

It's not possible to read this story without gaining a deep appreciation for the love Bev Halisky has for the people her service was targeted to help. Here was the true meaning for her, which continues to sustain her in spite of the hard work she puts into the business, at a stage in her life she might otherwise choose to slow down. Her dream continues to reinvigorate her as she continually remembers the purpose behind her endeavor.

YOUR TURN NOW—WHAT DID *YOU* LEARN FROM BEV'S STORY?

CHAPTER 3

CHERRY BROOK KITCHEN

A Conversation with Patsy Rosenberg, Founder of Cherry Brook Kitchen (www.cherrybrookkitchen.com)

Our waking hours form the text of our lives, our dreams, the commentary.

—*Anonymous*

This is going to sound hokey—my definition of success is not being afraid to follow your dream. I think the key is the following part because you could fail at it, but learn something even better in the process or (it) turns into something else you couldn't have even imagined.

—*Patsy Rosenberg*, founder of Cherry Brook Kitchen

It's one thing to be born with difficult allergies or to acquire them in early childhood. It's another to develop a life-threatening allergy as an adult. Imagine a person who highly values celebrating not being able to share dessert or birthday cake! Yet even so, Patsy Rosenberg took a difficult restriction and turned it into a business opportunity and a crusade that others have gratefully appreciated.

As Patsy learned the hard way, food allergies occur when the immune system mounts an attack on certain proteins in certain foods. The substances in the food that trigger this immune-system response are called allergens. In Patsy's case, she became life-threateningly allergic to eggs and dairy. Her sensitivity was probably a result of the aftereffects of viral meningitis and flu when pregnant with her daughters. It's likely her immune system became altered from the sicknesses and the pregnancies.

Being by her own admission a true chocoholic, Patsy turned her Boston kitchen into a testing area for homemade desserts she *could* eat. She thought it would be easier to attend a playgroup with her kids or visit someone's house if she could bring her own dessert with her and avoid making excuses for not eating others' treats. So she set about trying to create a tasty chocolate cake without the requisite normal ingredients. Not an easy feat.

She persisted with her quest, baking over and over again, even if the cake didn't rise, or even if it turned into a big bowl of mush. At least when the output tasted good, Patsy thought she had something to go on. She reworked her recipe 50 to 100 times, with many of the versions landing in the trash. But she was determined!

What kept Patsy going was her love of desserts, especially chocolate, and her abiding love for celebrating life with others. Losing pieces of her life to the food allergies and having to renew her view of food, she was determined to salvage as much of her life as she could. She also didn't want to depress dinner hosts, making them feel nervous or guilty when they were eating desserts in front of her.

Even though friends and family promised to make dinner and desserts carefully allergen free, Patsy couldn't rely on their good intentions. Socially, it became difficult to say that she didn't trust people and needed to prepare food for herself, but if anyone did mess up or if something did go wrong, it was Patsy's life on the line. Unfortunately, an allergy can creep into a social structure in untold ways.

Finally, Patsy's persistence paid off and she arrived at a workable, delicious cake she could eat. Her two daughters, Sarah and Caroline, five and seven at the time, had been by her side throughout the ordeal, tasting and watching her go through the process of coming up with a viable recipe. With success, all three became ecstatic and marveled at the positive result, exclaiming, "Look at this cake!" They admired how it looked like a real cake with frosting, and not only that, it tasted good too.

Patsy started bringing her cake to events and celebrations so that she could have something to enjoy. To her surprise, she noticed that some preferred to eat her cake, not even realizing it was allergen free and specially made for her. They just liked the look and taste of her confection.

PERSONAL SUCCESS LEADS TO AN IDEA
FOR A BUSINESS

Now that she realized her cake had universal appeal, Patsy began considering how to share her dessert with many people. She noticed children with food allergies at her daughters' school eating from a bag of Cheerios or crackers while others were eating cupcakes. Or worse, they would be handed a cupcake substitute that looked awful. Patsy's heart broke for these children who were excluded from enjoying what others ate. She hated that at this time of innocence, allergic children could not enjoy themselves without abandon.

Patsy shared her concern with her husband, Chip, telling him:

There has to be a way that I can get this out there to more people, because what's out there now that you can find doesn't taste good.

Patsy started to consider alternatives. Maybe she could start a bakery. But she dismissed this idea when she thought of herself as an example. If she didn't live near a bakery, it would do her no good, and what use would a local bakery be to her if she were on vacation or visiting friends or relatives in another city?

Then she thought of preparing mixes that could last in the cupboard longer than would a store-bought cake. If she had a mix handy, she could always open it up when she needed to use it. The more she thought about the advantages, the more pleased she became. Ideas started to pop:

What if I did mixes and, if I did it with a chocolate cake, why not a yellow cake? So then I went back into the kitchen and then it just started to snowball. I started to think of all the classic things of childhood: yellow cake, chocolate chip cookies, sugar cookies, frostings and just went sort of on a roll and developed a whole slew of recipes, gaining a few pounds in the process. Really sort of riding that high of, oh my gosh, look what I can create and how can we get this now to a consumer; how can we make this a business; how can we do this?

Patsy dived into creating recipes for all of these new product ideas in much the same way she had experimented with her chocolate cake. At the same time, she began questioning others about how to do a mix. She'd have people taste her variety of items, asking for feedback about the taste. She also questioned whether each mix she created could actually become a product.

Patsy had crossed the line from serving herself to creating a serious business. Once she believed she had a good idea on her hands, she solicited friends of friends in the food industry as well as appealed to her father-in-law for help. He had a particularly useful background because he had been in the grocery store business, having owned and operated as many as 17 ShopRite Supermarkets in New York and Pennsylvania. He had retired at 50 after having successfully expanded the one store he had inherited from his father.

Patsy's father-in-law introduced her to his many remaining connections in the food business. She had useful conversations and visited a food show. After collecting feedback and doing more research, Patsy sat down with her husband to relate what she had found:

Here's the feedback; here's what I think. And he took a look at it with me; and we decided, all right, if we're going to do this, we'll do it together. He said, all right, let's just go ahead; let's do this and jump with both feet in and see where this takes us.

Until now, Patsy had been a stay-at-home mom. Coincidently, with both daughters in school she had recently arrived at a point of questioning what she was going to do with the extra time on her hands. She had been thinking seriously about returning to school to get a doctorate in psychology, having a bachelor's in the subject. Now with the thought of a business, she wasn't entirely abandoning her plan. She thought perhaps she'd do the business for about a year. She envisioned it as a transition year.

A small business startup sounded like good fun. Patsy imagined she could create her own hours and simply transition into applying for a doctorate after she had accomplished something worthwhile.

At this time Chip had just completed three years' tenure as a director of an overnight summer camp. Prior to that he had been in the real estate business. He was considering returning to real estate, but he thought a business might be a good diversion for him as well. He agreed to join his wife in her venture.

LEARNING WHAT SHE WAS GETTING INTO

Patsy claims that if she knew then what she knows now, she might have been more terrified about what she was getting herself into. She didn't know what she was going to be up against, not having any experience in the food industry.

What supported her, surprisingly enough, when she met each hurdle in that first year was her spunk born of her determination to see this project through. Whenever she would sit across from a manufacturer or a label maker or a designer and they would respond to her with a "no," "you can't do this," or "that's not possible," Patsy would tell them she didn't care what it would take to make the situation work.

If I can't do it this way, what way can we do it? Meet me half way here; help me out!

Patsy remembered she was doing this negotiating on behalf of the friends of her daughters who had allergies. These children couldn't speak for themselves. She was there representing them. When she entered these meetings, she remembered the personal stories she had heard from people who told her she had a great idea, people with a son or a daughter or a sister with allergies as well. The more she had shared her idea, the more she had learned of the need and just how many people were counting on her to succeed.

With these people in mind, Patsy didn't find the push back she was receiving from the food industry experts annoying. She didn't tell herself she couldn't handle their resistance. She became resolute and believed "this has to happen!"

And I was just bound and determined for myself, but also I had all these other people waiting behind me who didn't even know how their lives were going to change yet, until this would come out. But if it didn't, their lives wouldn't change.

Patsy didn't even have the vocabulary to describe what she didn't know because there's a whole lingo in the food industry to which she hadn't been privy. Going into this business, all she had were her recipes and her desire to succeed. She had no background or previous business experience to rely on.

She knew she was smart, and she really wanted to make her business work. What she found that actually helped her were the connections she made—people who knew more than she and Chip did. If the couple didn't know something about sales, they would find the right salesperson. Their connections led them to the right people in manufacturing who were effective and trustworthy and willing to share what they knew. Patsy learned not to be afraid to ask for help. The more she put her hands out, the more the right, reliable people showed up.

Patsy is grateful her husband Chip was as interested in the business as she was. He was not the missionary she was, but he was the business analyst and number cruncher, with a natural talent for sales. She was the product person because she had her skin in creating the mixes. She found it comforting from the beginning that he was by her side; they were both in this together, and the business would not just rely on her failure or success. Actually, this was an entire family affair because the girls also were involved from the very beginning with their taste testing.

Fortunately, Chip had done well in real estate and the family had accumulated substantial savings. He continued with real estate part time during the first six months as Patsy ramped up the business. Even so, like Nancy Gruver and Joe Kelly, who started *New Moon*, Patsy and Chip wondered about the efficacy of using their savings for a business launch:

Do we want to use the savings and gamble on this? If not now, when would we take a chance like this? We're not in our 70s, where this would be as dangerous as a risk. It's sort of now or never.

Patsy's father-in-law was outstanding in his support. He took her with him to New York City to her first food show, where she literally carried around containers with samples of her cakes in them. He graciously introduced her to people he remembered from his years in business.

One woman in particular, who Patsy met at the show in the New England aisle, stood out because of her willingness to help at that early time. Her name was Lindsay Frucci. She ran a successful company based on her own recipe called No Pudge Brownies. Patsy found the woman's achievement an inspiration. When Lindsay heard what Patsy was up to, she encouraged her with, "You can do it!"

Lindsay was so generous, and offered organizations Patsy might want to know about. Patsy was amazed by what Lindsay had accomplished, and was grateful that she was still willing to share her knowledge and connections. To this day, Lindsay is on Patsy's board.

At the food show, Patsy sat down with salespeople and brokers her father-in-law had known who were still in the business. She gave them some cake, offered her spiel, and gained a positive response. All this was encouraging.

If this support weren't enough, as luck would have it, Patsy's sister-in-law had a degree in culinary arts. Patsy valued her opinion also and was forever asking her to try her recipes, asking her opinion and gaining information useful to putting the products together. She was a tremendous help.

Once Patsy and Chip decided to ramp up the business, they realized they were facing a 24/7 operation. It just wasn't in the financial cards to hire a staff of 20. It was going to be just the two of them in the beginning, and Patsy had to think long and hard about what she was getting the family into. She wondered whether she was being selfish taking everyone on the journey with her.

She questioned, "What if it's not successful? What if I lose all this money?" Those questions brought fear to the surface, but Patsy reassured herself that she could take this. She realized that it would take all of their energy, time, and savings to start the business, but she was willing to make the call. Even though her husband was by her side, she considered herself the front person for the business. Because of this, she had to come to grips with how she would feel if they failed.

Ok, it's going to be ok with me if I fail. It's either I don't try at all or I fail. What am I constantly telling my girls?

Patsy saw herself as a role model for her daughters, wanting them to see her pursuing her dream. As a result, she wanted her daughters to see her complete this process, as hard as it was. That was as important to her as her motivation to make a difference for people with allergies.

TEACHING THEMSELVES AS THEY WENT ALONG

Patsy and Chip had to teach themselves the process of putting their mixes into packaging that was safe, food grade, and allergen free. They had to figure out how to package their samples to send to buyers and stores. No one told them how to do this; they had to invent the process themselves.

Literally, they moved everything out of their dining room, bringing in large drums filled with flour, cocoa, and chips. They measured and mixed their ingredients, weighing them out on a scale. They bought a big roll of commercial plastic, cutting the proper sizes for their home-made bags and placing the contents into them. They purchased a food saver vacuum sealer from QVC to ensure the contents in the bags would be properly preserved. Again, everything had to be done with the greatest of care to prevent any contamination.

This was the process they devised to create samples, but when they were done, they realized next they would need to find a manufacturing facility capable of producing an allergen free product. No ordinary manufacturing facility would do.

Even when they found the facility, Patsy was careful to record herself a stringent protocol that needed to be followed. As a mother and a person with food allergies, she wanted to be certain that if anyone were to call the company and ask a question, it could be properly answered. She wanted to be assured that a mother with a one year old would be confident that her child would not be in jeopardy, that everything had been handled stringently. There was no room for deviation.

Above all, there could be no cross-contamination. They needed to have allergen testing and to obtain certifications from suppliers to ensure that they met allergen standards. It became an incessant hurdle to find the right suppliers who would follow Patsy's approach. She found herself continuously telling companies, "No, I'm sorry, you need to give me this paper. Trust me; this is what we need to do." Patsy held out until she found others with integrity.

When they were pricing their items, some people encouraged the Rosenbergs to skip the allergen testing because of the cost of the special labs and necessary records. Patsy was adamant that unless this step was included, she would not get into this business at all.

There were difficulties also with working with people in the food industry with these new products and protocols. People she encountered asked Patsy from where the protocols were originating. When she told them she made them herself, they seemed to back off with their questioning.

All of this was quite the process. But Patsy did find manufacturers who understood what she was up to, especially those whose personal experience with a son's or daughter's peanut allergies gave them sensitivity to her mission. They were immediately on board when the flicker of light dawned on them, recognizing the restrictions their own children had faced; perhaps they had not ever had a piece of birthday cake. These people became Patsy's natural allies.

As the Rosenberg family transitioned into the business of what was to become Cherry Brook Kitchen, all four of them got involved, preparing 800 cookies and 40 sheet cakes from scratch in their own kitchen for the first food show they attended as a company. The girls rolled all the cookie dough balls, pitching in with the baking process that lasted for 2 days straight. Everyone was tired.

Seeing their mother with blisters from holding the mixing bowls and exhaustion on her face, the girls asked their mother, "Why don't you just stop?" Patsy responded:

Because this is important to me, and I need to make this happen. It might not be easy and easy isn't the point.

FUNDING AND PROTECTING THE OPERATION

The Rosenberg's initial personal investment in Cherry Brook Kitchen was $120,000 in addition to their sweat equity. Manufacturing products is an expensive proposition to get off the ground. As much as this sounds like a massive amount of money, it was just the beginning of what they needed to invest to get the business going. Accordingly, they also had to go to banks for loans.

To get the banks on board, the Rosenbergs took out a few small loans, piecing things together. Funny as it seems, one piece of collateral that they used to secure their loans was the very first piece of equipment they had purchased. It's called a form fill machine. It collects the mix after it's been amassed and drops the measured contents into bags that are then sealed.

Patsy had insisted on purchasing this equipment to ensure they were using something 100% safe and reliable. Ironically, this very machinery in turn became one of the company's greatest assets. Patsy doesn't know what the bank would have done with the contraption if it had had to be sold, but every time she gazed at the machine, she saw what amounted to her life savings.

Sinking in their money and taking out bank loans amounted to a leap of faith for the Rosenbergs. Luckily they had gotten enough positive feedback and orders from major companies after their first food show that they realized they had a potentially viable business. They simply decided to gamble on themselves as opposed to investing their money into the stock market.

They learned quickly to insist that anyone with whom they spoke needed first to sign a confidentiality agreement. But even so, consultants told them that although this step was all well and good, would-be competitors could always claim that they had been working on a similar idea for years. Such a signature was not entirely protection from copycats.

Early on, especially in the first year, Patsy and Chip worried that bigger companies might take notice of what they were doing and undermine them. Fortunately, no great competition came along, perhaps because such organizations let the little guys do the leg work and are reluctant to get into a new aspect of food manufacturing until they are convinced there's a large enough market.

Patsy believes major companies *are* keeping tabs on them. She hasn't seen anyone dedicate a plant to mixes similar to hers yet, but with the trends in the population of people gaining allergic sensitivities, she believes it's a matter of time before other companies get on the band wagon.

So far at least, Patsy and Chip's investment has paid off. In their first year of business, 2003, they sold 50,000 cases. In 2008 they produced 200,000 cases. In terms of sales, at the end of the fiscal year 2008, five years after they started their business, they had $3 million dollars in sales. To gauge a range of their reach, Cherry Brook Kitchen mixes are found in 7,000 stores across the country.

SUSTAINING HER PASSION

Patsy admits that after the first initial high of starting a business she had to get down into the really tough stuff. There were nights when she'd be in the plant at three o'clock in the morning, standing over huge machines, watching that processes were being done properly. She would switch off duties with Chip, with one of them staying home with the girls. To her, having such a business was equivalent to having a third child.

This work was truly exhausting. There were days when they'd be in tears because what they were doing was so hard. But at such moments, she'd be buoyed by emails and phone calls from mothers.

Women would send their children's crayon drawn pictures of their very first birthday party where they shared cake with everybody else. These helped the entrepreneur remain dedicated to her business.

Although Chip makes business decisions through the lens of what the numbers dictate, Patsy says business is completely a personal affair. She sees herself raising the banner of those counted among the food allergy population; she is out there championing their cause and attempting to make changes in food presentation, quality, and taste. The more she gets involved and the more she interacts with people, the more she sees how much of a difference she can make.

Being a woman in this business has helped Patsy tremendously. Other women, such as Lindsay Frucci, have happily helped Patsy "push the boulder up the hill." When she encountered businessmen across the table, they too were supportive, perhaps because so many women had already done well within the food industry. Having these people behind her and the inspiration of the other women's success gave Patsy faith in herself to continue to pursue her dream.

And Patsy has done her part in supporting other women as well. The head of marketing for Cherry Brook Kitchen is a woman who came from Annies and Applegate. The head of sales, also a woman, came from No Pudge and had previously worked for Lindsay. Patsy doesn't believe she consciously set out to hire so many women, but little by little a network started to be created that rested on trust, honesty, and loyalty. When she went looking for a person to head up sales, Patsy believed that a recommendation from another woman could be counted on. She has found women to be unbelievably helpful to her, and in turn she has enjoyed doing her part to help other women.

Patsy believes this may sound hokey, but her definition of success is not to be afraid to follow your dream:

I think the key is the following [the dream] part because you could fail at it, but learn something even better in the process, or [it] turns into something else you couldn't even have imagined.

I really thought when we started this that we would be a great company. I couldn't wait to do this, but I could not imagine how widespread we would be at this point, and also how much we affect people's lives and the emotional responses we get in daily emails still every day from consumers. It's more than I could have ever imagined. I had to make up my mind just to go for it. To follow that dream was what I needed to have the courage to do.

THE FUTURE FOR CHERRY BROOK KITCHEN

Patsy wants to continue to grow the business and expand the product line. She would like to become a standard in the industry and make inroads into other grocery aisles. In this way people could prepare their meals by following Cherry Brook Kitchen throughout the day. At every turn, allergy-free products would be available from her company.

Today her products can be found in major stores such as Shaws, Stop & Shop, Super Targets, most major supermarkets, and also little gourmet shops. Patsy's attention now is on growing awareness for her brand so that she can continue to create more products for her market. She is forever discovering what products work and don't work for people. Additionally, she also has positioned part of her company to be focused on increasing food allergy awareness, educating people, attending related events, and championing the cause.

PATSY'S ADVICE TO WOMEN WITH A BUSINESS DREAM

Patsy suggests women with an idea should immediately surround themselves with those who will support their dream. There will always be somebody who will say it can't be done. Be sure to push that notion aside. Rather, listen to those who believe in you, such as friends and family. Then start to pull on your resources. Ask friends for connections. It doesn't matter where you start with the six degree of separation world we have today. Starting will lead to finding your way.

As an example, she cites what she did herself at the food show. She just started writing down the names of people who were willing to talk with her. In this way, early on she gained access to a public relations company run by a woman, Bullfrog and Baum in New York City. The agency took Cherry Brook Kitchen on as a client at a really reduced rate because they believed in what Patsy was doing.

People are always willing to help and lend a hand, Patsy believes. Just find those people. Maybe the initial idea you have doesn't work, but you'll learn a lot about yourself and how far you can take something. Then you can ask yourself what else you want to do; this starts to create a way for you to approach your life.

The right timing for starting a business is a personal preference in Patsy's estimation. It all depends on what stage you are in your life. When you start a business, be prepared for it to become an integral part of your life, as well as that of everyone close to you—your best friends and your family. You have to be ready for that.

If a woman asks herself, "Who do I think I am to do this business?" Patsy retorts she is somebody with a great idea! Of all the entrepreneurs she's met, there's not one set prototype that she's seen as the personality necessary to be in business. However, the one important factor is believing in yourself. If you can believe in yourself and you want to be an entrepreneur, Patsy says you can be. That one belief makes you an entrepreneur in her mind. You may make $20,000 or a million dollars, but in any case it's all about bringing yourself to the table.

ONE DREAM INSPIRES ANOTHER

Now that you have learned about Patsy Rosenberg's story and the emergence of Cherry Brook Kitchen, it's time to reflect on how this story can inspire you in your quest for your entrepreneurial dream. Take some time to reflect on what you've just read and allow the following questions to guide you. Use your journal to take notes so that you can ground your understanding and learning for future reference.

1. What's a challenge you've faced in your life that has the seeds of an opportunity within it?
2. What expertise is right out there in the open within your extended family that you could take advantage of in starting a business?
3. Who in your life would you like to be a role model for?
4. Name three things you have in common with Patsy. How can these common threads help you?
5. What collateral do you have that could be turned into an asset for a business?

WHAT CAN YOU LEARN FROM PATSY ROSENBERG?

Patsy Rosenberg turned a seeming life-threatening issue into a crusade to help other people with allergies. Her business evolved out of her value of celebration and the compassion she had for helping others, especially children, who were denied the simple joys in life of being able to share cakes and cookies with others at events with family and friends.

Her passion stirred her on to making a contribution and a difference, but she demonstrated a capacity to think things through when she moved her initial idea of a bakery into a more easily distributed goal of selling dessert mixes. She has an ability to look beyond immediate hurdles to ways in which her ideas can work.

Patsy also has a commitment to high standards and making sure that if she is going to do something, she does it right. A number of places showed up in which she could have been persuaded to cut corners, but she adamantly stood her ground.

She knew how to solicit help from others and actually had the good fortune of having people in her very family who could help her. She was willing also to ask for help every step of the way.

When the work became almost too much, Patsy found ways to renew her passion for the business. She was also willing to take calculated risks

Patsy was determined to teach herself what she didn't know. She did a lot of improvising, but she didn't seem to mind. She also didn't shy away from the hard work she had to put in to see her dream become a reality. Besides creating a profitable business with a meaningful mission, Patsy Rosenberg learned, like many scrappy startup women, how much more she could be as the business called the best of her to come forth.

YOUR TURN NOW—WHAT DID *YOU* LEARN FROM PATSY'S STORY?

CHAPTER 4

NO MONDAYS CLOTHING DESIGNS

A Conversation with Ingrid Matagne, Founder of No Mondays Clothing Designs for Girls (www.nomondayskids.com)

If you can DREAM it, you can DO it.

—*Walt Disney*

Any time can be the right time if you are ready for it.

—*Ingrid Matagne*, founder of No Mondays Clothing Designs for Children

Imagine traveling to a distant country, integrating yourself into a new culture, and biding your time until you could get back to your craft that you loved. It takes time to get situated, yet being a stay-at-home mother, there's much to be done caring for your offspring. Pushing a career ever to the back burner seems to be practically justified. Yet opportunity may appear sooner than you anticipated when the passion is irrepressible.

Ingrid Matagne had worked as a fashion designer in her native home of Belgium, but had given up her career to marry an American electronic engineer and emigrate to the United States around the turn of the twenty-first century. Now, with her children getting older, she was ready to start her own children's wear line, especially because she couldn't find clothes she liked for her daughter to wear.

She started No Mondays in earnest in 2007 when her daughter was 9 years old and her son five and a half. She saw her entrepreneurial venture allowing her to marry her interests with her ability, still being available for her children as she worked from home.

Ingrid claims it's easier to start a clothing design business in the United States than it would have been in Belgium. If she were still there, she probably wouldn't have taken the plunge because of the many barriers she would have faced. Many taxes need to be paid up front in Belgium, even before starting a business. Because of this, it takes considerably more money to start a business there than it does in the United States. Abroad there are few networks of support and little business startup help; entrepreneurs are entirely on their own as she sees it.

By contrast, to start her company in California, all Ingrid needed was a business license from city hall. She got her license, a seller's permit, declared a business name, and she was in business. All that remained was opening a business account with a local bank.

Ingrid was confident in her design skills. She had started working in fashion in Belgium with a well-known designer. He had created a small line of high-end women's wear—very haute couture and very beautiful. She had worked for him for 4 years, developing his line with him. As a result, she had become involved in every aspect of the work, which gave her a strong foundation as a designer. It was demanding, yet fun because she was able to go to Paris at least twice a year.

She had been interested in fashion ever since she was 16 years old. In those days she knew the French and Italian designers, the names of all the top models, and was up to date on everything. In school she only wanted to create and play with fabric, but in truth she recognized that she truly learned her craft once she collaborated with a designer.

Now, many years later, Ingrid was able to bring her unique flair to her own clothing line, which is decidedly European. Even if people don't know where she's from, they often remark how European her fashions look. They are distinctly different creations than what American designers produce, offering her an individual look and advantage.

A PURPOSEFUL FOCUS ON A MARKET NICHE

Ingrid has deliberately focused on designing for girls and not for women, especially because the field for adult design is so big and so competitive. She had sensed a need for tween designs, from age 7 to 14, particularly because of her experience with her daughter and feedback she's received from store owners who specialize in this age group, who find difficulty locating new and interesting clothing for their customers.

Ingrid targets fashion-forward parents who themselves are highly aware of dressing stylishly and wanting to mimic such style in their children. Many live in New York City and range in age between 30 and 40 years old. Such people have existed in Europe for years. Ingrid proudly counts herself among these people and so enjoys providing value to them.

She knows this unique style is not for everyone, though, especially because American mothers often prefer to dress their tweens in "girlie, frou frou clothes," in no way compatible with her own style. She's banking on those parents who *do* value her designs to provide enough of a niche to gain a foothold in the market. Of support to Ingrid has been a French female mentor living in New York who herself created a successful line of children's wear that is decidedly European.

The spark for the name of the business, No Mondays, came from a line printed on her daughter's clothing. At the time, Ingrid imagined she would start her business with a collection of children's loungewear. As she was putting her daughter to sleep one night, her eye caught the sayings on her daughter's pajamas: "sleeping beauty," "I need my beauty sleep," as well as, "I don't do Mondays." When she considered that last line, a light bulb went off. Kids don't want to go back to school on Mondays—that's a perfect name for a business for children's clothing! The response to the name has been great.

Ingrid had originally hoped to create lounge wear for girls, but as a designer she has learned that what emerges often is not what is intended:

You just design and you sketch and you sketch and you sketch. And I noticed that my mind was switching and was going just to urban clothes and then coming back to lounge wear and then urban clothes; and I said, "No, I don't want to do lounge wear obviously, I want to do something else." That's how it happened.

Her clothing has evolved into an urban line. She has retained her idea of using cotton jersey, however, determined to provide stylish yet comfortable clothing for children. Her two lines have comprised items in multiple colors with up to 11 items in each. She's followed her instinct in developing her clothing rather than making an analytical study of the market. She trusts her instincts implicitly.

GETTING DOWN TO BUSINESS

Secure in her ability to design, Ingrid at first was green on the business side of No Mondays. Consequently, she had to teach herself this aspect by doing research, going to workshops, and asking many questions of her accountant. Participation in several business and fashion networks has proven useful as well.

Two years into No Mondays, her business is still quite small, having finished the second season, which is the spring and summer lines for 2009. It can take anywhere from a season to several seasons until customers start recognizing a brand and business really starts picking up. It depends on exposure and acceptance of the designs.

As we've seen with every scrappy startup dreamer we've met, entrepreneurism means hard work. This story is no exception. Much sweat goes into designing a line of clothing and ensuring that it's interesting. At the same time, a designer must be mindful that others will be producing the items, so she needs to keep them uncomplicated. Simplicity also reduces the expense of manufacturing, so it's important to streamline the equation at every step along the way.

Once the design is determined, Ingrid must find sources for fabrics, trims, and patterns; whatever appears on the garment has to be found. Ingrid attends trade shows and does much research online to find her materials. This too takes much time.

Because No Mondays is still a small operation, Ingrid is challenged with needing to purchase minimum quantities of materials, which are at times beyond her economic reach. Consequently, she must negotiate with manufacturers to obtain the fabrics she wants to use. This requirement is both taxing and time consuming.

Fortunately, she deals mainly with U.S. manufacturers, primarily located in the Bay area—no more than 40 minutes from home. That's convenient and important for maintaining control of the production process, especially in the beginning. So many problems can occur in the production, and even the sampling process, necessitating the designer to be on hand to attend to them. Off-shore manufacturing presents minimum quantity issues as well as the necessity of hiring a manager to oversee the process. A designer can't be sure of the skill level of such a person, nor can she count on that person taking the job as seriously and personally as she might. Ingrid is grateful she lives in proximity to appropriate facilities for her business.

When it comes to promoting her line of clothing, Ingrid has realized she needs to rely on others. It's difficult to mix designing and other business demands with promoting a line as well, although at the initial stages she did conduct some door-to-door connecting with her target market. At first she went to San Francisco to meet the boutique store owners and introduce them to her line.

But as she moved further into her business, she couldn't continue that activity. A clothing line is seasonal, and every four to five months she needs to come up with a new line. Spending time designing means cutting back on other activities.

Ingrid has found some reliable showroom and road representatives to market her line. She has also been able to post her clothing on specialized Web sites, found by viewing competitors' Web sites.

Ingrid's daughter, Mara has become her "fit model," a person who handily tries on clothing to demonstrate what it looks like on a true human form. She also offers important advice to Ingrid, informing her when the pockets are too low for kids, for example, reminding Mom that children have small arms. Mara raves about the items she loves, insisting she wear the clothing on the spot and sharing her enthusiasm of the designs with her friends, thus helping to promote the business in her own way.

KNOWING WHETHER SHE IS ON THE RIGHT TRACK

Anyone who knows for sure when she starts a business that she's going to succeed is kidding herself, Ingrid insists. Certainty is not assured, even if this is a woman's field and even if she's been in business before. Too many unexpected events can occur.

At the same time, entrepreneurs can bank on their passion for their dream pushing them along so that they can handle more than they might originally imagine. What's important is taking whatever is facing you now and tackling it, without thinking about what will occur in the future. Wonder about that later.

I knew for the clothing part that I could pull that off easily, because it's what I do and I have experience here. And for the business part, my idea was ok, I'm here to learn in the same time. I'll try to make as few mistakes as I can. We'll see. You have to be open minded.

Any time is the right time to launch a business only if you are really obsessed by your idea and have done your research, this entrepreneur believes. Yet, it's important also to know that you can over prepare, postponing your entry, thinking you're not certain or you have to know more. This dynamic can be a delaying tactic. At some point you simply have to take the plunge and start.

FACING BARRIERS

Ingrid has had to confront many barriers as she grows her business. Daily she's faced with the problem of making minimum purchases. Generally she can't buy two zippers; she has to buy 100. It's not that a zipper is too costly, but when she adds up all her expenses, she can be overwhelmed if she has to buy in quantity.

She'll try to negotiate or see if she can get a higher price per unit or yards as in the case of fabric. She's forever trying to find a way to deal with her restrictions. Often manufacturers are willing to be flexible with her in hopes of getting continued business. Frankly, she finds it easier to deal with American companies than those abroad to achieve customized arrangements. All of this creative maneuvering takes its toll because she must spend considerable time focused on getting what she needs on a limited budget.

Money has been a challenge from the beginning because Ingrid started her business on a shoestring. Daily she's reminded of what she can't do because of being undercapitalized. That's hard, especially in the fashion industry. She imagines a service business allows faster sales to be made. In her case, she has to rely on seasons, when there is a defined period in which she makes most of her money when the orders come in. However, she has to pay her suppliers prior to that. What's hard for Ingrid is that she has to lay out money ahead of time.

Her initial investment of her own money was $10,000, which she insists was not enough to start this kind of business. But she's determined to make the best of the situation, doing as much as she can herself to save money. She takes advantage of as many free forms of advertising or marketing as she can find; marketing is a necessary element in the success of her business. Fortunately, the Internet has opened many avenues to gain free exposure, and she takes every opportunity to use it.

Yet learning to market herself remains a challenge for Ingrid. She sees it, frankly, as her biggest issue. Although some people enjoy being visible, she does not. Ingrid has to make an effort to reach out because she's by nature an introvert. She reminds herself it's not her but her business on the line. And she realizes people want to meet the clothing designer, so she does her best to go to trade shows and local events often.

A WOMAN WITH PASSION ADVISES OTHER WOMEN WITH DREAMS

Ingrid's definition of success is keeping a balance between her time with business and her family life. She admits she's not where she wants to be, but she's making progress.

She doesn't have to put much energy into sustaining her passion for her business because it's a constant. Her passion never leaves her because it's been growing for many years. She can spend hours getting lost in her designs.

As Ingrid imagines her future 10 to 20 years from now, she sees herself proud about how her business has been a solution and how many people she's been able to employ. She sees herself reminiscing about her first season, laughing about how she started her business in her garage. She hopes No Mondays will be a household brand by then, but she doesn't put too much energy into thinking about that. If it happens, she says, "Why not? It will be very, very nice!"

Ingrid Matagne echoes the chorus of every other scrappy startup dreamer we've met so far: if you have a dream, you are absolutely the right person to go after that entrepreneurial vision. If you've nurtured your passion over many years, or you just dreamed your idea up yesterday, in your mind you've already made it. Just follow through. Your passion about your product or service provides all the necessary expertise you need. That makes you the right person for the job.

ONE DREAM INSPIRES ANOTHER

Now that you have learned about Ingrid Matagne's story and the emergence of No Mondays Clothing Designs for Girls, it's time to reflect on how this story can inspire you in your quest for your entrepreneurial dream. Take some time to reflect on what you've just read and allow the following questions to guide you. Use your journal to take notes so that you can ground your understanding and learning for future reference.

1. What trends are out there that you are most intrigued about?
2. How could what you studied in school be the foundation for a business?
3. What's the business dream you have been harboring for many years?
4. What aspects of Ingrid's story do you find inspiring to you?
5. Ten to twenty years from now, what would you like to be known for?

WHAT CAN YOU LEARN FROM INGRID MATAGNE?

Ingrid offers a grand example of someone who has fanned the flames of her dream, keeping it sacred until she could act on it. In spite of the cultural differences she faced in her new country, she sprang into action at the moment she could, mindful of the advantage of doing business in the United States.

She was willing to stretch her comfort zone on behalf of her dream, engaging in activities that are not among those she favors. Although she's been challenged by being so undercapitalized, she's done what she's had to do to negotiate effectively with manufacturers. She's not letting any difficulty get in her way.

Ingrid has also used her support system effectively, calling on those both here and in Belgium to egg her on. She's relied also on mentors along the way, gaining guidance as she's needed it.

From Ingrid we learn the importance of holding the vision, of seeing where you want to be 10 or 20 years down the road. And although she has a passion for her vision, she also holds it lightly in her hand, recognizing there may be untold surprises along the way. She's ready for them.

YOUR TURN NOW—WHAT DID *YOU* LEARN FROM INGRID'S STORY?

— CHAPTER 5 —

APRON ELEGANCE

A Conversation with Rachel Hart, Founder of Apron Elegance and Gift an Apron (www.apron-elegance.com and www.GiftAnApron.com)

Don't be afraid of the space between your dreams and reality. If you can dream it, you can make it so.

—*Belva Davis*

Maybe you hear this a lot, but the business I started is actually me. It is a reflection of me.

What my dream was, when I step back, it wasn't to be a novelist, it was to be creative. It was to master something. I knew I would never master writing. Not the way that I wanted to. I wanted to be a Steinbeck, but I just didn't have it. And this, I can master an apron and walk away from it and say, "Wow, I just created something that didn't exist. I took it to its ultimatele level and somebody wants it."

—*Rachel Hart*, founder of Apron Elegance

Sir Ken Robinson, author of *The Element* (Viking, 2009) suggests that our ambitions are often compromised by personal restraints, cultural blocks, and family proscriptions. Imagine being the first in your family to graduate from college, being well on your way to a successful career in advertising and as a novelist, and walking away from it all to work at Starbucks! Starbucks literally saved son of privilege Michael Gates's life (*How Starbucks Saved My Life*, Gotham, 2008), but it provided Rachel Hart with nearly as much when she became a barista. The all-important health insurance Starbucks offered her as a well as a boss who wanted to promote her talents created a platform on which to launch her dream of creating unique and elegant aprons.

Rachel Hart demonstrates her love for people by cooking and entertaining. In her extended tribe, tradition was to partake of huge weekend meals served at her grandmother's house, where as many as 20 to 30 people congregated. With these fond memories in her soul and a mixture of Cherokee blood in her DNA, 36-year-old Rachel and her Irish husband Justus set out to replicate the ritual in their own home. Together they would host gatherings as often as twice a week for 10 to 12 people, encouraging guests to bring their friends.

A UNIQUE PATH TO A BUSINESS

More than three years ago, Rachel went looking for an apron to wear while entertaining that reflected the joyous energy she felt while preparing her large meals. Coming up empty on her quest, she resolved to sew one herself. Relying only on her semesters of junior high sewing, she invested in a sewing machine and ordered a collection of vintage 1940s patterns from eBay. With tears and frustration at having forgotten more about sewing than she remembered, she persisted until she had created a garment she could wear proudly:

It just took me a little bit longer to get started than I thought. But finally I conquered it and then I was a monster. These things started to take on their own personality.

They were no longer for cooking. They just got frillier and more feminine with satin, taffeta, and lace. People started to notice. In the back of my mind, maybe like many women do, when the idea first hit me, I thought, "I bet this would be a fabulous thing to sell." I didn't quite have the confidence to announce to the world this is my business idea.

As women filtered in and out of her house, they'd ask Rachel if she could make them an apron too. Or would she make one as a gift for a friend of theirs? Requests started trickling in.

Ironically, Rachel's domestic forays into cooking and sewing were in defiance of her mother, who had barred her from the kitchen as a child. As a woman who came of age in the 1960s and supported equality and basic rights for females in the workplace, her mother was concerned her daughter would end up a housewife, not utilizing the hard-won gains of her own generation.

Yet being among a new cohort of women who may not have reached equality, but have at least reclaimed their power, Rachel wanted to assert her femininity. Ironically, this urge may also be the impetus behind the interest in vintage aprons among those in their twenties and thirties.

As the oldest child in her family, Rachel conformed to expectations of her. Like many women, she was a people pleaser. But while staying within the norms, she had experienced some unusual turns anyway. Wanting to become a novelist, she had taken a class from a Pulitzer Prize winner and had spent three years writing for as many as six hours a day. At one point she had considered obtaining a Ph.D. In the long run, however, she decided this would not be the life for her.

At the time Rachel was experimenting with her aprons she was working as an account coordinator for a Duluth, Minnesota, advertising agency. She had followed this path after pursuing a dual major in journalism and speech and then a master's in rhetoric communication. Hers was a demanding job that had her "just flying every day" for 10 or 12 hours. For her it was a stressful, corporate environment, and she was tired of working so hard for other people.

I think a lot of people get to that point where they say, "I can't complain about my salary, because I know I'm making it better than most, but I want a future that's as fantastic as the effort that I'm putting into It."

Rachel had reached a stage in her job where she knew something had to change. She decided to start a business with her aprons, but she needed some training wheels first. So she quit her advertising job and went to work for Starbucks, which offered the all-important health insurance, even at 20 hours a week, and a chance to start her business designing and selling elegant aprons. Consequently, she calls herself a Starbucks startup.

Surprisingly, working for Starbucks during the two years she was there was among the most fun jobs Rachel has ever had. Her boss was supportive and encouraging, and with her tip money, Rachel bought fabric.

SUMMONING HER RESOURCES AND TALENTS

Her days, however, were grueling and long, although she didn't see them as negative. She'd start work before 5 AM when the store opened, put in a full day, and then come home and get right on the sewing machine. And it took Rachel a good 15 months of sewing, getting her "chops" on the machine, until she was satisfied that she had a viable product. She was relentless about mastering her skills and design and achieving her vision.

When all of that clicked my boss at Starbucks said, "Hey, why don't you put up a display of your art? This is as significant as painting or drawing or photography." I said ok, and so we did it and literally that was the match; people were curious, what is this? They didn't understand it, but they loved it and they wanted to touch it.

Even with all this early positive feedback about her aprons, Rachel was not certain she could succeed. But she happens to be a person with a strong faith. She believes adamantly that if you do the work, then God will take you to the next step.

Rachel claims that had she not been on a path of faith and had greater expectations about outward results, she wouldn't be where she is. If she judged her progress by worldly standards of what is important and valuable, she never would have considered taking her job at Starbucks, which led to her ability to start her business. As a matter of fact, when her father learned of her decision to leave her well-paying job, he called to ask her if she were on drugs!

Besides her faith, Rachel credits her ability to pursue her passion to having a talent of discipline. Each time she has discovered a new means through which to direct her creative energies, she has poured herself into it. When she steps back and takes a metaview of her life, she realizes that her dream was not so much to become a novelist but to be creative, to master something.

Ironically enough, Rachel has applied some of the very techniques she learned in novel writing to her apron designing. She has affection for narrative; she was on the speech team in college and coached competitive speaking, actively participating in forensics. Today she approaches her work from a narrative perspective:

I put the fabric on the table and I look at the fabric and the fabric looks at me and then starts to tell me a story about what it wants to be. I rarely sketch things out in the beginning—although I do, especially for clients, especially if I'm creating couture aprons especially for them. But letting go of expectations—all the things people say about flow or that main space.

HUMAN SUPPORT HELPS AS WELL

Besides her cheerleading boss at Starbucks, Rachel has received support from many others. Among the primary people has been a local photographer who has not charged Rachel for many of the services she's provided, resulting in a professional look in all her marketing materials.

Another important player has been a public relations specialist in Washington, D.C., who was among Rachel's high school friends when growing up in Kansas. Her friend has been instrumental in gaining exposure for the apron designer in key publications such as McClatchy Company newspapers as well as a stint on Donnie Deutsche's *Big Idea* television show in October 2008, prior to its cancellation later that year. All of this publicity enabled Rachel to have a rollicking, successful Christmas season, in spite of the doom and gloom in the economy.

Rachel's greatest support, obviously, has come from her husband Justus, an entrepreneur himself in a packaging business for trucking materials. Whenever she gets stressed out about her business, he reminds her that if she is bringing in more than she is spending, she's doing well. Everything else will work itself out. He's her voice of sanity.

What Justus also offers Rachel is an ability to listen to her problems without tying to fix them for her.

I've got to tell you. The first things I sewed. It was like trying to put a tutu on a pig! They [the aprons] weren't pretty.

WHAT IT TAKES TO BE AN ENTREPRENEUR

Rachel never imagined how hard she would be working in her business, yet it has been a labor of love. It's not just the sheer amount of hours she works, but it's the amount of coordination, problem solving, and decision making she must go through daily that amazes her. She realizes this effort may be a good reason why not everyone chooses to become an entrepreneur.

She's also learned that being an entrepreneur today requires a minimum level of professionalism in every aspect of the business. If you have a Web site, it can't look homemade. If you've got a tag on a garment, it has to look professional. As a manufacturer, wholesaler, and online retailer, Rachel has to present herself professionally within each of these three distinct operations.

Fortunately, technology allows for greater exposure and more specific targeting, evening out the playing field between big organizations and little ones. But it also demands fast turnaround. People used to take orders over the phone, promising to ship in a matter of weeks. Now customers expect results instantly.

Rachel's mother at one time disparaged her daughter's sewing as being beneath the level of someone possessing a master's degree. Yet Rachel believes her educational underpinning and business background have been foundational for her in her business. She doubts that she could have become an entrepreneur without the level of savvy accumulated through her learning and commercial history.

Rachel looks back in particular to when she was a coach for a speech team, traveling continuously while coaching daily. At the same time she was carrying a full load of classes and was teaching a freshman public-speaking class. The energy it took to coordinate all of that and the demand on her while attempting to perform at a high level academic level while conducting original research taught Rachel she was capable of more than she thought. She draws on this knowledge about herself daily in her business.

The flip side for Rachel has been restraining her otherwise stickler tendencies:

I tend to be a perfectionist. So I had to make a deal with myself and this would probably to the outside world sound funny, but I call it 70%. If I give 100%, then there's not one flaw in it in my mind. I could say, oh, you know I could hand dye all of my fabrics. Wouldn't that be great? Then I could [do] what I think of what I'm capable of doing. I suddenly have something that is impossible to deliver to the customer.

Rachel decided she would NOT pursue everything in her business to the extent that she could. Her "70%" rule protected her from the tendency that bogs down many entrepreneurs: if I can't do it perfectly, I won't do it all. It allowed her to pursue her dream, rather than spin her wheels. It also gave her a prescription she could use daily to steer herself away from her urge to perfect: 70% is my new 100%.

Rachel has had to relinquish much of the sewing of her garments to others. Although she started with haute couture aprons, charging $200 to $300 per item, the "sexy part of the brand" that brought people to her Web site, she has needed to offset these with a unique cotton line starting at $25.00 per apron. Whereas the expensive items have created a buzz for the business, the pedestrian aprons have brought in the revenue.

She hired five home-based women in Duluth, Minnesota, good Scandinavian stock with a strong work ethic, to manufacture the high-end garments, and she hired a representative in Shanghai to produce the affordable line. Although initially opposed to off-shoring, Rachel needed to bend to accommodate production costs, but she remains adamant that the cotton being used meet her specifications. Domestic sewing contractors double right before the holidays, when demand is at its peak, which is also when Rachel brings in 30% of her annual sales.

MONEY LESSONS

Rachel's husband taught her an important lesson in conducting business: don't spend money you don't have, even if this presents you with an uncomfortable situation. Actually, as her business has grown, hardship has come home to roost. She has literally taken over three rooms in her basement for designing and has been working her way upstairs, eyeing the dining room table as a potentially great place for cutting material!

Not paying rent somewhere has enabled Rachel to plow all her money back into her business. She's made do with machinery that's not top of the line. Fortunately, she has not had to make huge capital investments to get her business going.

Justus also advised her that one of the worst mistakes she could make would be to acquire retail space. Create the products, create the demand, and then consider retail space if that's what's warranted, he asserts. But frankly, with the Web as an alternative sales outlet, local bricks and mortar presence has been unnecessary.

He also advised her not to go after a small business loan. Don't buy for the sake of buying; that's the mistake that many entrepreneurs make. They accept money that they don't really need and then run the risk of digging themselves into a financial hole.

SUCCESS, PASSION, AND BALANCE

As with all other scrappy startup dreamers, Rachel has her own unique definition of success. For her it is making sure whatever she labors at aligns with her faith:

I'm not selling anything that's hurting anybody. I'm not cheating anybody out of anything. Everything about it aligns up with my faith and it's authentic to me.

A lot of people feel that the goal in life is to be happy and fulfilled. I feel like the goal in life for me is to stick to my core values and beliefs and to be authentic to myself and everything else will work itself out, because it's too uncomfortable for me to be outside either of those things.

What stands out in Rachel's prescription is her desire to be out in the world with her products in a way that resonates with her faith and her true sense of herself. Anything less would be missing the mark. Ironically, as she puts herself into her designs, her unique stamp does shine through and makes her products truly appealing. Who she is *is* what she does, which in turn leads to her success.

Rachel characterizes herself as a "nuclear reactor" for sustaining her passion. She's fervently curious, constantly innovating, and striving for what's next. Frankly, there's so much room in what she does to innovate that she never gets tired of her business, even at 10 to 12 hours a day. She gets physically spent, but she is so excited that she can't wait to wake up each day and start again. Every day is different.

As an entrepreneur, Rachel must be an agent of change. Yet in the beginning, she had to tolerate what was not changing. At first, nothing moves, time is spent simply exploring, getting in sync with the product before it is introduced to the world. She found it was important not to hurry that part, even though her tendency was not to be so patient. She believes many people give in too soon, rushing their product or business before it is ready.

ADVICE TO ASPIRING WOMEN ENTREPRENEURS

As a woman embracing her femininity and unafraid to include her domestic side, Rachel says the world isn't pink enough. Any woman who is getting her business out in the world is doing us all a great service. Many women have paved the way over the years to allow women to break out of the traditional roles they once held, so we owe it to them to do our part to bring our businesses into being.

Even so, Rachel cites Winston Churchill as an inspiring voice for women to consider when plunging into their business ventures:

Never, never, never, never, never give up! I just can't emphasize that enough. Because if you have aligned your passion and your skills with your vision, when you come out the other side of that you'll have something. It may not be the widget that you started out with, but you'll have something that the world finds interesting.

And at that point, you collaborate with the world. It becomes a dialogue. What do you think? Well, it's a little big. Ok, you take it home and you trim it. You dialogue a little more with the world. And it's the fear of rejection that prevents people from the dialogue.

Rachel turns to her master's thesis on vision and leadership, which taught her lessons she's brought to business. What she discovered is that leaders are people who can dialogue with the masses. They create a vision that catches fire. In a similar way, it's willingness to dialogue with customers that gets you the product that will sell.

If someone disputes what she is offering, she does not take it as rejection. She sees it as part of the exchange and sets out to modify her offer.

Rachel has demonstrated her own business philosophy in deciding to offer cotton aprons in addition to the taffeta ones she originally presented. She has taken a step further in the rhythm of her business by deciding also to put forward a home party format. She discovered almost by accident how much women coveted her aprons when they had a chance to touch them. She was invited to participate in an experiment with a Mary Kay representative and a chocolatier, collaborating in a successful Chocolate, Lipstick, and Aprons home party event. The success of this event has led her to wonder about new avenues for opportunities like those.

While she has explored collaborating with large companies to produce aprons that would be offered in much the same way companies offer home parties with Tupperware and other products, the alliances she's made to date have not worked to her satisfaction. Ever the optimist, Rachel is not discouraged. She knows that her dream will lead her in many new directions and she is willing to experiment with what those will be.

ONE DREAM INSPIRES ANOTHER

Now that you have learned about Rachel Hart's story and the emergence of Apron Elegance, it's time to reflect on how this story can inspire you in your quest for your entrepreneurial dream. Take some time to reflect on what you've just read and allow the following questions to guide you. Use your journal to take notes so that you can ground your understanding and learning for future reference.

1. What traditions have you inherited from your family?
2. What skill would you like to develop that you would doggedly stay with until you mastered it?
3. What role does your faith play in how you approach the world and business?
4. Whom do you know in your workplace who would champion your dreams?
5. What natural interests did you have in childhood that your parents discouraged you from because they ran counter to their ideals?

WHAT CAN YOU LEARN FROM RACHEL HART?

Rachel is our guide to starting a business based on knowing and living inherent values. She is our muse in defying the values of the outside world that say some work is more acceptable than other work, i.e., if higher education is required, the vocation is sanctioned, but handiwork isn't. She demonstrates a capacity to step away from work that is unfulfilling in favor of that which she was called to, literally by creating something out of nothing.

Her tenacity in teaching herself to sew, believing she could do so, and basing her whole business on an almost non-existent talent is truly admirable. She walks her talk in being determined never, ever to give up. Yet she has come to terms with her perfectionist tendencies and is willing to allow herself to operate at 70%, rather than 100%.

Listening to the counsel of her husband, Rachel reminds us of the importance of creating a demand for your product before spending money you don't have to sell more.

Rachel also teaches us an important lesson regarding the dance between having a vision and being willing to adapt that vision after receiving feedback from the world. Had she insisted that she produce only elegant aprons, she might not be enjoying the success she is having in these difficult economic times. Actually, she has allowed the times to create more of a market for her product, as people not accustomed to entertaining at home don her aprons. Her practicality in offering affordable cotton aprons has allowed her to grow beyond capacities she had initially dreamed.

YOUR TURN NOW—WHAT DID *YOU* LEARN FROM RACHEL'S STORY?

EXERCISING YOUR OWN DREAM MAGIC

Ok, now it's your turn to begin exercising your own scrappy startup dream magic muscles. You may not know where to begin. You may be thinking about all the barriers you face. All your gremlins may be popping out of the woodwork. To that I say, "Whoa, don't get ahead of yourself!" The courage chapter comes next. Let's take some time out here for dreaming. Take several deep breaths and a few steps back. I promise you, we'll get there. But you have to give yourself space to get to know yourself and begin to see what the possibilities could be—first things first.

Have you taken the time to answer the questions at the end of each of the women's stories in this first part of *Scrappy Startups*? Be sure to do so. I have included more questions for you to consider as well in this summary space for Section 1.

If you are the type of woman who does better when you have someone interacting with you, find a friend to sit down with you over a cup of coffee or tea to explore the questions. If you're into more virtual friendships, find someone to exercise this process of discovery over the phone, on your favorite social networking site, or with a video chat. Or hire a coach. If you're the type that does better alone than with someone else, set aside time to answer these questions by yourself.

It's important first of all to know yourself and how you like to operate. Shakespeare, as always, said it best, "To thine own self be true." But you absolutely must give yourself time to explore yourself and your dreams. If you spring into action before you've given yourself this gift of getting to know yourself, you're apt to create a business that may be great but will not be *your* business. It also may not be as unique as it could be without your DNA stamp.

FINDING YOUR PASSION, VALUES, STRENGTHS, AND PURPOSE

Passions

Going back to the center of the Magic Approach Venn diagram, where you consider the passion, values, strengths, and purpose underpinning, who you are is the very heart of the matter of finding the foundation for your business. Don't quibble with language here. Perhaps your word may not be passion—maybe it's what interests you or what captures your imagination. Nancy Gruver found hers to be about keeping young girls whole as they entered adolescence. Bev Halisky discovered she wanted older people and disabled people to be given the dignity they deserved. Patsy Rosenberg noticed how celebrations were important to her and that food became a means to express that. Ingrid Matagne knew from a young age that she loved to design clothing. Rachel Hart actually found her passion in defying her mother's own dreams—Rachel loved to express her domestic talents.

As you can see from these women's stories, we vary much in the time periods in which we make our discoveries about ourselves. Some find early on what their passions are. Others can wait a lifetime. Passions or interests can also be expressed in different ways. There's no right or wrong here, just uniqueness.

Sometimes you can find the threads of your passions from your earliest memories. It's ironic. Do we remember this early memory because it says much about who we are, or is who we are an outgrowth of the imprint the early memory has on us?

Clients of mine have found passions in everything from discovering hidden treasures to fascination with herbs. You name it; they've been interested in it. Sometimes it's a matter of putting several unusual interests together such as acting and travel or love for animals and music. Don't be afraid to combine interests that seemingly have nothing in common with each other.

Spend a week, or a month, studying yourself as an anthropologist might. Don't take anything for granted. Look at how you live, what you like to eat, who you tend to invite into your life. Everything you uncover could be a clue to your interests and passions.

Whatever you do, however, don't judge your passions. Don't put a lid on them. Don't think them silly or out of step or judge them in any way. After all, great anthropologists don't judge, they just observe.

Here are some more questions designed to help you develop clues about your passions:

1. What section(s) in a bookstore are you naturally drawn to? Why?
2. What's easy for you?
3. What would you do for free because you enjoy it so much?
4. What would you miss most about life if you were suddenly to die tomorrow?
5. What would you do if you knew you couldn't fail?

In the resources section of this book you'll find many more books and Internet information for finding your passions, values, strengths, and purpose.

Values

Next, take stock of what you value. It's been said, if you want to know what you value, take a look at how you spend your money and your time. What's important to you? What do you get angry about when it's not met?

Among my values are gaining insights—I call them my "ahas." I also value egalitarianism—no one is really better than anyone else, and we all deserve an opportunity to be heard and valued. So what am I writing about? Scrappy startups, not high-on-the-hog businesses—you can see my values inherent in the subjects I'm including in this book.

Some people value variety; others prefer stability. Meaning seems to be a value coveted by many people today. They want their days to be loaded with importance. Some people want to be acknowledged by others; they crave recognition for themselves and their work.

Your values will lead you to places in which you want to invest your time and money and will have great impact on your business. Nancy Gruver of New Moon appears to have an egalitarian value too. Otherwise, why would she invest herself in a magazine in which the girls run the editorial board? If she valued experience more than egalitarianism, she might have insisted adults be in charge of her magazine, and its uniqueness would indeed have been lost. Her passion provided the "what" and her value guided her in the "how" of her business.

You might be familiar with the process of choosing values from a list someone gives you. Doing so may tempt you into selecting values you *think* you should have, rather than ones that are truly aligned with who you are at your core. Better to think of those times in your life when you felt fully satisfied and consider what was going on. The more aligned you are with what fulfills you, the closer you will come to your values. Likewise, when you uncover what makes you angry, what makes the world not right, you'll find where your values are being dishonored.

Here are some additional questions to lead you to your values:

1. What would stand out to some who didn't know you well about how you spend your time and money? What would be most apparent?
2. If you were to reincarnate as an animal, what animal would you want to be and why?
3. When in your life have you been most satisfied? What were the circumstances?

Be careful of your faux values. It's important to be honest about yourself about your values. If you spend much time and money shopping, for example, you may not actually value consumerism. This could be a faux value that's hiding something more important to you. Be clear with yourself what the motivation is behind what you are doing. For some people, shopping is not what they value, but they love being out among other people, or they love color and texture and newness. Remember, we're on the hunt for what fulfills you.

Strengths

Marcus Buckingham has become an evangelist for people identifying their strengths. Perhaps you caught his visit on Oprah. If not, be sure to go to iTunes and download the free podcast of the *Take Control of Your Work and Life* program he conducted with Oprah.

As a researcher at the Gallup Organization, Buckingham and his colleagues have analyzed results of interviews conducted by Gallup of over 1.7 million employees from 101 companies representing 63 countries. In his strengths books, starting with *Now Discover Your Strengths* (The Free Press, 2001), Buckingham lays out 34 strengths that were commonly identified in his research. You can take a special code to the Internet and identify your top five strengths when you follow this course, which is included in the price of one of the related books.

Among my top strengths, according to his model, are ideation, input, and positivity. What this means is that I am oriented around appreciating new ideas (ideation); enjoy collecting things such as recipes, Web sites, books, podcasts, and business ideas (input); and am generous with praise (positivity). If I build my work and my life around my strengths, I'll find more ease.

Besides identifying your strengths using Buckingham's method, there are other ways to find your strengths. Again, your life holds clues.

Think about a story that's told in your family about you when you were a child. The tale may reveal some of your distinctive and quirky qualities as well as your strengths.

In my case, I'm told I used to fall asleep, standing up with my eyes open so I wouldn't miss anything. This was an early indication that I love to sweep the environment around me, taking in what's going on. This is actually how I collect information today and gives me the strength of input, as Buckingham calls it. No wonder I would write a book in which I collected stories about successful women! The process is aligned with one of my top strengths.

You might also send out an email request to people who have worked with you, friends and family who have played with you, or people who have served on volunteer committees with you and ask them to identify your top three to five strengths. Such an informal survey could bear useful fruit.

Businesses for years have been conducting what are called SWOT analyses. SWOT stands for strengths, weaknesses, opportunities, and threats. This technique is used to help organizations identify what is helpful and hurtful to them so that they can take the appropriate actions. You can take a page from this practice and identify your strengths as you begin to think of the business dream you are most disposed toward.

Try any and all of these approaches, and identify your top five strengths that you could employ in your scrappy startup.

Purpose

Steve Pavlina (www.stevepavlina.com) describes the simplest, most elegant way of arriving at your life purpose I've ever encountered. It demands that you get quiet and really do some soul searching; something we in this noisy, busy world really have to discipline ourselves to do. If you are willing to try this for 20–30 minutes, you can reap great benefits.

Open up a blank page on your computer screen or in your journal. At the top of the page, write the heading "My Life Purpose." Then start writing statements as they occur to you, without editing. Just listen to your heart and soul.

In the beginning you may get some standard answers pouring out as a reflection of cultural programming. Let yourself keep writing what occurs to you on the page. Keep going until what you write makes you cry. Then you have your life purpose! If you can be patient and quiet and listen to your inner guidance, you'll reap the rewards. I would encourage you to stop from time to time as you're engaging in this process and put your hand over your heart with your eyes closed—asking your heart to reveal your purpose to you. Be respectful and listen to the answer.

My life purpose that I arrived at with the help of a coach is this: bringing hope to the hopeful and reminding everyone they count. A longer version is the following: I share my own and others' learnings and discoveries, through writing and speaking, to bring hope to the hopeful and remind everyone they count. When I hold this book project up to this purpose statement, I have a direct match—no wonder I'm finding this project so satisfying!

Here are some additional questions to help you get at your purpose:

1. What is your sense of calling?
2. Where do you get the deepest sense of meaning in your life?
3. What is the impact you want to have? The difference you want to make?
4. If you achieve that, what will it give you?
5. And what will that give you?

PUTTING PASSION, VALUES, STRENGTHS, AND PURPOSE TOGETHER IN SERVICE OF A DREAM

All these elements work together to put substance behind what you want to do in the world as your business. A business based on these elements is truly united with who you are and therefore will be viably sustained. You will also discover the elements that will set you and your business apart from others in the world. Your combination of factors will be unique to you.

Give yourself the gift of discovering these aspects either by taking time away by yourself or by working with a friend, mentor, or coach or all of these.

Really pay attention to what you find, and take these elements a step further to consider what dream business startup would emanate from this unique collection of factors. Again, share what you know about your passions, values, strengths and purpose with other people and ask them what unique business dream would naturally flow from this mix of you. Others might see the obvious that you can't see because you're too wrapped up in yourself. Professional coaches are truly trained to help people in this area, so if you can, take advantage of working with one.

COURAGE

It takes a lot of courage to release the familiar and seemingly secure, to embrace the new. But there is no real security in what is no longer meaningful. There is more security in the adventurous and exciting, for in movement there is life, and in change there is power.

—*Alan Cohen*

You gain strength, courage, and confidence by every experience in which you really stop to look fear in the face. You must do the thing which you think you cannot do.

—*Eleanor Roosevelt*

There's a stretch of highway, maybe 15 miles long, leading to Thompson Hill in Duluth, Minnesota, where at night looms a view of this jewel of a city on Lake Superior. At various periods throughout the year, however, weather conditions create a trough of moisture that hovers low, just above the road. The fog that results can be tremendously thick in many spots along the road way.

Often, I'll be driving home from a trip from Minneapolis only to meet this foggy patch just at the moment I'm tired and bedraggled. All I want to do is get home and crawl into bed. Instead, I find myself white knuckled and wondering if I should pull over on the shoulder and wait the night out.

Trouble is, when this happens the fog is so thick I can't even begin to know where the side of the road is. I have no other choice it seems but to keep driving. So I slow down, move ahead, and hope for the best. At just the point where I've had it, I'm often greeted with a lifting of the moisture, and all at once there's a clear path ahead. Now I feel like I'm home free. What was I worried about? I start to relax and congratulate myself for staying the course.

And then again the fog thickens and I'm back in the soup. This can go on and on, over and over again. It's a trying experience.

I've often seen this episode as a metaphor for the courage it takes to step into the unknown. I see the patches of fog as fear and the clear spots as times we come through the fear. It takes courage to keep moving ahead.

WHAT IS COURAGE?

When voters at Yahoo Answers responded to a question asking what constitutes courage, they chose to express it as doing what was right, even when doing so would not produce as positive results as doing what was expedient. They also saw courage as putting personal goals aside while dedicating yourself to bettering the world. Courage, to respondents, included realizing your life's mission, taking a first step, and getting up again after being knocked down hard. Many saw courage as taking a stand for the future, even when your past makes that difficult.

When we apply the circumstance of starting a business to having the courage to do so, we recognize there is just no way around it— starting a business demands courage of us. We must take some chances. We must face the risk of failing. To a large extent, we train ourselves to do what we must to face our fears.

Especially in these economic times, we are asking much of ourselves when we consider putting our financial destiny in our own hands. And yet, in reality, we always have our future in our own hands. Anything else is false security. Imagine the dismay of the Detroit auto workers who thought they would be taken care of for life with their pensions and healthcare. How secure are they today?

Ironically, in some ways self-employed people may be more secure today than their corporate employed counterparts. Self-employed people rely on multiple streams of income; corporate employed people generally rely on one.

When you read the five scrappy startup stories ahead, you'll encounter women who have taken calculated risks to achieve their business dreams. Every one participated in courageous acts to launch and sustain her business. You'll find women who defied family traditions, family proscriptions, health problems, death, and war to bring their businesses, which contribute to the betterment of the world, into reality.

Stand in their shoes. Ask yourself what you would do. Use their shoulders to rest on as you consider the strength and confidence you must muster to make your business dreams come true.

CHAPTER 6

SOUNDS TRUE

A Conversation with Tami Simon, Founder of Sounds True (www.soundstrue.com)

All serious daring starts from within.

—*Harriet Beecher Stowe*

I can't fit into the game, so I'm going to make a new game.

—*Tami Simon*, founder of Sounds True

What do you do when you don't find your place in the larger culture? How do you find your way back to life when you defy the straight and narrow, tried and true paths? What can you do in the United States to succeed at life without the requisite college degree? How do you find your calling with the loud din of *shoulds* and *oughts* swirling around you? These are some of the questions young Tami Simon faced in the early 1980s as a young adult.

Imagine coming from a comfortable upper-middle-class family, where your father was a lawyer. Your parents sent you to Swarthmore College, but you don't fit the norm and feel the urge to leave after 2 years. Your own interests and curiosity about the world are stronger than the confines of the life around you, and you must be off on your own journey.

Such was Tami Simon's plight as she traces the roots of her successful media business founded in 1985. What looks courageous to us was a natural evolution for a young woman who needed to travel to India to listen to the unique language through which her soul spoke to her. She had been a religious studies major, learning about the lives of the mystics. But she concluded that any great mystic worth her salt wouldn't get a degree in mysticism; she would need to live the life of a mystic.

So Tami left the States to travel in India, Sri Lanka, and Nepal for a year, not knowing what she was going to do with her life. Actually, she was quite lost. She wanted to get "under the root of the root of my own being and of what wanted to come through me." She wanted to be of service and to use the talents she had been given. Like most young people, she was unsure within what domain she would exercise her gifts.

While in India, she attended intensive meditation retreats led by a Burmese meditation master and teacher named Goenka. During his 10-day Vapassina meditation retreats, Tami felt she had come home to her own being:

It was revelatory! For the first time I felt that it's actually possible to turn inward instead of turning outward and that there are techniques and reliable methods and approaches. And this really helps. I can actually ground myself, listen inward, find my own resources and from this place, anything is possible. These were the thoughts I was having: I'll do anything to make these kinds of methods and teachings available to other people.

These thoughts became a prayer that lived inside her being when she visited various temples and participated in full moon ceremonies, where she would prostrate herself, face planted downward into the earth with her arms above her. She would implore, "May I somehow be shown and given a way to bring these kinds of ideas to more people." She had a sense even then that she was seed planting.

Upon returning home, Tami did not want to continue college, but when her father implored her to do so from his hospital bed after suffering two heart attacks, she agreed at least to have a conversation with the Dean of the Religion Department at Swarthmore. Upon hearing her interests, however, the religious studies professor related,

"You know Tami, you don't belong at Swarthmore." Tami was relieved to hear his pronouncement and left.

Swarthmore is situated on the outskirts of Philadelphia, and Tami found herself aimlessly walking the streets of the city, asking herself what she was going to do. After a year of meditation, she was mentally in a very different place:

Having spent a year in India, I wasn't talking very much. I wasn't in an achiever mindset. I was still very much in the timeless realm.

Tami came upon a sign for a meditation room, part of something she didn't know, called Dharmadhatu, but she decided to enter and see if she could meditate there anyway. Greeters inside asked her to wait, and while doing so she noticed brochures about Naropa University:

I thought, "What is this?—you can study meditation and psychology?—that's so cool! Being in the mountains of Boulder reminded me of my experience in Nepal, which was important and even formative for me. At that time Naropa was not an accredited college, but I was continuing to think along the lines of, "Ok I'm going to go out to Boulder; I'll go to Naropa. This will make my parents happy."

With that, Tami moved to Boulder, Colorado, a place she found she liked. But she found that she still couldn't be in school, even an alternative university such as Naropa. She simply had a strong need to set out on her own. She alerted her parents she wouldn't be attending school, and they refused to provide any more financial support. She saw this as fair, so she took a job as a waitress and fulfilled herself hosting a volunteer radio show on community radio station KGNU.

Having seen her life to that point being one designed for academia, even having considered becoming a professor, Tami felt she had deviated from her life path:

I had decided to go to India to see what's true, what's real. It was as if I had begun a journey with only my knapsack and had jumped off the train of my life. My knees got a little bruised on the landing and I rolled over and I thought, "What the heck is going on?" And yet I felt compelled. Looking back, this was a journey I had to make.

Tami followed her intuition and continued with her life as she found it. On her radio program she interviewed various spiritual teachers and wisdom holders, such as Ram Dass, who happened to pass through Boulder, ironically furthering her education unconventionally.

At the rate of two requests per week, people started asking her for copies of her radio show. She used a small dubbing machine to duplicate recordings, earning $10 per cassette. To her, this wasn't a business; it was just something she did while waitressing and finding her way.

HER UNCONVENTIONAL MENTOR AND THE START OF HER BUSINESS

One of the people Tami interviewed, Czechoslovakian-born Jirka Ryssavy, had become a highly successful entrepreneur in Colorado. He started Corporate Express and later founded Gaiam, a publisher of many yoga videos. To her, he wasn't an entrepreneur but a curiosity.

She stumbled upon his store one night, noticing huge crystals in his window and a weird sign on the door, a yin yang symbol with a dollar sign through its center. It stood for Transecon, or transformational economy. Her curiosity was piqued.

Tami introduced herself, conducted a friendly chat, and invited Jirka to appear as a guest on her show discussing crystals. The more they conversed, the more Tami realized that this man actually was a sophisticated businessman who happened to have metaphysical interests.

Just at the time the two were becoming friends and meeting regularly, Tami's father died, leaving her an inheritance of $50,000. At 21 and idealistic, she didn't want to put the money in the bank, which might invest it in the military-industrial complex. Jirka urged her to put the money into herself, claiming, "Wherever you're putting your money is where you're putting your energy."

Tami thought that sounded like a great idea, but she didn't know "what me and my 'bad self' could do." He asserted she *did* know and requested she return in a few days with an answer.

She remembers walking from his office, having a strange whole body experience, feeling "this tingling thing going on."

I no longer felt myself walking entirely on the ground, but walking above it. It was a very weird experience. I then heard a voice that said, "Disseminate spiritual wisdom." I immediately began to question, "How was I going to do this?"

Tami weighed the thought of disseminating spiritual wisdom through books, recognizing that many people had published books quite successfully. She wondered how she could enter that world. However, she remembered having found reading laborious in college.

Then she considered video, but she had grown up in a family that watched a lot of television, which she viewed as numbing. Accordingly, she dismissed that medium as well. Then she thought of sound and her radio show, and she realized she loved sound, especially communication through dialogue.

In college I learned best when I was listening to a great teacher. I loved learning in this way so much—through deeply and actively listening—I would even go to extra lectures on campus after hours. I simply loved listening as a way of learning. It gradually became clear that if I am to disseminate spiritual wisdom, I should begin with audio.

People were already buying a few copies of her radio show each week. When Tami relayed this thought to Jirka, he was supportive and offered to rent an office to her. Sounds True was born.

At the time, Tami's expenses were minimal because she was living in a house with four others and didn't own a car. At 21, essentially she was still a kid. This business seemed like a noble experiment to her, one she could try for a couple of years to see where it would lead her. If it didn't work out, she could always get a job. That was about the size of her commitment.

Worst-case scenario, I'm back where I am right now. Best-case scenario, I've actually found a way to contribute using the talents that I have and I've created something unique and beneficial. It seems like there was significant upside and not much downside.

HER BUSINESS IDEA SOLIDIFIES

Tami felt she had been given much by her family and the world. She had a desperate need to give back and use her life effectively. She asked herself, "What does the world really need?"

The answer that came to her was that the world needs people to understand and be educated on the perennial truths of our interconnectedness; once that realization is inside people, she thought, then we'll be able to solve a lot of our other problems. This line of

thinking continued to inform the direction of her business of disseminating spiritual wisdom through audio.

All the wisdom traditions of the world agree on this point of understanding
our oneness. If people could feel that in their being the way that I felt it
through these meditation practices, we would have a different kind of
world. It was from this vantage point that I began to fully pursue what was
to grow into Sounds True as we know it today.

Tami planned to use her duplication equipment to provide services
to local musicians in addition to making copies of her talks with spiritual teachers. This could become another stream of income.

One local guitar player proposed that he build a studio for Tami.
He suggested she pay for the materials and he would put in the labor.
She could use the premises to record the teachers and he could use it
to record his albums.

Tami agreed to this simple arrangement with a handshake. He was
able to knock out the studio by himself with a bunch of egg cartons
and pink fabric that Tami purchased.

At the same time, Tami had begun recording conferences and live
lectures of leading spiritual teachers. She approached these guests on
her radio show, requesting they allow her to record their live ses-
sions. She would give the teachers a copy of the recording, enabling
them to do whatever they'd like with it. In turn, she would make
copies available on-site to the participants as a service.

She determined her costs, set a breakeven point, and beyond that
she proposed giving each teacher a percentage of the sales of the cassettes. Most everyone agreed.

At this stage, Tami wanted to attend these live events but didn't have
the money to pay the admission. She was thrilled to go for free. Even
if she didn't sell many recordings, she believed she was ahead of the
game. She didn't have to travel far because Boulder, Colorado, was on
the circuit of most spiritual teachers, drawn in by Naropa University.

Tami started amassing a library of recordings. She would carry a
Xeroxed sheet of offerings to every conference in the hopes that
someone at that conference would be interested in purchasing earlier
recordings.

At about two and a half years into Sounds True, Tami met Devon
Christensen, who had a background in direct marketing and catalogue design and strategy. He proposed she convert her Xeroxed
pink sheet into a catalogue with descriptive content to increase sales.

Devon visited Sounds True to look at the cassette masters Tami had collected, 500 to 800 of them by then, all sitting tucked on a wall.

He exclaimed, "Tami, you're sitting on a goldmine!" Shocked, I replied, "It's a bunch of live recordings." He assured me, "No, there are people that want this and yet have no idea how to get it. What we need to do is to create a catalogue. It will be a catalogue for people who don't have access right now who hunger for this kind of learning."

With a handshake, Tami and Devon agreed to work together for a couple of years. She paid him about $10,000 annually. They decided later they would draw up a partnership arrangement if their work together succeeded. Three years later, the catalogue was generating $1.2 million in sales and Devon became a 20% partner in Sounds True, based on his sweat equity.

GROWING THE BUSINESS AND MEETING OBSTACLES

From these humble beginnings, Sounds True had grown over the course of 15 years to become a $9-million-dollar company, quite a decent return of 18,000% on a $50,000 inheritance!

Eventually her catalogue had gotten into the hands of bookstore owners, whose customers would implore them to order tapes so that they could avoid paying shipping fees. As a result, Tami started working with bookstores, creating packaging for a bookstore-friendly format. She also began attending the big American booksellers' trade shows. There she connected with business distributors who dealt with bookstores. That was when Sounds True really started growing.

At the $9-million-dollar point in sales, about 15 years into the business, Tami and Devon began thinking about growing into a number of other mediums. Never having borrowed money before, they borrowed $1 million dollars from the bank, which was happy to lend to Sounds True.

Without much planning, they decided to move into video and create a children's series of world wisdom tales with music created by various international musicians. With the hubris that came with their success in the audio world, they naively thought they could easily grow the business in untold ways.

However, without cash flow or business planning, they learned sadly that they had tried to expand in too many different directions.

They didn't understand the capital it would take to become successful in diverse departments. After being profitable for 15 years, Sounds True lost three quarters of a million dollars in one year.

It was a hard lesson, but Tami learned that she didn't have the ability to scale up a small business on her own. She needed serious financial and strategic planning guidance from people who knew how to grow exponentially.

In over their heads, Devon proposed they sell the business. At the time, Tami thought he was right. It was pretty disheartening to lose that much money. They had staffed up to 85 people to have the resources to start their new divisions, but it was about 20 too many.

I agreed Devon was right; I was exhausted. I had shingles from the stress of the whole situation. My partner and I had broken up so here I was 38, 39—exhausted and having just gone through two rounds of layoffs. Finally, in a moment of desperation, I wondered, "You know, maybe it's time for me to get out."

Tami started talking to prospective buyers. She had only one real non-negotiable point, which was that she wanted to sell Sounds True to an individual or a business that would be aligned with its purpose and continue it in the world. If that intention were there and the money were reasonable, she'd sell it. Otherwise, she was not going to sell.

The problem was that none of the companies interested in buying Sounds True actually genuinely shared the purpose and the mission of the company. They saw Sounds True as a chance to reach new customers and make money, but Tami could tell that in five years there would be no Sounds True. The soul of the company would disappear. Tami couldn't sell to these people.

Devon's perspective was that this process was much like selling a car: you don't care who the buyer is, you simply sell the car for the right price.

Tami had a different perspective:

I relayed to Devon, when you and I began, we never started this business so that we could sell it and get rich. We started for another reason, namely to disseminate spiritual teachings! After 15 years, I wasn't about to make this suddenly about me. It was never about me; it's not about me now. It was about something else: It was about these life-changing teachings and their preservation, integrity, communication, and dissemination in the world.

At the same time she was going through these negotiations, Tami was getting involved in a new connection with a woman named Julie, with whom she continues a relationship seven years later. Julie innocently asked Tami why she was selling Sounds True. Tami admitted it was because she was exhausted.

Julie's advice was to change her relationship with Sounds True but not to sell it. She proposed Tami get out of the way and let some of her qualified employees pull more of the weight in the business. By doing so, Tami could rest.

Tami agreed. She told her staff she would not sell the company but would start working less. The employees were elated and said, "Watch us go!" As they did their part, Tami realized she had built her company around her own "centrality" and that she simply had to start to restructure it so that if she were off at a meditation retreat, the company could thrive anyway.

Tami told Devon the employee stock ownership plan that had been devised many years earlier would buy him out at his 20% valuation over a five-year period. He agreed to this arrangement and left.

From Tami's vantage point, buying back this 20% was a decisive moment in the evolution of Sounds True because there was a unique "energetic blockage" that existed with Devon there while truly desiring to leave.

Employees happily carried more of the weight, Tami worked less, and the company really began growing. Fortunately, they were able to recoup half of their losses in tax refunds and, going forward, took a more conservative approach to the scope of products they were offering.

Over the next 6 years Sounds True doubled sales revenue to $18 million. A good team of people who cared about the company and wanted to work made all the difference. Tami became happier as she learned to become less controlling.

HIRING A PRESIDENT AND CEO

As Sounds True became more and more profitable, Tami realized the business could increase its potential if it had leadership beyond what she could offer:

I excel at inspiring people around a vision. I'm good at helping generate and create content. When it comes to a lot of operational leadership issues and business planning, I don't enjoy those kinds of things, nor am I very good at them.

Tami hired a president and CEO who reports to her and assists her with the company's business. She found someone with strong managerial skills, who is able to be a day-to-day operational administrator and provide the necessary financial and strategic planning skills the company needs. This addition has enabled her to continue to function as visionary and purpose holder of the company, without carrying the piece that doesn't fit her skill set.

As Sounds True has evolved into a media company, even entering the book publishing business 6 years ago, Tami sees her way clear now to spend more time being the voice that broadcasts the organization. Now moving into podcasting and blogging, among other activities, Tami has the time and energy to put her attention here as she discovers new ways to leverage talents, such as hosting dialogues among various authors.

STAYING PASSIONATE ABOUT THE BUSINESS

Tami has created a variety of ways to stay passionate about what she is doing. All are related as much to whom she is as what she does. Because of her exposure to the perennial wisdom and her intrinsic belief in the values that it espouses, she knows she must walk her own talk.

She realized some years ago that she needs to spend several weeks a year, outside of vacation time, in retreat.

This is time for me to explore the meditative tradition that I'm part of. That's really, really important to me as without that I feel that I don't have a deep well to draw on; a deep well of inspiration, a deep well of commitment. I feel my life starts getting thin instead of deep. I wouldn't be willing to be engaged in the world at this point in my life unless I had that; to be by myself away in a meditative practice environment.

In addition to retreat time, Tami needs to be with her partner, whom she loves dearly. This association recharges her and refuels her desire to stay excited and passionate about Sounds True.

As she sees it, it would be ironic if she were just putting out wonderful teachings and not actually engaged in her own evolutionary path. She believes a disconnection would occur that her customers would feel at some level.

Tami sees herself as a conscious capitalist and social entrepreneur. The business exists for a reason, not just for a financial return. People who want to be successful entrepreneurs must have a purpose for their endeavor beyond their own self interests. You must be able to enable your employees, customers, and investors to believe in what you are doing. In actuality, you can't do that unless you yourself feel on fire inside about it yourself.

As a social entrepreneur, Tami believes a business must address some social problem. She believes that a business in a free economy can be so directed. A person who carries a sense of calling and is dedicated to solving a social problem has the energy and willingness to sacrifice to make the business work.

To her, success is feeling successful according to your own values. Frankly, it doesn't matter what anybody else thinks. Other people can think you are accomplished, but if you don't feel so yourself, who cares? For Tami, feeling successful means feeling loved and loving, feeling she has creative outlets and the ability to express herself, knowing she's making a useful contribution for others, that she's a truth teller, and that she has enough financial resources to be independent and well cared for. All of this summed together within a surrounding rich community sustains her and results in a feeling of success.

Tami believes that the values of the founder of a company in turn influence the values of the organization. Values become part of the DNA of the business.

ADVICE FOR WOMEN STARTING BUSINESSES

Tami believes a potential business has to pass certain criteria. First, does it really bring genuine benefit to others, to the world, and to future generations? Second, are you really genuinely passionate about it? Would you do it if you weren't being paid? Tami believes if you have those standards in place, you'll be successful. If you bring value to other people, there's a value exchange, and that's what a financial return is. If you'd do whatever you're doing even if you weren't being paid, you'll have patience and fortitude and the love and commitment for it. This is what you'll need to get something off the ground, especially because it may take time.

She also believes it's important to consider whether you have the ability to be patient about gaining a financial return. Some people may need to make a certain amount of money to support a family. Accordingly, this might not be the right time to start a business. Or perhaps you focus on the business half the time and the other half of the time you do something to earn money. As Tami sees it, sometimes startups suffer from having too much economic pressure on them to get off the ground.

Tami sees herself as fortunate for having started Sounds True in her early 20s when she could live on so little. She didn't know each weekend she taped a conference whether she'd be making $20.00 or $2,000 from her cassette sales.

For women who may lack confidence in their ability to start and run a business, Tami asks, "Whose voice is that?" All of us have the voice of the critic, the internalized parent, or the internalized teacher. We need to brush it away like we would a mosquito buzzing around our faces. As we do so, we must tune into our real longing and let that take us forward, trusting that when it is followed, something will flower.

COURAGE CALLED UPON YET AGAIN

Now the owner of a 24-year-old business, Tami has faced the need to call upon courage over and over again. In the beginning she had to chance losing her inheritance and defying her own and her family's ambitions for her to become a college graduate, even an academic.

Then, when her business got away from her with expansion beyond her means to handle it, she needed to face the loss of a goodly sum of money borrowed from the bank. She needed to release a partnership that no longer served her partner or her company, and then, as Sounds True recouped its losses and started to thrive, she needed to relinquish control and turn parts of her business over to those who were better equipped to handle those portions than she was.

Now she's at a point once again where she is being asked to summon her courage:

It is now time for me to go out and be more of a broadcaster and not hide so much behind all of the spiritual teachers whose work I've produced, but to come forward with more of my own voice in the world. This is requiring a lot of courage on my part. And part of me is questioning, "Gosh, why bother?" Why not just sink into some kind of more comfortable position? What I think about is what I'll feel like on my deathbed and what I want to feel in terms of fulfillment as a person.

Tami continues to ask herself what fulfillment means to her. What does she need? She answers, using her own metaphor, that she must express her own "snowflake of messaging." Otherwise, she won't feel fulfilled. She has to do it.

Even though it's scary and terrible and she can be humiliated, and she probably will suffer some of that, she's willing to take the risk. What is the choice? The choice is not being fulfilled. She can't take that. That's too big a risk. She'd rather have fulfillment than a kind of toxic ease. It's comfortable but, as she sees it, there's also the slight feeling of smoke building up in the room.

Tami believes there's no end to stepping out and being courageous.

It's not like I started my own business, check, done with that. It's just not like that. In order to keep growing and keep evolving and keep increasing that sense of aliveness, there's always a challenge, the next evolutionary step in each of our lives. I'm not sure how it's all going to evolve. We'll just have to see.

Tami also believes in taking a reasonable, measured risk at the right time. Rather than taking the whole family and spending every dime you have, it's considering the next step that is courageous, but is also intelligent. It honors the whole ecosystem that your life is in right now: your family needs, your financial needs, and the whole situation. What Tami did at 22 might not be what somebody's situation is. Buddhism would call it the karma of your life; it's being responsible to your karmic situation where you find yourself.

ONE WOMAN'S COURAGE INSPIRES MORE COURAGE FOR OTHER WOMEN

Now that you have learned about Tami Simon's story and the emergence of Sound's True, it's time to reflect on how this story can inspire you in your quest for your entrepreneurial adventure. Take some time to reflect on what you've just read and allow the following questions to guide you. Use your journal to take notes so that you can ground your understanding and learning for future reference.

1. What train do you have to jump off of to realize your true gifts for the world?
2. What do you know you need to do that you pretend you don't?
3. What do you risk by not following your truth?
4. What mentors could guide you through the scary passages?
5. What will you regret on your deathbed if you don't follow your unique "snowflake of messaging"?

WHAT CAN YOU LEARN FROM TAMI SIMON?

Tami Simon represents a woman of courage of the heart. From the very beginning of her journey, she touched her soul and her values and thereby had a compass that she could count on, even during those times when she was unsure how to move forward.

It's not easy in this culture to defy your parents or the norm of following a traditional path of college first and then career. But with the strength she gained in learning how to listen to her own inner voice while in India, Tami was able to hear that guidance above the din of other voices.

Fortunately, she was able, through her endless curiosity, to meet a mentor, Jirka, who was an entrepreneur disposed to the same idea of matching inner and outer lives, who advised her to invest in herself. To Tami's credit, she took his advice seriously and followed it.

Like many other women we have met, Tami Simon questioned her own likes and dislikes, and she found a means of adding value to the world through audio recordings. Ironically, by having a seat at the volunteer radio table, she was at the very place necessary to easily reach out to the spiritual teachers she wanted to capture.

Another piece of good fortune was connecting with Devon, who helped her transform her business through his understanding of catalogues and their affect on the sales of her cassettes. Then, Tami needed to be courageous to confront letting go of the very person who had taken her so far, buying Devon out rather than selling her business.

Tami believes that having courage is confronting your own evolution. If she stepped off at any point and succumbed to a life of comfort, she would be doing herself a disservice. Courage demands we continue to grow and keep asking more of ourselves. She believes in mixing courage with intelligence—not jumping off of a cliff, but recognizing what you need to do while being sane about it.

Tami also reminds us that courage demands patience. If we plant a garden, we must step back and allow that garden to grow. We can't ask a small garden to produce enough to feed an army.

YOUR TURN NOW—WHAT DID *YOU* LEARN FROM TAMI'S STORY?

CHAPTER 7

29GIFTS

A Conversation with Cami Walker, Owner of Creative Urge and Founder of 29Gifts.org

History, despite its wrenching pain, cannot be unlived, but if faced with courage, need not be lived again.

—*Maya Angelou*

My consulting business was dead in the water, because I couldn't function, and my marriage was under a lot of stress because of the financial strain as well as just being ill and my husband having to take care of me all the time.

—*Cami Walker*, founder of 29Gifts.org

Thirty-five-year-old Cami Walker juggles more than one business at once, which is not surprising—she comes from a long line of entrepreneurs. What *is* surprising is her stamina for both of her businesses, considering not so long ago she was so sick she was forced to leave her promising career in advertising and receive disability.

Her primary business is Creative Urge, a branding and marketing firm that specializes in helping women create bountiful businesses.

She acts as a consultant, coach, and sounding board for entrepreneurs launching their businesses. She's been in this business for more than three years. Currently, Creative Urge finances her other business, 29Gifts.org, and keeps her afloat.

Her other endeavor, a not-for-profit business, was conceived more than a year ago. 29Gifts.org includes a revenue model to be rolled out fully in 2009. From its inception it has existed as an online community that encourages people to commit to giving away 29 gifts in 29 days and then share stories and experiences on the Web site about how the process impacts their lives.

THE EXPERIMENT BEGINS

Ironically enough, this business project began because Cami was incredibly sick. She was dealing with a severe flare-up of symptoms from multiple sclerosis (MS) that left her incapacitated for months. Officially, she had been diagnosed with the disease 3 years earlier, but Cami suspects she had suffered from MS for 15 years.

As a result of her medical problems, her consulting business was "dead in the water," simply because she couldn't function. Her marriage was under a lot of stress because of the financial concerns, as well as because of her continuing illness. Her husband had to care for her all the time. She was a mess.

We actually had just moved from San Francisco to Los Angeles, so I was extremely isolated in feeling just really lonely and friendless and not being able to get out of the house and meet people. So there was a lot going on and I was not in good shape and I consulted with an African medicine woman who I had known for about a year. We had been working together. And she actually gave me the prescription to give 29 gifts in 29 days.

Cami doesn't understand why this woman, Mbali Creazzo, chose the number 29. An educated guess supposes it aligns with the moon cycle. The tradition had been passed down to this woman from one of her teachers, and likewise, she passed it on to Cami.

Initially, Cami thought the idea was nuts. She didn't think it was even physically possible for her to engage in this gift giving because she literally couldn't get out of the house very often. At the time the prescription was assigned, Cami was entering the hospital the following day for an eight-day stay.

I thought, you're fricking crazy. I can't even walk. How the heck am I going to give something to somebody every day for 29 days?

Just the same, Cami wrote the assignment down in her journal and promptly ignored it. Many weeks later, she was continuing to struggle with her life and her health. Her situation had improved, but she was still desperately distressed.

One night, she remained awake the entire night feeling sorry for herself. She pulled her journal out, intending to write about her despair, and surprisingly opened to the very page that instructed "give 29 gifts in 29 days." She was ready to try anything, and she figured engaging in the process wouldn't hurt. Who knew, maybe it could help!

It was 3 AM when Cami decided to commit herself to giving of herself. Losing no time, she offered her first gift at 6 AM. It happened that she called one of her friends who also has the disease of MS. This woman was the only person Cami knew who would be awake at that hour. Cami's gift was her supportive call. Mbali had made it clear that a gift didn't have to be material; it could be a kind word or positive compliment or a prayer. The two talked for an hour, and many "amazing things" coincidently happened to Cami that first day.

Cami hung up the phone at 7 AM. At 8 AM her phone rang with the Packard Foundation offering her a consulting assignment. The organization hadn't been a client in the past; the call occurred totally out of the blue. Cami had not been putting effort into getting any work for months. She took the coincidence as a sign that perhaps there was something to this giving.

That morning Cami then ventured out to breakfast. Her husband Mark, an actor, dropped her off at a little nearby café and departed for his auditions. She sat down beside a man who was eating while working on his computer. They exchanged hellos and engaged in a brief conversation. Not long afterward, the man left. Shortly, her waiter came over and said, "Oh. That man paid for your breakfast." Cami thought, "Wow, how nice!"

She finished eating and contemplated being there for two more hours, waiting for her husband to pick her up. Not wanting to stay that long, Cami wondered about calling a cab, but knew she didn't have enough money for a ride. She thought she'd just try walking home and see if she got tired or weak. She had her cane with her, so if she felt unable to continue, she figured she would sit down on the ground and summon a taxi. When she returned home, she would find change to pay the driver.

With these thoughts in mind, Cami began walking the six blocks home. To her amazement, she made it all the way! For months she had been afraid to leave her house to venture more than a block because she feared she would be unable to return.

At this point, Cami had given exactly one gift, the phone conversation with her friend in the early morning. She didn't see the conversation with the man at breakfast as a gift from her but to her. She claims the exchange with the man would not have occurred had she not given the gift in the morning. Up until then, she had simply been immersed in her own struggles, completely focused on her own drama. Talking to strangers was not her habit; something had now opened up inside of her.

Needless to say, this was an amazing first day of gift giving. She thought, "Wow, if all these good things can happen in one day after just making a phone call, I think it's worth trying this." So she decided to commit to the 29 days.

GIFTING GROWS EXPONENTIALLY

In the following days, Cami gave quite a bit of money. Mbali had suggested giving at least one thing that Cami felt she could never part with or couldn't live without. The medicine woman also told her to give items that felt scarce. Money fit those prescriptions.

Cami doesn't remember how far along she was in the 29 days of giving before she decided to give money. Starting small, she gave spare change to people on the street, bought them lunch, or simply gave them food. Then one day she decided to give a real amount of money that felt challenging to her.

That was the day she decided to send $100 to a woman she knew who was leaving for a volunteer trip, requiring $5,000, to either South America or South Africa, Cami wasn't sure where. Cami's donation was a large amount of money to her, which she had to put on her credit card.

As Cami gained strength, halfway through the month she also went to the house of the friend with MS to assist her. As she gave, Cami noticed her body becoming dramatically stronger.

I was able to walk without my cane. I was feeling so much better by the 14th day. And so I decided to go visit my friend whose MS is much further progressed and has trouble doing a lot of basic things around the house. So I came over and helped her clean out her closet. It took two days to do that actually because it was a pretty big job. Physically I couldn't do it (clean) for eight hours straight.

By the 29th day, Cami no longer needed a cane. Her health was back. She had made new friends because she had been able to get out of the house. At least once a day, she gave something to someone, which usually required her to leave her house. This activity led her to make new connections in LA, her new home.

At the same time, unexpectedly, she had brought in about $8,000 in revenue, literally with no effort. The clients and opportunities just arrived in her branding and marketing consultancy. Looking ahead, she saw her next five months full of work; her client roster was brimming.

Cami put up the Web site for 29gifts.org on day 13 of her program. She threw it together quickly with a basic [Microsoft] Office tool. That initial site is now the community page. She announced her Web presence with an email to 30 of her closest friends.

I just said, "Hey guys I'm doing this thing, so far this is what's happened and it's been really inspiring and I think it'd be cool if some other people did it with me, so sign up."

The first week, 120 people signed up, and it's been viral, word-of-mouth growth ever since. Many writers have taken part in the gift giving, sharing their experiences in turn on their own sites and blogs. That has led to much mainstream press.

Months into the 29gifts.org Web site, Cami saw the membership soar to 1,600 participants. Less than a year later, she's on her way to her goal of 29,000 registered members. She also has a book contract, focused on the 29 gifts story, with an October 2009 publication date.

THE BUSINESS PLAN

Cami's business plan includes a book, a documentary, and a screen play for a feature film. Each of these has occurred from people approaching her. Two publishers vied over the rights to the book, and a member of the community, also a close friend, is collaborating on the screen play. In addition to her initial site, a nicer site was designed, created, and donated by a member of the community.

In progress now is a line of eco-friendly gift products, including an array of reusable gift cards and reusable gift boxes and gift bags. Cami emphasizes the eco-friendly aspect of these items because sustainability is important to her. Gift boxes are all handmade out of recycled materials. To create these items, Cami is working with artists who themselves are on disability because she is passionate about helping these people become productive again.

As products on the site emerge and are sold, Cami hopes to gain a salary for herself as well as the 14 other people engaged in running the site. She sees all of the operating expenses being covered. The vision, however, is that 100% of profits are donated.

Reserves are set aside to cover emergency situations, such as rebuilding the site if necessary. Cami is intrigued by the not-for-profit business model, which is different from the traditional charity 501c3 model. 29Gifts.org is established as an S corporation, not a 501c3. An S corporation is incorporated as a business. The difference is that it donates profits instead of collecting them in its coffers.

Cami is an entrepreneur who believes in the power of conscious commerce. Traditional nonprofits are restricted in ways that prevent them from operating efficiently. Cami is not interested in having to deal with all the rules. She is headed in another direction, encouraged by people who have been successful with this alternate model.

She cites as an example a company in San Francisco called Wildlife Works. All of its profits go to supporting a village in Africa. Another store in Palo Alto, a shoe store called In Her Shoes, sends 100% of its profits to the Global Women's Fund. With these successful precedents, Cami does not think she is doing something revolutionary.

Cami has ambitious goals for 29Gifts: it will become the largest, kindest movement on the planet. She believes it entirely possible for this to happen. However, her financial investment has been minimal. Cami started 29Gifts with less than $1,000 because almost all of the major expenses were donated: People gifted the Web site, all the design work on the branding, and the video production.

BEING READY FOR BUSINESS

Cami believes there is no *right* time to start a business.

Well, if you had looked at me at that time, no one would say that was the right time. No, I don't think there is a right time. It's simply a matter of, are you willing to make the commitment and take the daily action required to follow through?

A lot of times my Creative Urge clients come to me while the idea (for their business) is still very much in the idea stage. There's still this nucleus of a creative spark but they haven't put any kind of strategy or plan around it at all. But what I've seen consistently is that almost always the person comes with an idea that's several years old, that they've been holding inside of them. And for whatever reason, now they're feeling capable and ready to take some action.

Cami prides herself in still being naive about her businesses. She's found that if she gets to a place where she thinks she knows what she is doing, she's in trouble. She experiences more success when she is just in the moment and dealing with what's going on rather than in the times where she's planning the next five years and thinking about how it's coming together. A plan is helpful, but it's important to remember that a big wind can come along at any time and change the direction that you're headed. Illness teaches that lesson. She has learned it well.

Before she became sick, Cami used to be able to predict what her day would be like. Now her life is different because she doesn't plan more than one big activity a day. She wakes up in the morning and she sees how she's feeling and judges from there whether she's even capable of doing that one thing. That's so dramatically different from the overdriven Type A approach she took when she was a creative director in the advertising world. Then she lived an intense life; it's just not that way anymore.

A BLESSING IN DISGUISE AND A SENSE OF PURPOSE

When Cami became sick, she was forced to leave her job and go on disability. She spent 3 months crying about her life being over before she woke up and realized it was actually the best situation that possibly could have happened to her. It was a blessing in disguise. The circumstances were a catalyst for launching her business.

Before leaving her director job, she had been working on the side for 3 years on her branding and marketing business, Creative Urge. She always had at least one client. When she left the advertising world because of her illness, she spent 3 months not working at all because she simply couldn't. When she felt more up to it, Cami decided to pick up Creative Urge and move forward with it.

To start this business more determinedly, she sat down and made a list of every woman she knew who owned a business, who had talked about wanting to own a business, or who was miserable in her career. Then she called every single one of them:

Hey, I'm going to be consulting now, helping women start companies and I'm offering an introductory session, an hour for $30 bucks.

As a result, Cami had about 15 clients within a week. She didn't even have a Web site for Creative Urge for her first year, even though she was creating Web sites for other people!

Today she charges $200 an hour for her marketing and branding services. As 29Gifts expands, Cami still consults with clients in her primary business, Creative Urge, but she is becoming more selective and working with fewer clients.

Cami feels successful when she is aligned with her own personal sense of purpose. She defines this as being here to inspire and motivate people. Doing so doesn't have to be in their business, it sometimes occurs on a personal level, as with 29Gifts; through her writing or speaking; or through the one-on-one work that she does with people. The moments when she feels frustrated are times when she's not in alignment with that purpose.

Cami finds no difficulty in sustaining her passion for 29Gifts, because all she has to do is log onto the site and read a few stories from people who are members of the community. Her email box is full every day with people thanking her for what she's started. She receives much external validation for what she is doing.

ONE WOMAN'S COURAGE INSPIRES MORE COURAGE FOR OTHER WOMEN

Now that you have learned about Cami Walker's story and the emergence of her businesses, it's time to reflect on how this story can inspire you in your quest for your entrepreneurial adventure. Take some time to reflect on what you've just read and allow the following questions to guide you. Use your journal to take notes so that you can ground your understanding and learning for future reference.

1. What's a piece of advice you've been given that you've stuffed away and forgotten?
2. What fears keep you in inaction?
3. Would you be willing to take the 29 day gift challenge and see how it changes your life?

4. What excuses do you repeat to yourself that get in your way?
5. If you were no longer afraid, what would you do?

WHAT CAN YOU LEARN FROM CAMI WALKER?

When you consider the courage it takes to become an entrepreneur when you're healthy, you can imagine how much more mustering is involved for someone who suffers from a debilitating disease such as MS. However, the businesses that Tami participates in seem to be so life-giving that she thrives from their very existence.

How many people do you suppose were given the prescription of 29 gifts in 29 days before that challenge was put before Cami? How many turned away from it or laughed it off as she initially did? But here, right under her nose, was a gift to her and her very soul—something she lovingly nurtured and gifted the world. We can be inspired by Cami's willingness to bring gift giving with meaning to untold numbers of people.

It never ceases to amaze me how many opportunities present themselves that are truly resident in our lives already if we would just look at what's there with new eyes. How many opportunities do we miss because we don't take into account the most obvious? We take the ordinary occurrences for granted.

Once again we see a woman who allows the organic nature of business to take hold. As she reached out to others, others responded.

Cami also raises the possibility of looking into a not-for-profit business that gives back to the community as opposed to a nonprofit or even a for-profit business. There are indeed other forms to consider. She also demonstrates a dedication to providing outlets for others who suffer disabilities of all kinds, wanting to provide jobs for artists making products for her site.

Cami Walker is a remarkable young woman hell-bent on a mission to change the world. She is truly living her purpose as a shining light to all who know of her existence.

YOUR TURN NOW—WHAT DID *YOU* LEARN FROM CAMI'S STORY?

CHAPTER 8

TARA SPA THERAPY

A Conversation with Tara Grodjesk, Founder of Tara Spa Therapy, Inc. (www.taraspa.com)

Courage, it would seem, is nothing less than the power to overcome danger, misfortune, fear, injustice, while continuing to affirm inwardly that life with all its sorrows is good; that everything is meaningful even if in a sense beyond our understanding; and that there is always tomorrow.

—*Dorothy Thompson*

I think that people go into business for different reasons and I think even though women can behave like men, I think that the feminine model of business is different than the masculine model. It is more emotional; it's more gut level; it's more with passion and inspiration.

—*Tara Grodjesk*, founder of Tara Spa Therapy, Inc.

Tara Grodjesk's business was an evolution. It wasn't that she set out to create a product brand or go to market with buzz. It really was an outgrowth of filling a need, a gap she discovered in spas many years ago, focused more on pampering and less on therapeutic treatments for guests, which she chose to provide. However, the gutsiest, most courageous aspect of her business occurred because it took off, flowered, and grew right smack dab in the midst of one of the darkest hours of her life: when her husband whom she loved with all her heart was dying of brain cancer.

Up until this point in her business, Tara had been repackaging, promoting, and selling Ayurvedic treatment products manufactured by others to recognized spas, such as Marriott Desert Springs Resort in Southern California, Sonoma Mission Inn, Watercourse Way, Lake Austin Resort and the Claremont Hotel and Spa. These products were good and sound, but building her business using others' items only made Tara vulnerable to her suppliers' whims and willingness to collaborate with her.

It was literally—practically—on Mark's deathbed that he said that you can represent other companies and you've helped to put them on the map. You've put them in world class spas. But at any time they can let you go— you have no security with that, at any time they can let you go. And so he infused me with some energy as he was leaving, literally. I felt infused with something, because I don't know how I did what I did, but I was able to launch the Tara brand literally a few weeks before Mark left the earth.

This is the exceptional part of Tara's unique story. She truly believes Mark infused her with his life force energy, enabling her to move forward with her business of manufacturing her own unique spa treatment products. This was the blessing as well as the curse of his terminal illness and death. At the time, 1996, she and Mark had traveled from their home in California to New York's Sloan-Kettering Hospital for clinical trial treatments. Yet the doctors didn't give the young man much hope of surviving. While in treatment, Mark needed time to rest and sleep. During that time, Tara would ride the subway down to SoHo, with her infant son, Jacob, on her hip, to her graphic designer's office, where she worked on the packaging designs of her spa products.

Tara doesn't know how she survived through this period; it all became a blur. Yet something drove her forward. She equates her experience to that of Olympic athletes and feats like marathon running, where good training is important. She did what she had to do. Ironically, Mark's passage seemed the very impetus behind her success. He wanted her to rely on her own strengths, not those of the companies he believed had no loyalty toward her. This was his legacy to her.

The initial launch of the Tara line of products occurred while Mark was dying. When he passed on, while she experienced a tremendous amount of grief, Tara immersed herself in her work, trying to figure out what she was doing. She wouldn't suggest such an approach for everyone, but it worked for her. Immediately, Tara took the products out there and marketed them generously.

Among them were her own formulation of professional massage oil; an aromatherapy neck pillow, filled with cinnamon bark and orange spice and "hard" herbs to hold moist heat; and pre-blended aromatherapy massage oils called "Aromablends." These were therapeutic products with more healing efficacy and a higher, naturally pure, quality than those typically being used in spas at the time. Such products led her, in fact, to name her business Tara's Spa Therapy.

LAYING THE FOUNDATION FOR HER BUSINESS AND CHANGING THE INDUSTRY

Years before, in the late 1980s, Tara had been a massage therapist in private practice as well as a certified Ayurvedic practitioner and a holistic health educator. Even though her business was successful, Tara realized she could reach only a certain number of people. As well, this work was physically demanding on her. Tara wondered how she might reach greater numbers of people.

With that question, Tara began to develop the idea of going beyond her clinic, reaching out to spas and training massage therapists so that they could pass on her unique techniques.

Tara saw how she could grow, not just through her "little clinic" but by training massage therapists and other spa therapists around the country.

So now all of a sudden I realized not just through my little clinic, but I can train massage therapists and other spa therapists around the country. I could train a few hundred and then those several hundred therapists are going to touch how many thousands and thousands of individuals? And so all of a sudden I realized I could touch in some way a larger population and to touch them with something that's pure and healing and nourishing for their body and soul.

However, as she traveled to spas around the country, Tara saw a gap and a need for higher quality and more natural products. There was also a need for more therapeutic efficacy. Consequently, she studied extensively with master aromatherapists and also studied a variety of therapeutic spa treatments, including thalasso, pelio, and hydro therapies.

She also wanted to bring a more holistic philosophy to the spa industry. When she had visited spas in the late 1980s, she had found many to be more about beauty and pampering than about wellness and lifestyle. Today these words of healing are common for people in the spa industry, but back then, this was a relatively new direction for spas.

STAYING CLEAR

Tara never questioned whether her new business venture would succeed; she just kept going down the path. She could see the opportunity clearly. She didn't have the business experience to put a business plan together and get working capital, but she didn't have to, as she sees it. Even though she had no business experience, she took her enthusiasm, passion, commitment, knowledge, and experience in her field and just went for it. Her clarity kept her going down the path.

Tara believes it's easy for people excited about something not to see outside of that and see whether it's a realistic possibility for them. She was fortunate that she was not blindsided; people can lose sight of whether their idea is realistic, doable, or practical because they're so caught up in what they are doing in the moment.

It's like a boyfriend, a new boyfriend—you're so jazzed about this new boyfriend that you cannot even see anything beyond that, any of the potential flaws or traps. And you tell your friends and either you've got the friends that like jump in and support you with that or they ask wait a minute, are you crazy?

Tara knew she was on track with her business expansion, not only because she was jumping in and doing it but because the feedback she received from others was so on target that she knew she had hit something. Every door opened, and there were very few nos.

And so—what I'd say to other women pursuing their businesses is it is good to chunk it off. You take each step and if you hit a green light and a door opens, you go the next step, then the next one. The doors kept opening so I kept going. The feedback from others was so positive. Also acknowledgement from mentors I have to say, like people in the industry and my industry that were very successful, very large business, owners and they were looking at me admitting wow, you're really doing something.

INSPIRATION, PASSION, FOCUS, AND PLANNING

According to Tara, some business success is predicated on preparation and planning, and some on passion and staying focused on the outcome. This combination is what she believes propels one forward. With most great feats, people will comment that it was something beyond themselves that made it possible. That is the case that Tara makes.

Tara started her product line with 18 to 20 products. She began with her massage oil. As a massage therapist, she knew what oils she liked to use and what wasn't greasy and sticky on the skin but had a good texture for the therapist. Then she added moist heat neck pillows, and she built her product line from there.

Tara used money from her former business to fund her product line. She didn't take out any loans at that time. It was quite a few years later before she got an SBA loan. Sales were coming in, and she used that money to fund more product development and more packaging and label printing. She just kept plowing money back into the business.

Tara was totally naive about getting into this business. She had no business plan. She had no clue what it took to establish a business, establish a corporation, and file all the paperwork. She had no exit strategy. What she *did* know was to follow the demand and respond to it. She calls this a "yes we can" attitude.

It was yes I can, yes I can, yes I can, or yes we can. I was following the demand and responding to it and so fortunately—I wasn't pushing a cart up hill.

Tara believes the times were on her side because she was attempting something unique, filling a gap others hadn't recognized. She has a friend with a marketing background who started a fancy gourmet chocolate company. Unfortunately, entering a competitive field, this woman is contending with many other companies. She's had a tough time of it. Tara sees herself as fortunate because she entered her niche at the early stages of the trend in the spa industry.

Is there a right time to launch [a business]? My right brain says the inspiration and passion has to be there, but the left brain says that you really do have to look at market trends and [ask] is it the right time for that market? And that's very important because coming into an already competitive marketplace is a lot tougher quite honestly than coming into an opportunity where it's a wide open field.

Tara's business was undercapitalized from the beginning, but she really didn't know anything about the importance of capitalization until a few years down the road. Looking back, she would insist on much more planning if she had to do it over. At the time, she also wondered whether this was what she really wanted to do forever. Tara is a spontaneous and creative person, and so it has been a challenge for her to remain in this business for the long haul.

MAINTAINING AND SUSTAINING PASSION

Tara periodically asks herself whether what she is doing continues to make a difference. She dove into the business for certain reasons, yet she believes people need to have checkpoints and need to reflect periodically to decide whether they are still in it for the right reasons. Women need to ask themselves occasionally, "Am I still doing what I wanted to do? Am I still being effective?"

If I say I wanted to touch hundreds of thousands of people and bring wellness lifestyle into their lives, I have to ask that question, am I still doing that effectively? Sometimes when you get bogged down with the tedium of sitting behind the desk and putting out fires each day and dealing with employees, or dealing with cash flow crunches and all that stuff ... [you need to ask the question again.]

All the day-to-day operations can sometimes bog the entrepreneur down because she is the one who has the vision, the creativity, and the passion. The founder needs good people around her to support her with the structure. That's a big lesson Tara learned: It's of paramount importance to have people who support you because the entrepreneur is not always the person who has the structure to execute the vision.

And so part of this thought is reflecting and saying am I still making a difference, am I still doing what I set out to do? Because if you're off track you're [wondering] okay, why am I doing this?

Being undercapitalized has created a pervasive struggle for Tara's business. She would describe her operation as a bootstrap company. Being such a scrappy startup has made it more difficult for her to grow faster and stay competitive in the marketplace. Catching up requires proper strategizing, planning, and strategic alliances. It also requires big-picture planning.

To sustain her passion, Tara taps into her creativity and vision. Over the years she has admitted to possessing a strong vision—to really being able to see ahead and see clearly what can be manifested or what can be created. She sees creativity as her strength and believes we need to tap into our strengths to keep our passion alive. Strengths vary. For some it could be crunching the numbers; that's how they keep going because they can analyze situations from various vantage points. For Tara it's tapping into her creativity and her vision.

Another way Tara sustains herself is by meeting customers. She also keeps up with other massage therapists and aestheticians, service providers in the spa, spa directors, and even spa customers.

When she's out in the field, she receives incredible feedback. She hears how people love her products, and she believes them. She discovers they are so happy she's doing what she's doing because they really can get behind the products. There's a loyalty that provides a connection. All of this feedback and loyalty feeds her. As a result, Tara finds being out there more productive and sustaining than staying behind the desk.

Although Tara does pick up negative feedback as well, she always turns the negative into lessons.

I always say I want people to speak honestly and give the feedback because we want to learn and improve. So even if it's negative feedback it's important. But find whatever it is that feeds you that says go get 'em, you're on the right track, this is so great. And stick around that, because [it] keeps you going. You don't want to hang around people and energy that pulls you down and tells you that it can't work.

Of greatest importance to Tara is connecting with the people who use her product daily. Doing so reminds her how good the product is and how much she should keep going because her customers love it, want it, and need it. You've got to stick with your customers to keep momentum going.

MEASURING SUCCESS BEYOND THE DOLLARS

Tara also counts financial stability and liquidity in her success equation. Product sales amount to about $1.6 million per year at this point. In the early years, sales went from $300,000 to $500,000 to $700,000, a steady progression of revenues.

However, success for Tara has never been a monetary valuation. Her business has always been driven by her passion to serve and make a difference. She sees herself as leaning more in the philanthropic direction than anything else. She measures her success by respect and recognition among her peers. It is gratifying for her to be among other longtime industry leaders, and even newcomers, but it is also rewarding to continuously be acknowledged and respected for her accomplishments and her success.

What's strange and sometimes challenging is seeing the copycats of her innovation. Yet it is important to take note of them. Entrepreneurs can run the risk of having tunnel vision. Tara had a business advisor who reminded her to pay attention to what her competition was up to. However, like a race horse with blinders on, in the early years, she didn't care about her competition at all. She was focused, and she knew where she was going, what she wanted to create, and what products she wanted to launch.

Over the years, though, her particular market has become more competitive. As a frontrunner, Tara has seen companies looking to her. They've identified what her company does with its style, packaging, color-codes for products, and messaging. She's seen companies literally copy hers. That can be pretty unnerving! She wonders, "Can't you come up with your own ideas?"

On the other hand, people remind her that such "flattery" is a testament to her innovation and success. She's had huge company executives, such as the former CEO of Bath and Body Works, shower her with accolades about her products besides being steady customers.

BALANCE COUNTS

An infant when her husband Mark died, her son Jacob is now 13. Tara's had to balance the time and effort she's devoted to her business with the dedication she has to her son.

These aren't so measurable, but success is also a balance in your life where the company is not running you, but you're running the company.

Accordingly, Tara has led a women's retreat every year for the past eight years. Hers happens to be for spa professionals, located at a top spa in her industry. Yet Tara believes balance is important for all women.

Tara leads her annual retreats because even women in her own spa industry struggle with the balance of work, personal nourishment, and family responsibilities. She's realized over the years that a component of success that is hard is maintaining and sustaining. Tara believes success ultimately is about sustainability.

The sustainability of the company and the financial stability directly correlate with the sustainability of one's energy. It involves the sustainability and maintenance of the balance of personal and professional, and making sure to take care of yourself so that you can take care of others.

Women struggle with this proposition. Maintaining balance is one of the strongest messages Tara has within her company, yet she sees that women constantly are struggling with this issue. Women are tapping out, becoming depleted, and finding they have nothing left.

ADVICE TO WOULD-BE WOMEN ENTREPRENEURS

For women with an idea for a business, Tara admits that planning is key. She sees this even more so in retrospect: Planning is paramount to laying out a strategy and achieving your objective. Tara draws an analogy with women training for a triathlon, a marathon, or other event:

I'm actually going to hike Half Dome in Yosemite Friday. It's a 16-mile climb and it's a lot of elevation. To do that with grace one has to prepare for it and train for it. Now I can do it and struggle and suffer through it and maybe if I wasn't prepared, barely even make it.

Same thing in business: by planning and training and mapping out the strategy and what the objective is, it really, really helps staying on track and being successful.

Part of the planning is projecting out into the future. Not being so myopic and focused on just today but really looking ahead. Doing so is important because trends ebb and flow.

It is also important to have working capital.

You hear all kinds of stories, great stories [such as] in Inc. Magazine, all kinds of stories of a guy from Under Armour started selling clothing out of his suitcase and his trunk and all those kinds of stories. The guy started the Limited brand same thing, out of his car. You know I would definitely say I'm in that bootstrap category, but ideally having working capital really eases the stress.

Tara also believes in understanding the life cycles of business. She has read business articles that told her that some of what she was going through at various points in her evolution were normal and natural.

She stresses the necessity of not making yourself wrong or thinking that you've failed. If you can learn about business cycles, you can anticipate them and not fear that you're failing or on the wrong track.

Tara also insists that business will be successful only for women who believe in themselves. "If you go into it with doubt, that's what will come out of it." Although there are exceptions, sometimes people will say "I never thought I could have done this" and all of a sudden they're in *People Magazine* and getting a hundred calls, you have to believe in yourself and you have to know your success to be true.

To know business success to be true means putting the intention into it with the sense that it's already happened. Tara thinks it may sound esoteric, but she insists that you have a calling of a higher order. You have this calling and it's bigger than you are.

I think that people go into business for different reasons and I think even though women can behave like men, I think that the feminine model of business is different than the masculine model. It is more emotional; it's more gut level; it's more with passion and inspiration.

Not all businesses are going to be like this, but getting into a business that does serve a higher purpose, like that is socially responsible or is the cause, those are the types of businesses that I'm more interested and excited about. It's like someone can make a pet rock and make a gazillion dollars and that's great. But okay then if they take that money and do something good with it, that's even better. So I guess my focus is really on businesses that make a difference and not everybody wants to go that route.

ONE WOMAN'S COURAGE INSPIRES MORE COURAGE FOR OTHER WOMEN

Now that you have learned about Tara Grodjesk's story and the emergence of her business at the height of her deepest grief, it's time to reflect on how this story can inspire you in your quest for your entrepreneurial adventure. Take some time to reflect on what you've just read and allow the following questions to guide you. Use your journal to take notes so that you can ground your understanding and learning for future reference.

1. What do you need to risk to reach a larger audience for what you could offer?
2. What field is unsaturated, so it's not such an uphill experience to create a business in it?

3. If your partner were on his/her deathbed, what would he/she urge you to do that you're not doing?
4. What security are you resting on that's not really secure?
5. What keeps you "small"?

WHAT CAN YOU LEARN FROM TARA GRODJESK'S STORY?

Imagine losing your life partner, right in the midst of a time when you are expanding your business to create your very own products! It takes much courage to keep moving ahead under those circumstances—not to mention having a baby on your hip at the same time.

Tara represents another woman with a long-lived business who has tons of advice for other women considering a business for themselves. Like Ingrid Matagne of No Mondays, Tara built her business on her well-developed background in a field in which she was an expert.

But Tara took chances. She was a woman who was out front, a pioneer in a new element of spa treatment, long before others caught the significance of wellness and lifestyle for women. She was actually a trendsetter.

We would do well to heed her advice to combine planning with creativity and innovation. And although Tara understands the plight of a bootstrapping company, she proposes that if women can enter business better capitalized, they should do so.

Tara also reminds us of the importance of recognizing how saturated the field may be before you launch into a business. Obviously, it's may be easier to enter without having to elbow the other competitors, but it is just as important to know that those who are too far out in front may have to conduct a lot of education among potential customers.

Obviously she is a woman dedicated to balance and caring for herself, which may suggest why she entered such a field in the first place. Like a wise older sister, Tara reminds entrepreneurs of the importance of finding life outside of business to sustain them and keep them enthusiastically rejuvenated.

YOUR TURN NOW—WHAT DID *YOU* LEARN FROM TARA'S STORY?

CHAPTER 9

TARYN ROSE

A Conversation with Taryn Rose, Founder of Taryn Rose International, Inc. (www.tarynrose.com) and Haute Footure

The best way out is always through.

—Robert Frost

When you're passionate about it, it's hard to have a rational reason. It's like falling in love. And if I ever write a book the title would be "Feet First."

—Taryn Rose, orthopedic surgeon and serial entrepreneur

Taryn Rose truly loves being an entrepreneur. She enjoys creating new products and new brands. That's where her passion shows up. She is what is known as a "serial entrepreneur." Theory has it that her zeal for business invention and reinvention may actually lie in her genetic heritage.

A Vietnamese refugee in 1975, Taryn arrived in the United States at the age of eight, speaking no English. She cites one hypothesis that America teems with entrepreneurs because so many immigrants live here. According to this theory, immigrants genetically have a higher tolerance level for risk. Such people are able to overcome their fears, leave a familiar environment, and face untold challenges. They bring their risk tolerance to business as entrepreneurs. Consequently, they have much to teach the rest of us about courage.

Taryn Rose is an orthopedic surgeon by training, encouraged by her father to follow in his medical footsteps. She left medicine in 1998, to her parents' dismay, to enter the shoe business as an entrepreneur because she wanted to pursue her passion for fashion. The business also allowed her to take advantage of her technical understanding of footwear. Although she sees the marriage of passion and technical know-how as a winning combination, she believes her success in business has stemmed equally from her genuineness and authenticity.

Aside from her love of footwear and fashion, Taryn saw no "rational" reason for stepping away from her surgical career to become an entrepreneur.

When you're passionate about it, it's hard to have a rational reason. It's like falling in love. And if I ever write a book the title would be "Feet First."

No pun intended, that's really her motto—stepping into her creative endeavors without fear. She believes you have to think about what you're doing and you have to look at the project from different angles, but ultimately, you must follow your passion.

THE ADVENTURE BEGINS CREATIVELY
WITH UNLIKELY CONNECTIONS

Taryn began her shoe business adventure determined to travel to Italy, the international mecca for high-quality leather shoes. She wanted to manufacture her unique line of women's shoes there. Unfortunately, she was at a disadvantage because she didn't know anybody in the shoe industry, or anyone from Italy. But since she shops a lot, she asked her salesperson in the shoe department at Barney's, "Hey, do you know anyone from Italy who may have ties to the shoe industry?" Ironically enough, this woman had two Italian friends who travel to the States every August; one had a factory and one had a tannery in Italy.

Through phone calls that these Italians arranged, Taryn gained an invitation to meet up with people who could help her at the shoe trade show in Milan. Taryn excitedly made her arrangements to go to Italy.

I called my travel agent and I said, I need to find a hotel room during this time. And she responded, "Oh you've got to be the Pope to get a room in Milan during this time period because there are several trade shows going on, there's fashion week, and forget it. I can get you 100 miles away is the closest. And I said, "No, that's not acceptable."

So I visited my salesperson at Gucci. And at that time I was only buying sale items, but I love people. I love to get to know people so …

She said, "Okay, let me see what I can do." She called corporate. She got me a room in Milan at one of the best hotels at the Gucci corporate rate which was at half the price.

Taryn arranged to meet with the Italian friends of her Barney's salesperson at the shoe trade show in Milan, and they helped her get all the resources she needed.

That's another lesson, you just never know who you will meet, so you've just got to talk to everybody.

Through her shopping relationships, Taryn managed to get connected and set the stage for her shoe business. She manufactured her first samples through her contacts in Italy. Yet at the beginning, she was the one selling the prototypes to vendors. Here's where another retail association comes in:

So I get my samples . Now I have to sell these, but I don't know any buyers.

Next she visited Neiman's and asked her salesperson there, "Is there a sales rep here that you really like that you think is really nice?"

The Neiman salesperson gave Taryn the phone number of a woman named Barbara. Thankfully, Barbara agreed to meet with Taryn. Unfortunately, however, the sales rep looked at Taryn's shoes and told her she had a great concept but, "Honey, you can't afford me. I make over $100,000 a year, and there's just no way you can afford me."

Rather than leave Taryn high and dry, Barbara agreed to share names of other reps so that Taryn could get started. One was a buyer at Nordstrom's. With that name in mind, Taryn went to Nordstrom's and started looking at all the nametags on the shoe floor until she found a match.

I walked up to her and I said, "Hi Suncho, Barbara recommended that I talk to you and I have this new line. Would it be possible at all for you to look at the line? And she gave me my first $25,000 order.

From that beginning, Taryn was able to get other names of retailers and to truthfully say that her shoes were going to be sold at Nordstrom's. Five other accounts signed on because of this association. Taryn built a multi-million dollar business from that very foundation.

Being scrappy from the start, creative with her connections, and a complete "babe in the woods" about business made it easier for Taryn to run her business. She didn't worry about what she didn't know. She just tried whatever avenues occurred to her. Her approach also made her unique. Over the years people in the shoe industry commented that Taryn didn't think like somebody from the shoe industry.

And I said, I think that's part of my success. Because I think like a consumer; I think like . . . consumers today think. And I understand what they want. Whereas, people from the shoe industry are handicapped by what they've been told has always been done. They're kind of stuck in their old shoebox.

A SERIAL ENTREPRENEUR

Taryn proved herself in her business. Ten years after the launch, she sold her shoe business for many millions of dollars. That was just the beginning. Today she's launching a whole new entrepreneurial endeavor in foot skin care and sees herself as a serial entrepreneur, as well as a renaissance soul:

I've always thought of myself as a renaissance woman because, I just met with my close friend who was the manufacturer for me for six years now for the shoes. And I told her what I was doing in skin care and she responds, "How are you doing this; what do you know about skin care?"

And I said, "Nothing, but I'll learn." And that's part of the fun is that I get to learn something new and it's not scary, it's fascinating. So that's why I think I love it. I get bored with the same old routines.

Taryn remembers finishing her orthopedic surgery residency and seeing what she faced as looking like death when she realized for the next 25 years she would be doing the same 10 procedures over and over again. She didn't want to spend so many of her days engaged routinely. She didn't want to regret not taking the risk; instead, she wanted to spend her life in as stimulating a manner as possible:

It's not that you don't understand that there isn't a risk or that you're not afraid, but to be able to overcome your fears you have to take on the risk. That's where the courage is. And sometimes it helps just to start moving, just start doing it and it'll start to flow.

RISK TAKING IS PART OF HER NATURE

It's not that Taryn wasn't aware of the potential for failure, neither the first time as an entrepreneur or now, as she launches her new products. It's that she has been determined not to allow failure to happen. She knows that whatever she is up against, she has to prevail, even if she can't predict the course along the way.

Realistically, Taryn knew that big potential pitfalls were out there, but she told herself that whatever came up, she was going to overcome it. She didn't enter business saying, "This is going to be a piece of cake; there's just not going to be any problems." Her mantra was, "Whatever comes up, I'll overcome it." She simply had to figure out a way to succeed.

And if you start thinking that failure is not an option, then you will steel yourself for any problems. Like for example that $25,000 first order. The shoes came in and the soles were completely wrinkled. It was unacceptable. So I ran around L.A., found leather, had somebody make a custom dye. I drove to the Valley to get this done and then stayed up all night gluing soles onto the shoes, because I wasn't going to call up Nordstrom's and say, oh I can't deliver on a client. That was not an option.

There is no such thing as smooth sailing; entrepreneurs must have the ability to problem solve and think quickly, often under pressure. That's where Taryn's surgical background definitely was helpful to her because there she functioned in an environment where she was continuously problem solving. Many factors in surgery are thrown into the mix that can't be controlled or predicted and demand decisions on the run. Taryn took this background and training into business.

RESISTANCE, NOT SUPPORT, FROM HER FAMILY

Taryn's parents are traditional Vietnamese who thought she was crazy. For about a year, they were quite angry with her for leaving medicine.

Yet by the time Taryn was in her 30s—she started her first business at 31—she had gained some sense of who she was and told herself that acceptance wasn't what she was after:

I'm after realizing my dream. And basically nobody else has to walk in my shoes but me. So, I've got to be able to feel comfortable in them.

Originally, Taryn had wanted to become a writer, but her parents had prevailed on her career choice. Even though she's an independent woman today, at 18 she didn't know better than following her parents' dictums. She doesn't regret doing so. She doesn't think there's a pure right or wrong when it comes to career. In her mind becoming a doctor was a logical option for her because of her natural giftedness in science. It was an easy path for her, and it gave her a convincing platform for her shoe business.

THE CREDIBILITY OF BEING AN ORTHOPEDIC SURGEON AND A WOMAN

Being an orthopedic surgeon brought Taryn credibility for her shoe business. Her brand distinguished itself, not only with its fashion but also with its structure from someone who truly understood the foot. From her vantage point as a doctor, she could see the potential in the marketplace from looking at the shoes that were available and also knowing what women needed. Her shoes were soundly constructed AND fashionable.

Working all day and busy, many women need comfortable footwear; like it or not, though, they are still judged by their appearance. They need both fashion and function. According to Taryn, these elements were missing in the marketplace at the time she started her footwear business because most shoe companies are either run or owned by men.

Being a woman has enabled Taryn to understand completely what her target audience wants. The scale has tipped in her favor because of her gender. She advises other women to first figure out if their idea would appeal to other women because they must have consumers. An idea may sound great to the entrepreneur, but if it doesn't resonate, it's not going to work.

Many women helped Taryn along the way in her business, from the saleswoman at Barney's to her banker. These mentors have contributed to an urge for her to want to give back. She strongly believes women should help each other, just as they did when they lived on farms and shared tips about child rearing and housework. Women have always been very connected to each other, and we shouldn't lose that sense in business, according to Taryn.

Her advice to women entrepreneurs is even if you do have the expertise, you can't just rely completely on others to do your business for you. You have to stand alongside, guiding the process and making the final decision that you feel is best for your dream. Additionally, she encourages women to trust their intuition.

Your intuitions are not the female voodoo. It's that sense you get from all of the factors that you are considering all at once.

You just know in your head. There's a voice that says that's the right packaging. And I think what a lot of us do, and I do the same thing—I almost have to practice saying to myself listen to that voice [rather than] start doubting ourselves.

INNER AND OUTER BARRIERS WERE A FACTOR FOR HER

Taryn admits that her inner barriers were definitely her fears. For her, particularly, it was the fear of failing in front of others, that her parents would be able to tell her, "I told you so." Her colleagues would be able to say, "Gosh, what a crazy pipe dream that was, right?" In spite of this, she got to a place within herself where she realized that it didn't matter.

I would rather fail and face the embarrassment than to face the regret 40 years from now and think back, what did I do with my life? Why didn't I pursue that dream?

The external barrier for Taryn, as she imagines is the case for most women, occurred on the financial side of creating a business. The funding and the capital world are oriented toward larger corporations. As a result, women have a more difficult time getting their hands on startup capital. At the same time, money is a factor in every successful business.

Taryn secured a loan for startup costs from the SBA, but she believes the organization has changed its criteria for lending today, making it more stringent. She also got lucky because she had a female banker who understood the product.

ADVICE TO OTHER WOMEN

Taryn insists that if women run into a person who says no, this refusal does not mean that the business isn't valid or doesn't make sense. It just may mean the person may not understand it. She didn't realize when she entered the business world that banks are like people: they're all very different and looking for something different. Women should persistently approach a variety of lenders.

Some women are lucky to find the right fit the first time, but they need to keep moving if they don't. Just because the bank says no does not mean the business isn't right. The profile simply may not be right for their risk tolerance.

There's no right time to start a business, according to Taryn. It's just like having children; it may be the greatest thing you'll do, but there's no right or convenient time. The only answer to the question would be when you feel such a burning passion for what you do that you can't stop thinking about it. That is the right time.

Taryn's caution to women is that if you don't have the capital equity, you're going to have to put sweat equity into your business. You can't get out of that. Even if a woman is very creative but doesn't like the operational side of business, she'll have to take on most of the activities herself. When Taryn started her business, she had to do it all. There's just no way around it, unless you have the money to hire someone. That's why you have to pick something you're really passionate about.

To women who say to themselves, "Who am I to do this?" or "Who do I think I am?" Taryn retorts:

You've got to get rid of that voice. You should be asking that voice, "Who are you to be talking to me like that?" I mean, there are some great female entrepreneurs who just use their smarts and their problem-solving abilities and shear gut to make something out of nothing.

SELLING HER BUSINESS OPENS UP NEW CREATIVE OUTLETS

Taryn sold part of her business along the way, and in 2008 she entered negotiations for a complete buyout. She is now thinking of other products to create. Her shoes are expensive, and she wants to create more affordable items for women. Women complain often about aching feet, and so she formulated a product that she calls the stiletto stick, which sprays on for immediate relief from shoe discomfort. The product contains a combination of benzocaine, lavender, and peppermint to help with the swelling and the inflammation and soothe hot, red toes. Her next project involves skin care products for feet.

Her second time around in entrepreneurship, Taryn has accrued the proper capital. The business ideas still require networking, however. To that end, she has found and retains a consultant who knows the cosmetic industry and works with direct-to-consumer channels. Being able to pay for the woman's consulting fees has shortened Taryn's learning curve.

Taryn still goes to the trade shows to discover what the new ingredients are and works directly with chemists. She looks at different packaging companies and works alongside the graphic designers for the branding. She is still very much involved, but she feels fortunate to be able to afford to have a person actually designing her logo instead of doing it herself as she did the first time around.

Even though it's a new ball game, she cautions she still has to be quite involved; if she were not, she would diminish her business' authenticity.

It loses something in the message. And especially when you market to women there has to be an emotional connection; there has to be an experience that involves the heart as well as the experience that involves the brain.

I think that women are very holistic in their approach to buying. And I do believe that it's neuroscience-based, because we know that women's brain connections are in a web-like pattern instead of a linear pattern. So women are taking on a lot more data at the same time and they want that stimulation.

For Taryn success is measured in freedom: freedom to pursue her dreams, freedom to walk away from situations that are not healthy for her in emotional and psychological ways, and freedom to really chart new territories.

She still doesn't like the operational side of business, and what she's been able to do her second time around is focus primarily on the activities she's passionate about. She's negotiated ways to get the operational side of business off her plate. Taryn indulges her urge to write by creating much of her own marketing material, collaborating with a female copywriter.

THE NEW LAUNCH

Taryn plans to launch her skin care products in 2009—all for feet—under the business name of Haute Footure, with the tagline: "We make products that worship your feet." She wants to offer fashionable footcare products because she believes women want to feel they are purchasing presents to themselves. In this way they can feel feminine and worshipped. She also wants to create a fashion image for this brand, believing Haute Footure definitely spells fashion.

She expects her products to appear on the Home Shopping Network as well as in department stores. Initially she'll begin this venture with five products, adding more items every few months. Among her products she includes the stiletto stick for aching feet and a moisturizer containing peptides, which increases collagen because aging women lose cushioning at the bottom of their feet.

Taryn doesn't plan to address feet exclusively as she expands her new business. She is also experimenting with a new way to construct undergarments, based on *Grey's Anatomy* (the book), so that the areas of compression are based on muscle insertions to make women look better. She sees this product being on the drawing boards for two years.

Although medicine was her father's choice for her, Tara sees her experience as a physician actually paying off. She has never regretted going to medical school and encourages others not to feel like, "well, you know I went down a path that had nothing to do with what I really want to do." Not so—if you apply yourself and try to live a life of excellence, you are going to gain skills and habits that will help you in any field.

As she matures as a businesswoman, Taryn believes in her own judgment and follows her gut more often than she has in the past. For her, business has been an arena for learning, growth, and experimentation. She prides herself in the contribution she has made to women's lives and looks forward to providing even greater impact as time goes on.

ONE WOMAN'S COURAGE INSPIRES
MORE COURAGE FOR OTHER WOMEN

Now that you have learned about Taryn Rose's story and the emergence of her businesses, it's time to reflect on how this story can inspire you in your quest for your entrepreneurial adventure. Take some time to reflect on what you've just read and allow the following questions to guide you. Use your journal to take notes so that you can ground your understanding and learning for future reference.

1. How could a background in a field you no longer enjoy provide a foundation for a successful business?
2. Who in your life would think your business ideas were crazy? How might you mitigate their opinions?
3. What would you need to move away from in order to move toward what you want?
4. What do you fear you'd have to give up to succeed in your business?
5. Who will you disappoint if you don't succeed? If you do succeed?

WHAT CAN YOU LEARN FROM TARYN ROSE?

Taryn Rose offers a loud, clear reminder to be courageous. Imprinted in her DNA is the history of an immigrant who moves among cultures and fields to claim the land that resonates with her true being. She is a woman who takes what she has and spins it into greater gold, mindful of the people she is serving.

She is a woman willing to be foolish or crazy in the mind of her family, weighing that against the lifelessness of a repetitive future. It's not easy to walk away entirely from the prestige of being a surgeon. But she did that indeed to follow her true passion. Ironically, her parents may have taught her this lesson themselves when they gave up their life in Viet Nam and came to America.

Taryn reminds us to be inventive and creative in the way we go about our business. You don't know anyone from Italy? Ask your shoe salesperson. You can't get a room in Milan? Go to another salesperson. Want to meet a sales rep to present your line to the public? Walk through the store until you find the name tag that matches the name you've been given. Use your imagination to find what you want without ever allowing yourself to be defeated.

Although well-educated and you might say well-heeled, Taryn saw no job beneath her. The shoes came wrinkled from Italy, but she wasn't about to let that stop her. She did whatever she had to do to right the situation, even if it meant gluing the soles on herself.

It's not that Taryn Rose never knew fear or was not plagued with doubt. It's not that she didn't have her losses along the way; she saw her first marriage slip away as her business blossomed. But she did not let her doubts define her. Fear was not the leader in her life. Although saddened by the dissolution of her marriage, she continued on.

Once again we are reminded of the currency of authenticity. We see from Taryn's success how well she converses with her sense of herself and that she recognizes its importance in the marketplace. Who she is aligns with what she does and the products she offers. This essence becomes irresistible.

YOUR TURN NOW—WHAT DID *YOU* LEARN FROM TARYN ROSE?

CHAPTER 10

ARGHAND COOPERATIVE

A Conversation with Sarah Chayes, Founder of the Arghand Cooperative in Kandahar, Afghanistan (www.arghand.org)

I long to accomplish great and noble tasks, but it is my chief duty to accomplish humble tasks as though they were great and noble. The world is moved along, not only by the mighty shoves of its heroes, but also by the aggregate of the tiny pushes of each honest worker.

—*Helen Keller*

You're going to start a soap factory in an active fear of war, right? Tell me a worse climate for starting an entrepreneurial enterprise!

Our soaps, colored with local vegetable dyes and hand-molded and smoothed till they look like lumps of marble, and our oils, elixirs for polishing the skin, sell in boutiques that cater to the pampered in New York, Montreal, and San Francisco.

—*Sarah Chayes*, founder of the Arghand Cooperative in Afghanistan

Where in the world could you lay down a foundation for a company that would be more unstable than Afghanistan? Why would *anyone* consider such a spot for a business cooperative? What courage it takes there just to stay alive each day! But historian and free-lance American journalist Sarah Chayes makes a convincing argument for her chosen adopted spot in an *Atlantic Monthly* article in December 2007:

In the wake of 9/11, getting Afghanistan right seemed terribly important—important to the direction history would take in the 21st century. Slogans urged us to cut up the world into two opposing blocs, to align ourselves with one or the other of two irrevocably hostile civilizations. That thinking would get us nowhere, I was convinced.

What better place than Kandahar to give in to the nudgings of a conscience that had been telling me for some time: "Stop talking about it already—do something."

—*Sarah Chayes*, The Atlantic Monthly, December 2007

Sarah had made her way to Afghanistan in 2001 while covering the fall of the Taliban for National Public Radio. When she decided to stay, she accepted a leadership position within a non-profit organization. Multi-lingual and fluent in Pashto, a native Afghani tongue, Chayes found herself listening more often than speaking.

Throughout her time in the country, the native people consistently asked why foreigners didn't engage in economic development on their behalf. To them economic development meant starting factories, hiring people, and creating jobs. Sarah took heed.

She ventured into an existing dairy cooperative in Kandahar, which the owners gave her to run. Eventually, however, she became dissatisfied with their motivations and ethics. At the same time, the people from whom she had been collecting milk encouraged Sarah to do something commercial with their fruits. They saw milk as a sideline offering no more than pocket change. To them the real staple in this southern area of the country was fruit.

Sarah wondered what could be done with fruit. It's heavy, perishable, and, in an ordinary state, challenging to export. Since her objective was to focus on exports, because more money exists outside Afghanistan than within the country and she wanted to bring in currency, Sarah contemplated what she could do with the native fruit.

Then Sarah remembered an exchange several years before with an anthropologist researcher who was raving about the value of rose oil as a commodity. Could oil be extracted from fruit, she wondered?

That's when Sarah also began thinking seriously about natural skincare products. She especially liked soap because she doesn't use cosmetics and was keenly aware of the huge market for skin-care products in the West. With these notions in mind, she began a fascinating process of moving forward with a commercial endeavor.

Still running the dairy cooperative, Sarah started crystallizing the idea for a new business venture. However, in the midst of her considerations, she took a six-month break from Afghanistan. She left partly to keep from burning out and partly to finish writing a book. She realized her tome could become a reality only if she could dedicate herself to it fully.

The idea for her business truly came into its fullest development while outside of Afghanistan. Back in the United States, Sarah visited a natural soap maker in New Hampshire to understand the production process for creating soap. The woman owner kindly allowed Sarah to hang out with her while she mixed a batch of soap. Watching the process, Sarah realized, "I can do this!"

And not only can I do it, but the idea was how can I actually create formulas? In other words, modify or focus the production around things that are specific to southern Afghanistan. The whole point is to expand the market for licit local agriculture. So you want as many as possible of your raw materials to come locally. And also it helps in branding, frankly. You can really focus on what southern Afghanistan is all about in terms of both the cause, but also the mystique.

THE LUNACY AND EXCITEMENT
OF STARTING HER BUSINESS

The stumbling blocks Sarah confronted starting her business were not for the faint of heart. For one she had no economics or manufacturing business background. Second, she had no money. Third, she was considering undertaking this business in one of the most dangerous cities on the face of the earth! And fourth, the skincare market, which looked quite saturated, led most people to discourage her, saying:

Sarah you're out of your mind! There's an Origins and Body Shop on every other street corner. How can you possibly break into this market?

In spite of all of this, Sarah was undaunted. She focused more on the contribution she wanted to make than on the obstacles she was confronting. Her long-term objective was to contribute to the process of weaning southern Afghanistan off of its dependence on the opium poppy by manufacturing skincare products using indigenous items. Actually, she found a benefit to working within an active arena of war: here people think if you stay alive, you've succeeded, so the measure of success in Afghanistan is much different than that in California, for example.

Sarah established her business, Arghand, in 2005 as a nonprofit cooperative, offering skincare products for profit. With this structure, for startup capital she could look for donations and grants, public money, and private donations, thus greatly reducing the financial risk. Assets, revenues, and risks were to be jointly owned by those who contributed their efforts to the company's activities. Planning and decision making would be carried out by consensus.

Sarah's first product goal was to create a soap using the oil from pomegranate seeds. At the time, the pomegranate craze was just gaining momentum around the world because of the perceived health benefits from the fruit. Sarah's hunch, based on local lore, was that the skin of the pomegranate was good for human skin. Later she found medical research proving that the oil from the pomegranate seed is well suited for skin care.

The cooperative's first major purchase was a $2,000 hand-cranked seed oil press ordered from Germany. It took days to assemble and two or three days of patient operation before oil could be extracted from the pomegranate seeds. No one had ever attempted this feat before, but Sarah was certain oil could be obtained.

Afghans collaborating with Sarah and their ancestors had been working with pomegranates all their lives. Yet they had never imagined extracting oil from the seeds. As the native people gathered around, their excitement was palpable, and they almost couldn't believe their eyes when pomegranate oil *did* finally flow from the press.

Sarah and her group also wanted to develop the esthetics of the product. They groped through a trial-and-error process to discover the right balance of ingredients to prevent the soap from turning blue; the alkaline of the soap could affect the magenta color of the pomegranate under certain circumstances. A labor-intensive procedure they engaged in resulted in a marble/granite-textured soap, but the amount of skin-nourishing oils within the product inhibited unmolding. Sarah was unflappable:

Then I said, hey, what if we hand-mold the things deliberately to look like rocks? And my own mother's bathroom has a marble top, and so I started picturing this thing. You know, what if you had soap that looked like marble and it would look just dynamite. A lot of people like the look of stone and have stone bathroom fixtures and things like that, but particularly in the market that we were aiming for, which was a relatively high-end and luxury and esthetic market. And so these things were really beautiful, and what was kind of exciting too was wow, we were producing something that was visually gorgeous.

With the production hang-ups solved and the product marketed worldwide, the quality of the soap proved to be a boon to business. Many customers have reported becoming addicted to using Arghand's soap, claiming they won't use any other.

FINDING A NEW SOURCE FOR PRODUCTS

As the Afghan Arghand cooperative members sprung into the fun of the business, they would bring unusual, new raw materials from the bazaar to Sarah, insisting the items be included in the skincare products. One example is something called *shneh* which the Afghans proposed extracting oil from as well. Shneh are a turquoise-colored, pea-sized snack food with an evergreen taste. The shneh plant grows wild in the area.

Curious about shneh, Sarah turned to an Afghan agricultural specialist. She asked, "Atiqullah, what on earth is shneh?" Even though Sarah trusted that shneh was not poisonous, because people ate it, she also believed you have to know what something is before you can use it. They would have to put the ingredient on their labels and to know what the botanical name was. Additionally, they needed to test the oil.

So I asked him "what is this stuff?" And he says, "oh let me check my notes from Kabul University in the 1970s," or something like that, and I'll call you back.

So he calls me back and he says, "Well I think it's Pistacia khinjuk." And I wanted to say God bless you again, what is Pistacia khinjuk? Well thank God for Google, right? I spelled it phonetically and put it into Google and that is the botanical name, it's Pistacia, p-i-s-t-a-c-i-a, and then the second word is k-h-i-n-j-u-k.

These items turned out to be wild pistachios, a close cousin to the pistachio nuts we eat. As a result of this find, Arghand now has created soap and oil whose base is Pistacia—wild pistachio oil, found in Pistacia khinjuk.

Also through Google, Sarah found someone at an American university doing his Ph.D. in botany on Pitacia khinjuk. She reached him and asked what he thought about their extracting the oil from this wild nut for soap. He declared, "I have been waiting to see when the oil of these seeds would be used for skincare products; it's an absolute natural." That kind of connection was really exciting to Sarah: to realize Arghand made discoveries not only for their business, but in botany and chemistry as well.

ACHIEVING INTERNATIONAL EXPOSURE
AND COMMUNITY

What kept Sarah and her employees going were new discoveries, as well as the success of the product. Arghand has never done any deliberate marketing or advertising. However, Sarah is somewhat of a public figure, and when she gets interviewed on radio and television about Afghanistan, of course Arghand comes up. For example, she's been a guest on *Bill Moyer's Journal* twice in the last year and on Rachel Maddow's popular MSNBC show in 2009. In that sense, Sarah's created a degree of free advertising.

One of the first excellent pieces of media exposure Sarah had at Arghand was from the French version of the Canadian Broadcasting Company. Since Sarah speaks fluent French, this interview was conducted entirely in that language. Fifty emails arrived in Sarah's email box the next day from French Canadians.

As a result of this exposure, people immediately wanted to carry Arghand's products in various parts of Canada, including Montreal. By responding to the interest in Canada, Sarah discovered she was actually creating a community in the West as well as in Afghanistan.

So where we thought that we were focused on Afghanistan and the whole point was to help develop the economy and develop collective decision-making processes in a business environment and all of that kind of thing. Suddenly we were also finding that we were filling a niche in a way in the West, fitting in in a really interesting way into this whole small but very important and growing economy of people who care about the raw materials that go into the products they use: the working conditions, they're interested in natural products, they're interested in the esthetic of their product—of the products they buy—and they're willing to spend a little bit more money on something they use anyway, like soap, in order to get a higher quality product that also is contributing to human dignity and the environment rather than destroying it. There are a growing number of people who take that into consideration.

Specialty shop owners, hearing these interviews and through word of mouth feedback, began approaching Sarah and her cooperative about carrying Arghand's products. Return business occurred because customers became intrigued with the story of this business and truly liked the product.

Shops in the West have been enthusiastic. Obviously they need to meet their financials, but they're not driven exclusively by a short-term profit motive. By the same token, the survival of some of these shops depends on Arghand's existence, because in 2007 alone these merchants purchased $30,000–$40,000 worth of product. The shops need Arghand and Arghand needs the shops, resulting in mutual benefit.

In the early days actually it was UPS's fault, it wasn't our fault, but a shipment didn't get out fast enough and some of the shops were getting impatient. Where's our orders? And things like that. And I remember writing a letter to the retailers, explaining to them what had happened in Kandahar that week. And telling them that you're on a voyage here.

And all this stuff you read in the newspaper about what's happening in Afghanistan, well we live it! And that's the conditions under which we are producing this stuff. And they were incredible. And most of them posted the letter on their own Web sites and have never bothered us about supply or speed of delivery or anything like that since then. And so it's been this incredible process of discovering that there is a different economy out there that's operating under different principles than the mainstream, mass market.

THE PEOPLE BEHIND THE PRODUCTS

Three and a half years into the business, in addition to Sarah, there are 13 Arghand cooperative members in Kandahar. Purchasing raw materials directly from local producers, the company contracts with four additional people who gather herbs and other materials to be included in the products.

At the same time, a whole other dimension of activity exists around packaging the product. In Harat, another Afghan city, nine weavers produce hand spun and woven materials that are formed into strips. These strips, in fabrics similar to the famous turbans Afghans wear on their heads, surround the soap fastened with a bow. Scaled down versions of turbans are created to be sold as women's scarves, also sold by Arghand. All of this production has increased the need for more weavers from an original number of three.

Arghand also purchases almonds from five different families. With all of this industriousness, Sarah proudly tallies up the people employed in one way or another with Arghand: She counts 15 full-time employees, including herself, and as many as 25 part-timers. Most are located in Afghanistan, but a few are found in the United States and Canada, not to mention volunteer retirees who take care of shipping.

In addition to the workers and volunteers who make the viability of the business possible, Sarah has relied on her family for moral support. At the outset, however, members were totally skeptical of the endeavor. They had to come to terms with her obsession.

Sarah's mother, an energetic 80-year-old professor at Tufts University has found it psychologically difficult to imagine her daughter in the dangerous situation in Afghanistan. Despite her worries about Sarah's safety, she has not issued an ultimatum for Sarah to return to the States.

You're going to start a soap factory in an active fear of war, right? Tell me a worse climate for starting an entrepreneurial enterprise!

OPERATING A PURPOSEFUL BUSINESS UNDER EXTREME CONDITIONS

In addition to reducing dependence in southern Afghanistan on opium by expanding the market for licit local agriculture, Sarah hopes to continue strengthening the economic fabric of the country, providing dignified employment to cooperative members and encouraging their taking ownership of the business.

To Sarah, the social ownership of the business could be seen as social entrepreneurship. Yet this is not a bake sale. The cooperative is making products that are commercially viable. The business represents the culmination of goals and aspirations she carried inside of her.

In some ways the business has evolved beyond what she could have expected. Having lived in Afghanistan nearly 4 years before launching Arghand, Sarah knew the harsh realities she was facing.

Even so, the area around her has deteriorated from when she began, a circumstance she unfortunately foresaw.

The security challenges have prevented Arghand from expanding. Ironically, commercially the demand for products is greater than what the cooperative can handle. They could triple their production and easily expand if they weren't living in such dangerous conditions. If the situation were different, they could also diversify their product line further as well.

The reality is that within the backdrop in which they operate, people are continuously being killed. Sarah sees her employees struggling with their physical integrity and the psychological pressure of living daily in mortal danger:

So I guess that although I did with one side of my brain predict the deterioration and the situation, it's hard to know how that's going to feel. When you're doing business planning, you don't plan for no longer being able to buy the piece of land that you were planning to buy to build a factory because you're going to get killed if you build a factory. Because you can't make that your production site because it's too dangerous for your cooperative members. We have had to constantly adapt and what's been extraordinary has been, for me, our adaptability. It's just been amazing to see how (when) this challenge arises, or this constraint arises, we hitch up our trousers and figure out a way around it. But we really pretty much are now at the point where we can't. We can maintain our current operations, but we can't expand the way we normally would if we were a normal business.

Dealing with the psychological damage of her cooperative members has also required more bravery than Sarah expected. Managing people is always a tremendous challenge. But basically, the population of Afghanistan is suffering collective post-traumatic stress disorder.

These are people who have lived through 3 decades of combat. That experience has lasting impact on peoples' psychology. Any textbook on this syndrome will cite the toll this takes: lack of trust, short tempers, and inability to plan into the future.

Cooperative members experience all of this, and Sarah experiences it as well. She has found herself to be more short-fused than she understood herself to be, and she tries to handle that and also give her staff warning when she feels one of those moods approaching.

On the flip side, when the situation started severely deteriorating in the fall of 2007 to the point where Sarah had to minimize her presence on the site, she was overjoyed to see how her folks took the challenge on. They achieved what she expected to be a years' worth of evolution in a month. That experience became a blessing in disguise for the development of the organization.

One day there was a suicide bombing against a van-load of interpreters who worked on the military base. The women who worked at the cooperative came to work through a maze of body parts.

Workers are continuously subject to intimidation and danger:

None of my women can tell anyone they know, apart from their immediate families, that they work at Arghand. They have to lie and say that they are domestic servants in somebody's household or something like that.

One of my cooperative members was laid in wait for by Taliban in this village, and thank God he was on duty that night at the cooperative so he didn't fall into the ambush and die.

Electricity also has been a massive problem. Arghand has one machine that needs a decent amount of electricity, three kilowatts, which is actually not much by Western standards. The town receives electricity only up to 5 hours out of every 36. Nor do people know when they're going to receive those hours of electricity.

Consequently, workers sleep with light switches on so that if the electricity returns in the middle of the night, the lights turn on and awaken them. And that means they work the machine from 1 AM to 5 AM if that is when they have electricity. It's beyond one's imagination the constraints they've had to work around!

SUCCESS WITH POSITIVE INTERNATIONAL
IMPLICATIONS

In spite of having crazy limitations and continuous setbacks, Arghand produces products people love. Sarah credits this success to the men and women of the cooperative working in conditions beyond comprehension.

Often orders expand because Arghand soap was introduced to people as gifts and they like the product so much that they approach their local bath-and-body shop or health food store with a request to carry the item. Accordingly, shop keepers respond.

Last Christmas a friend of ours was in one of our retailers in Manhattan which was sold out and somebody else came in and asked for some of that fantastic soap from Afghanistan. Now this is Manhattan where the Twin

Towers fell down. That people in Manhattan were connecting Afghanistan with fantastic soap instead of with terrorists was to me an incredible achievement.

Another mark of success for Sarah is that people look to Arghand as a beacon for the whole situation in the country. The Afghan diaspora avidly follows what Sarah and her employees are doing. As long as the brand is surviving and continuing to do what they do and speaking out about the issues, the exiles have hope.

As a nonprofit with a revenue-generating for-profit business within it, Arghand continues to attract donations, primarily for equipment purchases. For example, to deal with their electricity problem, the cooperative has purchased a large, expensive solar generator, costing $70,000 with shipping. Sarah received help with this from the Canadian International Development Agency, called CIDA. This agency is the Canadian equivalent of USAID, which is the government overseas development agency. Private donors fill in the rest of the gaps.

Being a nonprofit business in a war zone gives an entity access to financing that a normal business wouldn't have. If Sarah didn't have the option of operating as a non-profit, she could not have started Arghand at all because the constraints are so monumental.

In addition to donations, the organization also gets help in kind. Their Web site is designed by a French Canadian Web designer who reached out and said she'd like to donate her time to their business.

Sarah finds it uplifting to discover how many people really *do* want to get involved, but many don't know how. She provides people a gateway. After all, not everyone can drop their lives and move to Afghanistan.

BUSINESS AS HOLY WAR

To Sarah and her employees, Arghand is not just a business, it's a mission. Taking that a step further, when the members discuss the company's purpose together, the Afghanis characterize their work as a Jihad or Holy War!

Jihad has been twisted by the extremists, where they see it as all the things that Al-Qaeda stands for. Afghans do not support that—the vast, vast, vast majority of Afghans do not support Islamic extremism. And I don't want to get into a whole political conversation about how the Taliban came to be in Afghanistan, but my cooperative members call this [business] Jihad. It's struggle for the good of people. That's what they understand Jihad to be.

This struggle sustains Sarah because she sees her role and that of Arghand as demonstrating how interconnected and interdependent we all are, no matter where we live on the globe. The Afghan members understand our synergistic relationship as much as the Westerners do, even though the Afghans are not educated, and some are even illiterate.

Of the 13 at Arghand, at the most 4 can read and write, but they all recognize the importance of their business. They say that Arghand is a bridge between Afghanistan and America. Part of their mission is to improve the image of Afghanistan in America, while at the same time improving the image of America in Afghanistan. Sarah sees this mirror understanding crucial to what the twenty-first century will become:

And I can't think of a better place for me to be doing it. It's not the only place to do it, but for me, Afghanistan was the place for me to take my stand.

Sarah hasn't found any reason she should stop doing her mission there. The only situation that's really starting to restrict her is security. Sarah believes she's the only Western development person left on the ground in Kandahar. Periodically, she leaves Afghanistan for her own safety.

Even though it's counterintuitive, being a woman helps Sarah in her work. Although Afghanistan remains an anti-feminist society, particularly in the conservative South, as a Western female she is not treated as a native woman would be. Setting aside the violent extremists, the regular society members see Sarah as a third gender. That gives her a huge advantage because she can interact with both men and women. In Afghanistan nobody else can interact with both men and women. Women can interact only with women and men can interact only with men, aside from one's immediate family.

Fortunately, Sarah is treated as a man by men. For example, she will sit down and hold meetings with tribal elders. This license seems crazy under the circumstances we know about women in this country. Yet she has carte blanche or laissez-passer—French for moving around without restriction. On the other hand, because she is female, she can, of course, interact with women as well. In essence being female has been a tremendous boon to her in her business and in Afghanistan.

SARAH ADVISES WOMEN WITH ENTREPRENEURIAL AMBITIONS

Sarah advises women with business ideas to follow their passion and their inner urges. She believes that you should be doing something that you want to do because life is going to be hard no matter what you do. What's likely to carry you across the rough times is knowing you're doing what you care about. That may mean resisting the advice of those near and dear to you; in their eyes your vision might be a bit off base, unusual, or iconoclastic.

That doesn't mean you should be rash or irresponsible either. You need to lay the careful groundwork for whatever you decide to do, but what you do should be something that lights you up.

Because we've only got one life and why waste it on anything that's any less than that?

For women who question themselves about their capacity to become entrepreneurs, Sarah says, "Bullshit!" And she doesn't think you should ever second guess yourself. If you think that you have weaknesses, set about improving in those areas. For example, Sarah didn't know anything about accounting, but she sought help from an American reservist whose job was to support small businesses in Kandahar. She visited him every Friday, and he gave her accounting lessons. She was dedicated to learning what she needed to absorb.

Sarah advises women to recognize their weaknesses and then do whatever it takes to compensate. Either learn what you don't know, or if you really hate that part of the business, find somebody else to do it. Sarah insists women are truly capable of doing whatever they put their minds to and proves it by walking her own talk.

ONE WOMAN'S COURAGE INSPIRES MORE COURAGE FOR OTHER WOMEN

Now that you have learned about Sarah Chayes's story and the emergence of Arghand in the midst of a world of war and conflict, it's time to reflect on how this story can inspire you in your quest for your entrepreneurial adventure. Take some time to reflect on what you've just read and allow the following questions to guide you. Use your journal to take notes so that you can ground your understanding and learning for future reference.

1. What courageous stand do you take about what goes on in our world?
2. What natural products are waiting to be extracted in your area?
3. What local artisans exist around you? What are they producing that you could bring to market?
4. Is there a natural nonprofit organization that would gain from having a for-profit arm? If so, how might you approach them with your ideas?
5. What do you care about so much that you'd possibly be willing to risk your life for?

WHAT CAN YOU LEARN FROM SARAH CHAYES?

Sarah Chayes must be much admired for the courage of her convictions and the dedication with which she carries out her mission. When she says that life is hard anyway, so why not do something meaningful with your life, she challenges us to consider what that could be.

Starting a business in Afghanistan has meant existing in the most difficult conditions, but Sarah reminds us of what it is to take calculated risks. She's a woman of hyper-vigilance, perhaps out of necessity from living in a war-torn area. Yet she eloquently uses her senses to scope out the possibilities far and wide. This is a woman with her antenna up. And she uses her know-how to take best advantage of what is around her.

Sarah is patient and persistent. Imagine what it took for her to continue to believe that she could extract oil from pomegranate seeds when no one had done so previously. How many would be willing to push through several days without results? She was persistent and inventive when her molds proved to be ineffective for the soap.

This is a woman with high values and standards who also makes do simply, drawing example from the surrounding culture. Recognizing that the uniqueness of the Arghand story could open the door for people to become intrigued enough to purchase the company's skincare products, Sarah made certain that the quality of the products would demand repeat business.

Sarah is a person who creates a groundswell of quiet excitement wherever she goes. She demonstrates a capacity to both lead and collaborate. She is smart, yet willing to do what she needs to do to improve her skills and abilities. No task is beneath her.

We cannot come away from hearing Sarah Chayes's story without being inspired. Whatever each of us might attempt in business will seem doable in the shadow of her example.

YOUR TURN NOW—WHAT DID *YOU* LEARN FROM SARAH'S STORY?

Exercising Your Own Courage to Start and Run a Business

Now that you've read the stories of these inspiring women who launched their businesses as their own creative acts, it's time to see how their examples of courage can support you.

When it comes down to it, mustering courage is a head trip. Often it's the inner demons that will deter you more than whatever else comes at you from the outside. You can see from these women that they found ways to conquer their own fears.

The **Magic Approach** (see Introduction, p. xxi) can be your secret weapon for conquering your inner beasts. When you consider the **Magic Approach**, you'll see that what the model offers to solidify your courage are beliefs and strategy. They are found on either side of courage in our Venn diagram. Fortunately, there are effective ways to combat the strongest of the gremlins, saboteurs, monkey minds, little inner rascals—whatever you might call the parts of yourself that hold you back from what you want to achieve. Their job actually is just to keep the status quo going. It's nice that there's a part of you that wants to protect you, but it becomes dysfunctional when it truly holds you back from your dream.

It is therefore necessary to identify the beliefs you have that are holding you back. Some may be in your conscious awareness; others may not.

WORKING WITH YOUR DISEMPOWERING BELIEFS

Take out your journal and make a list of all the reasons you think you can't have your dream business.

Really. Go do it. Make your list. This is your golden opportunity to confront your fears. I challenge you to fill up at least a page or two with your negative beliefs.

If you can get these on paper (or on an electronic page) and really force yourself to purge them from rolling around in your head, you're apt to see how silly many of them are. These beliefs are like rats that are leaving their drippings in all the dark corners of your soul. When you shine the light, the rats scurry away.

DISEMPOWERING BELIEFS WITH "THE WORK OF BYRON KATIE®"

Another way you can "defang" disempowering beliefs is by truly engaging them—questioning them. Byron Katie has developed a simple process for this that she calls "The Work."

Let's demonstrate how this can function, using her process to "defang" the belief "I don't know where to start."

I don't know where to start.

Is it true?

Yes.

Can you absolutely know you don't know where to start?

No.

How do you react when you believe that you don't know where to start?

I feel scared. I can't think. I get anxious. I worry I could never be an entrepreneur.

Does this thought bring you peace or stress?

Stress.

Who would you be without this thought?

I would be someone with an idea for a business. I would be excited about the next step. I could start by doing some Internet research.

Turn your thought around—what's the opposite of *I don't know where to start?*

I do know where to start.

Now give me at least three specific, genuine examples of how the turnaround is true in your life.

Well, I've already started! I have the idea, and that's a big start. Two, when I'm not feeling confused or afraid, I know where to go on the Internet to do my research. Three, I know how to go to friends and colleagues who know more than I do about business and ask them for help.

Another way to look at this is the following: When you believe your stressful thoughts, your mind doesn't know where to start. It's blocking you out of fear. When you question these thoughts, you may discover an openness of mind that makes the unknown a great adventure.

By simply questioning your thoughts and looking at their opposite, this process reduces the bottleneck in your mind. It allows you to see options other than the one your head is telling you.

If you'd like to find a worksheet you can follow to do this work with your beliefs, go to www.thework.com to get your own, more specifically, http://www.thework.com/downloads/onebelief.pdf

I recommend you do this work with your disempowering beliefs daily. It could be like brushing your teeth.

USING THE BELIEF TRANSFORMATION MATRIX

Jeff Staggs (jeff@jeffstaggs.com), a master certified coach and colleague, created another powerful process useful for transforming negative beliefs. He calls it the Belief Transformation Matrix. It works well in seeing how closely our beliefs can be tied to our actions or inactions.

Here's how you do it: Take a page from your journal and draw three columns. In the far left column, put the heading: **Disempowering Belief**. In the middle column, **Related Behavior**. In the right hand column, **Related Result**. And below the Disempowering Belief, let's choose the one we used earlier, *I don't know where to* *begin.* Below the other columns ask yourself what your behavior is and the result you're getting related to that belief. It will look something like this:

Disempowering Belief	Related Behavior	Related Result
(Start Here) *I don't know where to begin*	• *Spinning my wheels* • *Consider any activity as too hard* • *Don't start my business*	• *Feel guilty, worry and procrastinate about doing anything*

You can see the direct connection between the thought, the behavior, and the result. One leads logically to the next.

Now, work this process in the opposite direction from right to left with a new set of three columns, starting with the **Preferred Result** you are after:

Empowering Belief	New Behavior	Preferred Result
I have what I need to get started	• *I'm using the Internet to research* • *I'm finding what I'm doing is easy and pleasurable*	(Start Here) • *Feeling good about what I'm doing* • *I'm getting new leads every day*

By working from the preferred result, you are able to begin with the end in mind—what you want to accomplish. You can write as many results as you'd like. From there, you can ask what behavior you would have been engaged in if you had accomplished that, which leads you to the answer for the middle column. New activities you would engage in related to the result would be listed here. Again, you may want to list a number of them. Finally, ask yourself if you had the result you wanted and you were engaged in the behaviors that would make that result possible, what would you be thinking? That answer becomes your empowering belief. The more you tell yourself this belief, the more the activities and results begin to flow from it.

The reason this process is called a Belief Transformation Matrix is that you are using the columns to lay out your thinking and see how your beliefs are tied to what you are accomplishing (or not accomplishing). By working the format from what you want to accomplish until you achieve a new empowering belief, you have a chance to get unstuck—you really do have the opportunity to transform your experience.

No matter what process you choose, writing out all your negative beliefs until you tire yourself, doing "The Work," or working the Belief Transformation Matrix, you now have useful strategies that will enable you to gain the courage you need to move forward on your business.

If you remember from Tami Simon's story when Jirka tells her to invest in herself with the inheritance from her father, her first reaction was she didn't know what she and "her bad self" could do. Had she stayed stuck there, she wouldn't have listened to her inner voice that told her she should disseminate perennial wisdom. Cami Walker dismissed her medicine woman for the task of 29 gifts in 29 days. If she stayed with the belief that this activity was beyond her, she wouldn't have discovered the riches awaiting her in her renewed health and business. Had Taryn Rose listened to her parents about not giving up medicine, she too would have negated her dream.

Each of these women, like all of us, had to confront her mind demons in order to have the courage to step out to her dreams. The reason I am able to tell their stories is that they confronted their internal voices and brushed them aside. You can too, with a set of strategies to do the job. Now get into action!

—— SECTION 3 ——

ACTION

It is common sense to take a method and try it. If it fails, admit it frankly and try another. But above all, try something.

—Franklin D. Roosevelt

I've found that luck is quite predictable. If you want more luck, take more chances. Be more active. Show up more often.

—Brian Tracy

Don't you wish you had a million dollars for every idea you could have put into action, but didn't? Years ago when I was just getting started with a personal computer and a printer, I thought how great it would be to have my own unique clothing pattern that I could print out with my own measurements so that I could create a custom fit wardrobe.

Did I find a programmer to collaborate with me on this idea? No—I just sat on it. And wouldn't you know, someone did act on it and created a thriving business from which I ended up buying software—LivingSoft—You can find it on the Internet today as Living-Soft NW. They have been selling software for years that helps women whip up their own perfect-fitting clothing.

A friend told me about a woman who at 50 years old wanted to fulfill her dream of becoming a lawyer. Rather than listen to her inner gremlin's message that she was too old to do this, she took another tack. She told herself, "It wouldn't hurt if I investigated what law schools are in my area." After doing this search and finding a school matching her criteria, she then told herself, "It wouldn't hurt if I went over to the school and picked up an application." And then, "It wouldn't hurt if I filled out the application; it wouldn't hurt if I took one class." And on and on, one class, one semester at a time until, five years later at the ripe old age of 55, she graduated from law school. Somewhere out there, this woman is practicing law!

Imbedded in this true story are the myriad of individual action steps amassed that led her to her ultimate goal. Had she thought of everything that she'd have to do to graduate from law school and start her practice, she probably wouldn't have bothered. But taking each small step allowed her to gain enough confidence to go on to the next, until ultimately she had triumphed.

Many people beat themselves up by thinking they are procrastinators and doomed to not get into action. But we coaches like to call these people out on the lie they're telling themselves. Getting into action is not rocket science—it just requires an ability to put one foot in front of the other—motion begets more motion.

The women you'll meet in this section all qualify as people who saw the value of their business idea and got moving. Let their examples spur you on into action related to the business dreams you want to manifest.

CHAPTER 11

MOXIE TRADES

A Conversation with Marissa McTasney, Founder of Moxie Trades (www.moxietrades.com)

Dreams pass into the reality of action. From the actions stems the dream again; and this interdependence produces the highest form of living.

—*Anais Nin*

And so I thought that's crazy, then where are the pink boots? Why aren't we making them? 'Cause this is so easy. It's just a change of color; it's not a big deal!

—*Marissa McTasney*, founder of Moxie Trades

When we think of boots and women in the same breath, we are reminded of the song popularized by Nancy Sinatra: *These boots are made for walking!* Yet one Canadian woman thinks pink when she considers women's boots. She couldn't understand why tradeswomen would be expected to wear ugly, ill-fitting, men's work boots instead of ones uniquely designed for women, and she set out to do something about this gap. Marissa McTasney, a real woman of action, saw a need and ran with it.

Thirty-three-year-old Marissa began her company in Canada in 2006 with the name Tomboy Trades Limited. So as not to be confused with a U.S. company named Tomboy Tools, she changed the name of her company to Moxie Trades. Her company provides boots, hard hats, goggles, and t-shirts for women who work in trades or traditional blue collar environments. Her items are distinguished from their male counterparts not only because of their feminine colors but also because they come in shapes and sizes more suitable to women's bodies.

Prior to starting her business, she worked in an administrative function in IBM's management software business division in Toronto—a good job for a high school graduate with no more than a year of art college.

Yet during a year-long maternity leave with her first child, Carter, Marissa began considering alternative careers. While she raised her family, she wanted independence and time away from the office. However, after the leave ended, she returned to IBM because she still hadn't found a direction.

Two years later, she was out a second time, giving birth to daughter Frankie. Again, Marissa faced the question of what to do next. Having a year to consider her future, because of Canada's liberal maternity leave policy, she gained an opportunity to mull her options.

HER PHILOSOPHY SPURS HER TO ACTION

While home with Carter the first time around, Marissa had begun writing and illustrating "a cute, sweet little book" on the philosophies of life, meant for her children. She completed and self-published the project while on leave with Frankie. In writing that book, Marissa realized her destiny was not to return to a desk job; doing so was not aligned with what she professed to her children. Still she couldn't figure out what else to do.

Clues did abound for Marissa. By her own admission, she loves building stuff. Being artistic, she often visited a local 24-hour Home Depot, sometimes at 3:00 in the morning because she "totally screwed something up." She prefers learning by trial and error. She loves painting textures and faux finishes and painting peoples' homes. Because of this passion, she thought about launching into a house-painting business:

Why not do that, because it might give me the life balance I want. I can own my own business and I can be close to home. And maybe one day I could have a crew of construction women. I thought I would love to renovate and flip homes. I thought this is really what I want to do.

With this spark of an idea, Marissa began searching for a course for women in skilled trades about which she had read. She found the program and discovered it was being offered over the next eight weeks. The course, foundational for a trades career or apprenticeship, covered a wide range of topics: construction, electrical, plumbing, tiling, and house framing. Marissa, however, wanted to stay with her goal to start a house-painting company.

Supported by her mother, who moved in to care for the children, Marissa took the popular course, luckily avoiding the normal waiting list. She deemed herself fortunate also to be supported by her husband's income from his telco sales management position. At the same time, she took a leave of absence from IBM.

SHOPPING FOR EQUIPMENT LEADS TO AN IDEA

At the start, students received a coupon to redeem for their work boots. The entire class of women trooped to the store to discover that their only choice was men's work boots. Facing this reality, Marissa jokingly asked the sales manager to show her where to find the pink work boots. Without missing a beat, he confessed that question arises all the time.

And so I thought that's crazy. Then where are they [pink boots]? Why aren't we making them? 'Cause this is so easy. It's just a change of color; it's not a big deal!

With this notion, Marissa lost no time; she began conducting her own research. She pounded the pavement, visiting stores such as Canadian Tire, Mark's Work Warehouse, The Bay, Zellers, and Wal-Mart. She spoke with the sales associates, querying them about frequency of requests for pink boots. What are women saying? She wanted to know. She then looked up the sales statistics for work boots in Canada. She also investigated how industries were broken down among white collar and blue collar and percentages of women in each sector.

Marissa discovered a huge disconnect between what women were asking for and what was offered to them. She found an opportunity when she counted the number of women utilizing work boots in a vast range of settings. She thought of women in factories, women working as architects, and women environmentalists. She also counted women at Home Depot on the sales floor; realizing that it was not just women on construction sites who needed the product.

At that same time, Marissa just wanted a pair of pink work boots for herself. In true form as a woman of action, she located a Chinese factory through a manufacturing Web site, Alibaba.com. Her friends cautioned her about engaging such a factory sight-unseen, but Marissa was confident because of the specific questions the owners posed about the product she needed.

Marissa ordered her boots from the factory in China. Ironically enough, her local bank teller had to learn how to wire money to China. The first time Marissa conducted business with the factory she had to contend with those around her thinking, "this is crazy; are you sure you want to do this?" But her perspective was that she wasn't risking much; it was only $700.

Her first order was for 30 boots. Normally, minimum orders were 1,000, but she had negotiated a smaller number. She would have been happy with one pair, but she said to them, "The deal is that this is a sample, and I'll see if I can start a business here."

BUSINESS BEGINS ORGANICALLY

As with many scrappy startups, Marissa initially didn't look too far down the road. At the beginning, she had no real business plan for selling boots. She still was determined to paint homes, busy keeping many balls in the air. By day she was enrolled in the trade course. From 3:00 or 4:00 in the afternoon until her children fell asleep, she was mom. Late at night, she logged onto her computer to conduct research.

Continuing her research, Marissa thought of the boots as a potential sideline business. At best, she hoped some of the "girls" in her course would buy the other 29 pairs she had ordered from China. Maybe if others were interested she could start something.

Marissa had no idea what she was getting herself into. She had no notion of the scope of responsibility she would face working with giant retailers, such as Home Depot, who eventually bought her boots in a big way. She had no training in the legal details, the business paperwork, or the number crunching.

As she sees it, no books can prepare you for what you face in a business such as Moxie Trades. Marissa found that she was capable of drawing up a business plan, but she also found that her business plan would work for three months and then it would change. Now not only does she modify her business plan every six months but she completely changes her strategy along the way.

As a novice at business and startups, she operated in her favored trial-and-error mode. What *did* work was gaining relationships with retailers in Canada, such as Home Depot. Marissa would have found it impossible to start a product-based business without at least one big retailer's support so that she could meet her minimums and purchase the inventory she needed.

LANDING THE RETAILERS AS HER ACCOUNTS

How Marissa created a business relationship with Home Depot of Canada is a story in itself. She deliberately attended a luncheon where the President of Home Depot Canada, a woman named Annette Verschuren, spoke. Annette had grown her company's chain of stores from 30 to 150. What struck Marissa about Verschuren was how she had changed the business, seeing a man's business through a woman's eyes.

Not only did Marissa want to hear her hero Verschuren speak, but she was determined to meet her, particularly "because not many women can do what she's done."

So I harassed the team at Home Depot for a private meeting, but the intent of my private meeting was not to sell my boots, because I hadn't had my product line solidified yet. It was so that she would then through their services organization offer jobs to the girls in my course. They were getting crummy jobs.

So that was my first reason. And I said to her, "And I'll just need you, in a few months I'm going to need you, just need your advice." I didn't think they'd pick up the product line. But after I got the 30 boots, then women said well now I want a matching tool belt, and now I want a hard hat and wouldn't it be cute if you had safety glasses?

Marissa quickly sourced all of these items, some from North America. Her China factory offered to fashion the tool belts for her as well the boots, using the same dye. Once she had the whole package together, she then gave them to Annette Verschuren. A week later, Marissa was in the Home Depot office with the buyers and the executives. A week after that, she signed the buyer's agreement, and four months later the products were in the store and available online.

Moxie Trades introduced its products to Wal-Mart at a trade fair. Marissa was summoned to a hotel room where a mass of buyers sat at numerous tables. The review process began when a buyer rang a bell to invite the would-be vendor to approach with her products. After she offered a short "pitch," the buyer again rang a bell to signal the conclusion of the period. The buyer then announced whether Marissa would be invited to continue the process with a further appointment.

Marissa made the cut and has been building her relationship with Wal-Mart for the last two years. The relationship has demanded her to be both persistent and patient. The road has been long and time-consuming, but nonetheless a great learning process.

By the time Home Depot agreed to sell her products, Marissa had painted three or four houses in her original business. The good news about the retail placement of her products couldn't come soon enough because painting houses nearly killed her.

She was getting up before the kids woke up and coming home after they fell asleep, and then working on the boot business at night, exhausting herself in the process. It gave her more reason to pursue her products, which, after all, were unique. Yet she figured if *that* business didn't succeed, she could always return to the original house-painting business. She stopped painting houses but felt a tinge of sadness at giving up the spark for her entrepreneurial adventure.

FUNDING THE BUSINESS

As the process was unfolding, Marissa and her husband had decided initially to personally fund the manufacture of her line of products, remortgaging their house several times. The trade's course had finished, and Marissa was still painting houses. Her mom was taking care of the kids, and she and her husband were juggling all their appointments.

When she received the call that Home Depot was going to buy the product, Marissa needed a loan to secure the deal. She conducted some online research and learned that the Business Development Bank of Canada would fund small businesses, provided they had good business plans.

She visited other bankers who offered to loan her money for her business, but she believed her safest route would be with the Business Development Bank because its loan would be unsecured. This meant she didn't have to present any of her assets, such as her house, as collateral to obtain the loan, which was important to Marissa and her young family. As she put it, "I want pink work boots, but I want to have a roof over my head!"

Marissa did not have a silver spoon in her mouth. Even though she had the long maternity leaves to consider and research her future, and her husband's income, she still had to remortgage her house to get started. That entailed a certain amount of risk. But she didn't ask for money until she had a client, which she thinks is a really important factor. She thinks people often ask for money too soon.

It's much easier to ask for money with someone like Wal-Mart as a client. Even if the bank knows it's gambling on you, it's a pretty safe bet that it's not going to lose all the money it invested because you've got a pretty good opportunity behind you.

At the same time, Marissa believes you can get the client without spending a fortune. If you have an invention that requires a lot of money to get into, you probably have the technical expertise to figure out how to make that item frugally. You may be able to provide prototypes and technical documentation.

Marissa figures she and her husband invested $20,000 of their own money into the cost of the startup. Additionally, she counts the earnings she lost by giving up her job at IBM as a portion of her investment. Leaving a job, though, is not necessary, she believes. Someone working full-time can devise a product and start a business plan at night. It's simply a matter of working hard. It's demanding but feasible.

Moxie Trades has needed a fair amount of money to grow. The company ate through the first loan in about a year. After that, Marissa worked with investors to finance the cost of goods for each order. She found investors through networking events, press exposure, and great coverage throughout Toronto. The story of her company has evoked interest among people, some of whom have also approached her about partnering with them.

She's been careful about partnering because doing so has meant giving away half of her business. Yet having investors and partners has enabled Marissa to bring home a salary for herself.

EXPOSURE BRINGS INVESTMENT AND GOOD PRESS

To promote her business and raise money, Marissa appeared on a reality show named the "Dragon's Den," airing on Canadian television, where contestants ask investors for money. As with most reality shows, this one had a reputation of being critical of the entrepreneurs appearing to pitch their ideas. Rather than set herself up for failure, she wanted to protect her retailers. So to put herself and her product in the best light, she agreed to participate on the show *only* if she could bring women wearing her products with her.

Over the course of five days, Marissa emailed customers, including members of women's organizations such as the Company of Women and the Canadian Association of Women in Construction, inviting them to appear with her on the show wearing her products. She received a great response. Hundreds wanted to participate; eventually she negotiated with the show to bring 65 women along.

On the show, Marissa wanted to be articulate and not look like a "stupid" mompreneur who has this cute little gimmicky idea. She wanted to appear intelligent, demonstrating that real women out there were doing real jobs and nobody was providing them with appropriate equipment. Men, who had been dictating the market, were simply reducing items made for men to smaller sizes, missing the opportunity.

On the day of taping the show, all the women came to support her, many taking vacation or forfeiting a day's work. Marissa knew this demographic because she had researched it and read all the statistics about it. But on this day, many women she didn't know showed up in force to verify what she believed. It was one thing to share statistics with retailers. It was another to see these women on stage with her.

I go into my retailers and I give them the statistics and I sell them. But then I went, oh my God, I was right; it was true! You don't know it's true until you see the people.

On the show Marissa was actually offered $600,000 for a 75% stake in her business, which she turned down. But "the good looking billionaire cowboy, an oil and gas tycoon," she met there told her to call him anyway, that he would help her. As a result, they arranged to become 50/50 partners, which was captured on the show, one of the most popular in its history.

ABILITY TO HANDLE RISK AND CHALLENGES

Marissa didn't know what she would be facing in her business, yet that didn't scare her. She advises women who want to follow a passion and start a business to take stock of three things they "really, really, really need to think about." First of all, financially how are you going to survive? Number two, have you done your product research and done your business plan? And third, how much risk can you handle?

Marissa personally can handle considerable risk, and her family supports her in that. She claims she was just born with this capacity. She's a free spirit. She makes decisions and then deals with situations as they occur.

Women who approach her for advice about business feel bad they can't handle risk. She's pragmatic:

I say to them don't feel bad, you cannot pursue [the] business opportunity you're talking about unless you can handle a tremendous amount of risk.

Marissa takes calculated risks, though. She arranged a leave of absence from IBM and knew, leaving on good terms, that she could return to her old job if her business didn't work out. When she finally said goodbye to her previous employer, she knew she had learned much and that her skills didn't fit with her position at IBM. With what she had learned about launching a business, she figured she could get a job anywhere. It was scary to leave, but recognizing she could succeed elsewhere led her ultimately to see her exit as manageable.

Marissa has experienced time as a hurdle for her as an entrepreneur. Although an entrepreneur may be poised to act overnight, client companies are not. As much as six months to a year can pass before a vendor agreement is realized because of all the necessary levels of approval. For example, it's taken her a year and a half to work with Wal-Mart.

Dealing with clients can require tactfulness. Entrepreneurs have to prove the added value of their products because companies can decide to manufacture products themselves, skipping the startup altogether. However, the entrepreneur must be able to provide value without bankrupting herself in the process.

Negotiations and press exposure takes time. People told Marissa not to expect to make money until the third year. Although outsiders think she's made it, because of having landed the clients she has, such as Home Depot and Wal-Mart, she sees herself still in process.

She claims you cannot relax because you need to deliver substantially to your clients. You can't sell millions of dollars worth of products at the outset. Everybody starts the relationship with a pilot, during which the entrepreneur needs to prove herself. If that initial test succeeds, then the company will slowly increase the orders. It's not until the reorder stage that the entrepreneur really starts to see the profit.

SUCCESS AND SUSTAINING HER PASSION

Marissa sees success as being happy on a daily basis and having her kids happy. She likes achieving goals large and small and having them in front of her as challenges. She's also achieved her hope that her children would see the world—they now have an opportunity to visit China every year.

Marissa sustains her passion for Moxie Trades with the response from the clients and her customers, the people who wear the product.

They're crazy, they're crazy excited about it. It's a symbol to them and so they make it easy. And I love it; it is fun. It's a challenge working with Wal-Mart but you know you can read the book about it, you can watch the documentary. But to live it, it's a cool story to say I've lived through what they talk about.

She also purposefully meets with an entrepreneur of a successful company every few weeks to glean what she can from their experiences. She asks for help and takes as much advice as she can—finding people have generally led her in the right direction. She admits that sometimes if you ask for help, people will say, "I don't know, but I know somebody who can." Following up with such contacts results in arriving at the right place.

ADVICE FOR WOMEN WHO WANT TO
GET INTO BUSINESS

Women with business ideas need to do their research, write a business plan, and interview many people, advises Marissa. She counsels women to pound the pavement, look online, read books, and use as many government resources as possible. Both the Canadian and the

U.S. governments offer useful Web sites where they post free business plan templates. Women should also tap into their Chambers of Commerce. Many free resources exist to be tapped.

Next, Marissa suggests conducting market research—walking into a store, showing the manager your idea or your "trinket," and asking if the person would buy it. Many women are afraid to do this because they worry somebody is going to steal their idea. But since it's such hard work to bring an idea to market, it's unlikely somebody else is going to undertake the process. If you don't trust the person, then don't ask them, but if you get a good feeling from somebody, go ahead.

Marissa claims she tells everybody everything. In the process of talking she sees what sticks. Her problem is everything sticks for her!

I put it out there and somebody grabs onto something to help you get it to the next stage. Every single time it has amazed me. People want to help you. People's intentions generally are very good.

Do the product or service and don't make the jump from full-time to your new business endeavor until you know you can sustain the business for six to nine months. And have a backup plan just so that you have some emotional security there.

Marissa is dumbfounded when asked about the advice she would give to women who ask "Who am I to do that?" For women who lack the confidence to take their idea to market, she offers the following.

Do women ask themselves that? Well who's the next person? That's what I would say, well who else is going to do it? Who's the next person—why not you? I don't know the answer to that because I wouldn't understand that question.

This is why Marissa is the woman behind Moxie Trades. Her confidence hasn't wavered and she's gotten into action from the moment the idea occurred to her. "Who do I think I am?" doesn't even compute with her!

A PURPOSEFUL BUSINESS

With her business, Marissa was not dreaming about making millions. She was dreaming about setting a good example for her kids. Yet at times she wondered about the merits of selling pink work boots. After all, she isn't saving lives. She also found the process of establishing the business overwhelming and difficult at various junctures.

Whenever she would waiver, though, she would remember her little book and her philosophy and remind herself about all the life lessons she was teaching her children through her example. That thought always brought her back to the task at hand and kept her moving along. Marissa claims she couldn't have launched her business without the support of her mother and her husband.

All indications keep telling Marissa and her family that following through with Moxie Trades was the right direction to take. It has never received any negative feedback. On the contrary, women email her regularly about feeling empowered using the products.

They relate stories about how they've been injured onsite previously. Receiving welders' gloves or boots sized to fit women saves them from further injury and discomfort. Aside from fashion, such stories remind Marissa about the mission and the need for what she is doing.

Marissa fills a void, providing women's products as well as information to women who are hungering for more about entering territory long limited to men. Each of her products has its own personality: "Betsy," the original pink work boot, was joined by "Lola" (pale blue), "Stella" (dark red), "Lizzie" (forest green), "Sandy" (tan), and "Frankie" (black). Despite the female names and stylish colors, each pair of boots is designed for demanding work and meets both Canadian and US safety standards.

Marissa believes she entered her business at just the right time. Her actions have paid off not so much in spades as in pink work boots!

ONE WOMAN'S ACTION INSPIRES MORE ACTION FOR OTHER WOMEN

Now that you have learned about Marissa McTasney's story and the actions she took to launch and succeed with Moxie Trades, it's time to reflect on how this story can inspire you in your quest for your entrepreneurial adventure. Take some time to reflect on what you've just read and allow the following questions to guide you. Use your journal to take notes so that you can ground your understanding and learning for future reference.

1. What gap have you encountered that is waiting to be filled?
2. What calculated risks could you take?

3. What action have you been sitting on that you could perform for the sake of your future?
4. Who would you go out of your way to meet?
5. What complaints have you heard from others lately?

WHAT CAN YOU LEARN FROM MARISSA MCTASNEY?

Action comes from clarity. For two years, Marissa knew she wanted to make a change, but she didn't spring into action until she had clarity. Once she had the idea of pursuing house painting, based on her desire to create her own business and her ability to work with her hands, she looked around for what could support her in this endeavor.

Then, when Marissa realized she wanted pink boots, she didn't take her desire as being silly but pursued her hunch that others might have a similar need. She dedicated herself to conducting research at the local establishments catering to the trades people to confirm her instincts of having uncovered an unmet need.

Marissa demonstrates the positive effect of action begetting more action. Once she started down the path of taking a trades course, that led her to the need for boots, and that in turn introduced her to the gap that existed in equipment for women.

She also handled her interaction with the woman president of Home Depot smartly. Rather than approaching her with neediness, she decided to help the other trades women she had met to get better jobs. Marissa's patience paid off and allowed her to develop a relationship with this hero she admired, paving the way for further exchanges about her products. Landing the Home Depot account opened up other doors for Moxie Trades, both with lending institutions and with other retailers, such as Wal-Mart, which were more disposed as a result to do business with her.

To keep herself in action, Marissa turned to her own writing to her children to motivate herself to keep going, especially at those times when business was hard. She remembered she wanted to set a good example for her children. Doing so kept her on the path to her own success.

She was willing to trade 50% of her business to the right partner, one she sized up as providing the leverage she needed to expand her business as she needed. She claims she has burned through more than $600,000 of her partner's money, but she's been able to expand as far away as Australia and is expecting to enter a relationship with Penney's as well. She's a woman who knows a good deal when she sees it and responds accordingly.

YOUR TURN NOW—WHAT DID *YOU* LEARN FROM MARISSA'S STORY?

CHAPTER 12

ECO-ME

A Conversation with Robin Levine, Founder of Eco-Me (www.eco-me.com)

You cannot change anything in your life with intention alone, which can become a watered-down, occasional hope that you'll get to tomorrow. Intention without action is useless.

—*Carolyn Myss*

Everything we do affects the impact of our home, our health, our environment, our family.

—*Robin Levine*, founder of Eco-Me

What can be more shocking than to learn that your 36-year-older sister, an especially health-conscious person with no family history of disease, has been diagnosed with breast cancer? Needless to say, the diagnosis was a shock to the whole family, especially to 33-year-old younger sister Robin Levine.

When this situation occurred in 2005, Robin took a hiatus from her job as a producer in television and feature animation for preteens. She decided to spend time with her sister, Leslie, to help her through this ordeal. At the same time, Robin began conducting research to uncover the root of a medical condition such as this in a young, health-oriented woman.

Most people assume this disease occurs in postmenopausal women or rests on a genetic predisposition. Robin learned, unfortunately, that 8 out of 10 women diagnosed with breast cancer today do *not* have genetic-based cancer. In addition, as she dug deeper in her research, she learned the age at which women were being diagnosed with cancers in general was getting younger.

So it started me on the path of researching it and just digging into the why's because when you're touched by something scary and traumatic you look for answers. And I looked to scientific data and research for my answers. And what I realized is that the cleaning products and the body care, personal care, that are on our shelves in all the stores have no set regulations.

No government guidelines exist from the FDA, the Food and Drug Administration, or consumer safety committees for cleaning and body care products. These agencies have left regulation up to the manufacturers, and consequently, no checks and balances have been put in place. Much as lack of regulation has resulted in disasters in other areas, such as banking, consumers have been hurt by government laissez-faire.

RESEARCH UNCOVERED POTENTIAL LINKS BETWEEN ORDINARY PRODUCTS AND DISEASE

When Robin dug further into the labels of household products, she found chemicals such as formaldehyde or benzene and phenol, all derivatives, and even more chemicals with multiple names that stem from those that are known carcinogens. These chemical carcinogens are found in most of the cleaning products on our shelves, whether in large or trace amounts. Products are tested for single use, not for the substance that builds up on surfaces, such as on bathtubs. Yet people bathe in hot water week after week, lingering in chemicals that then accumulate in their bodies.

Robin also discovered that many of the preservatives used in body care products are parabens—Methylparaben, Propylparaben, Butylparaben, Ethylparaben, Isobutylparaben, and Isopropylparaben; there's a whole series of them. These are called hormone disrupters, estrogen-mimicking compounds, which some believe play a role in promoting cancer. No wonder so many women are getting non-genetic breast cancer and other cancers at such young ages when we consider the products to which they are exposed!

As she uncovered this information, Robin admits to experiencing "a giant aha moment" and becoming "incredibly fanatical and crazy about this." Immediately, she removed all chemicals from her and her sister's houses and began insisting to everyone she knew not use store-bought chemicals.

ROBIN FINDS A SOLUTION

Instead of using chemical-laden household cleaning products, Robin began to use white vinegar to clean and kill bacteria and germs. White vinegar kills. Our great-grandmothers knew this. Even the Heinz vinegar Web site states that the product is simply a liquid distilled from a grain. And it does the job.

Robin believes we've been tricked and trained over many years to believe that cleaning products need to be at chemical-strength and harmful in order to clean our homes.

This is a total lie; it's a total misrepresentation. And we've been duped at the cost of our health.

Every time she talks about this subject, from 2005 until today, Robin gets goose-bumps. It makes her want to cry, scream, yell, and share what she knows as loudly as she can.

Because of her determination to set an example and find alternatives to the deadly chemicals the public was using, Robin started making her own cleaning products. She simply mixed white vinegar, baking soda, olive oil for wood, and some essential oils. Actually, she didn't even consider starting a business; she went right back to her work in animation as Leslie returned to health. Her only "light bulb idea" at that point was that she needed to change her life and the lives of those around her whom she loved. She wanted to help others stay healthy.

Visitors remarked how pleasant her house smelled, wondering what room freshener she was using. She admitted to none, simply having cleaned her house. That comment raised more issues because her friends claimed that after cleaning they opened their windows to get rid of the accompanying toxic and chemical odors.

Robin elicited curiosity when telling people she no longer used chemical products. She would then show her friends a bottle of her concoction, suggesting they take it home and report what they thought after using the mixture. She admonished them to remove the old stuff and use only what she was giving them. People found that her mixtures worked well, and they loved them and asked for more.

A lawyer friend suggested she verify the results of her products and offered to help her send the blends to a lab. Robin agreed, and off to the lab the concoctions went. The results of the testing of her all-purpose cleaner, composed of water, white vinegar, and her central oil blend made of tea tree, lavender, rosemary, and lemongrass, was that it killed 98% of bacteria and germs. These are pure plant concentrates with nonsynthetic food-grade natural plant oil. Robin found these results to be pretty darn good!

A BUSINESS IS BORN

Robin realized she was onto something. Her sister encouraged Robin to start a company and put her products on the Web.

You've got to do something Robin; you're so passionate about this. You've opened my eyes up.

At the same time, Leslie was sharing her story with as many women as she could because *her* mission became "check your breasts." Robin proposed that should she start a company, she would want to use her sister's story to promote her products.

Leslie agreed. Unfortunately, Leslie's situation wasn't uncommon. This knowledge increased the importance of bringing the issues about household chemicals and personal body products to the public eye.

With this determination, Robin built a Web site, had labels made, and spruced up the look of her products. She gave her business "a little name," Eco-Me.

The name evolved with the help of her friends and family from a desire to find a word or words that evoked environmental and ecological health as well as brought the responsibility back to the individual or personal experience.

Everything we do affects the impact of our home, our health, our environment, our family.

Robin remembers taking out a ratty, spiral notebook and for weeks writing down word associations within it. She then returned to the words, selecting promising ones with a highlighter and noting which domain names were available on the Internet.

She then conducted a quick trademark search on her own, without hiring a trademark attorney. Such a lawyer became more important down the road, but not when considering if somebody had the category cornered with a certain name. She crossed words off and pulled up new ones. She knew the concept she was after.

THE BUSINESS RESTS ON A KIT AND INTERNET EXPOSURE

Robin was curious whether it was just her friends and family who were interested in her idea, or if people outside of that circle thought she had a viable option. She wasn't so interested in making a cleaning product as she was educating with a tool kit. She figured people owned these common items present in her concoctions.

She would give patrons the essential oil as well as the bottle and ask them to make the mixtures themselves. Simply, the kit enables the user to make an all-purpose cleaner, a wood cleaner, and a scrub cleanser, using water, olive oil, vinegar, baking soda, and essential oils. That's it. People can clean their entire houses, top to bottom, with these natural ingredients, using this reusable, refillable kit. The customer contributes the household ingredients.

Most people admit they already have the necessary items on hand, or can pick them up in one aisle in the supermarket. Additionally, people can save anywhere from $40 to $60 a year in cleaning costs by reusing and refilling the kit. They'll save their health, as well as the environment.

For Robin, Eco-Me became a mission to empower and educate. Amazingly, three or four months after she launched the Web site, *Women's Health Magazine* found Eco-Me. One of the editor's children had an extreme allergy, which prompted an Internet search for safe home products. As a result, a glowing, full-page article appeared; the magazine wanted to help Robin get the word out about her kits.

Exposure grew from there. Robin realized her passion and interest was shared by others who had the same need and interest. They understood the genesis of her business came from honest marketing, not a gimmick. Eco-Me was not looking to sell false information, and people appreciated that.

Robin admits her business would have been difficult to launch without the Internet. It would have taken much more time to launch, and she frankly doesn't know if she would have been able to get it off the ground without the access. The Internet has been huge for Eco-Me, not just because of retail sales on their Web site but also the research opportunities it provides for connecting with people.

The fact that *Elle Italy* magazine contacted Eco-Me and that a large distributor in Australia saw the company on Springwise, a Web site that tracks entrepreneurial trends worldwide, and wants to bring the products Down Under are two examples of responses that most likely would not have happened without having the international reach of the Internet.

ECO COMPETITION

Often Robin attends trade shows where people tell her they use her concoctions on their own already. She's happy about that and tells them to spread the word, because it's important to buy products whose brand and ingredients can be trusted.

Clorox just came out with a new green cleaning line. Hats off to them, Robin says, for removing some of their chemicals, but even though the cleaning product is green, there's nothing natural about a synthetic dye that's used within it. These companies are not teaching people why they're avoiding certain chemicals, or what the issues are.

In 2005 and 2006 when Robin was launching her company, not much competition existed because the green movement really hadn't started. And Eco-Me was not looking at what they were tackling as an environmental issue so much as a health issue. As she sees it, we can save the environment, but until we save ourselves through our own health, then we're not helping the environment anyway.

So Eco-Me's initial drive was health-oriented. The fact that the green movement started was a bonus. People began to see that we shouldn't be pouring chemicals down our drains because that action hurts our water, which in fact hurts our fish, which hurts our food, which then hurts our health again.

Robin is happy that the green movement has occurred. Its existence helps her business grow, which is great. But the phenomenon also has brought in companies who are doing what is called "green washing," which is just getting on the green, eco-friendly trend and selling a bunch of junk to the consumers. Situations like this happen whenever there's a big trend.

THE UPS, DOWNS AND ACTION OF BUSINESS

Robin launched her initial Web site in the winter of 2006. In the spring, she launched her current e-commerce site. At the same time, she left her animation job to focus fully on Eco-Me. To this day, she rereads her letter of resignation periodically to remind herself of her mission in her business.

Still in the early stages of her business, Robin feels like she's on a see-saw. One day she's feeling good, and the next she's feeling overwhelmed. She swings between believing "it's happening" to "I don't know if it's happening," back to "it's happening."

Yet, she finds the core group around her keeps her grounded. There's Joyce, her office manager, who helps her run everything. She also has a VP of sales and marketing, Jen, who works from New York; she is Robin's "clean spirit soul mate on this mission." Robin has known Jen for years and believes she's a genius at global sales and marketing. They raise each other's spirits daily.

However, business can be a roller coaster. At the end of the day, unfortunately, much rests on the bottom line and the bank account. And as much as Robin and her crew would just like to send many samples out and share a message, they still must feed their children and pay their mortgages. Fortunately, Robin has managed to operate with a low overhead. In addition to the office team, she supports two people in her warehouse and an accountant.

Robin sees herself as a doer. Action is her middle name. She'd be the first to create a product if one of her friends complained of a gap in what she needed to accomplish a task. Robin's response would be, "We could make this [happen]!"

That's me, I'm the "let's do it. We can do this" [person]. And I think it's why I was successful in animation because to put together an animated TV show or movie you have hundreds and hundreds of people, most likely internationally, that you're pulling together the tiniest minutest of information to make this hour- or hour-plus–long movie.

Her years of training and working from the bottom up in that career helped Robin realize that it's feasible to make something happen. It is doable.

Robin didn't think of Eco-Me as a dream because it hadn't been in the works for years. To her, it was more of an idea left on the table. She spotted the idea and wondered, "Is anybody interested in this?" As she gathered feedback and interest from others, she moved forward with her idea. As she did, interest grew.

For example, young women Robin hires and trains to demonstrate at trade shows excitedly return with numerous new orders because they can't stop talking about the products. Robin scratches her head wondering how these young college graduates can care so much about cleaning products.

However, having just moved into new apartments, many are jazzed to be on their own for the first time. As a result of what she has learned from these young women, Robin has recognized a whole new demographic she previously hadn't realized existed. Effectively, she has seen the Eco-Me idea take on a life of its own in what marketing calls a "sticky factor," where people attach ideas and interest to it. They start talking about it, and it empowers them. In that way the concept has gone from idea to action to reality to even a crusade.

Robin's husband, an architect, is also a doer. Not being the one cleaning house, he admitted to having little understanding about what she had been discovering. Yet he encouraged her to do something about her idea, especially when he heard about the reaction she received from others. He knew that when she put her mind to something she was serious about, she would put all her energy into it and succeed.

STAGES OF BUSINESS GROWTH

Robin believes there's never a right time to start a business. You just organically have to feel as if this is what you need to do right now. In her case, a situation appeared in front of her, she felt passionate about it, and it took on a life of its own as soon as she took it out into the world. The business evolved from there.

First it was her and her pantry; then it was her and a little office with tons of public storage; and then it turned into two little offices, a warehouse, and a small staff. Today she feels she can work at home occasionally because she no longer has to be on the road all the time. She can divide the work among herself and the others on her staff, giving her a bit of her life back. As a result, she can begin to consider also raising a family.

Looking back down the road she has come in her business, Robin had no idea what she would be facing—and still doesn't have any idea of what lies ahead. Not knowing has helped Eco-Me greatly, she believes.

For instance, they thought their greatest market would be the natural products market; they thought stores such as Whole Foods and Wild Oats and all the food co-ops would love the product. In reality, these companies looked at Eco-Me's kits in their drawstring bags and declared they couldn't put them on their shelves.

I ask, why not? They say, it's not a product. I respond, of course it's a product. They insist, no it isn't. They, the buyers of these stores, think very much within the box. So if I had early on known better I probably would never have done it [created kits].

Yet even so, Robin proudly declares that her products are to be found now in over 400 stores in the United States and Canada. She just picked up distribution in Ireland, the UK, and New Zealand, and next they're working on Australia and France. Robin believes "with the Internet the world is completely flat and we're all neighbors." She points to the story of *Elle* Italy:

And they contacted us and said we're running a whole article and we want to cover you guys and your products. I said that's great, we have no stores in Italy. They said well we're going help you with that because if we run this we really want a local store to run it and we think it's fabulous.

Robin concedes she's been free to break the rules because she's making up her business as she goes along. Although the "green" stores and the co-ops resisted her products initially, she has made inroads, but still finds them more difficult to break into than she had imagined. She's been delighted to learn also that Canadians are ahead of Americans, hungry for products off the beaten path.

Rather than dwelling on those who refused her products, Robin and her team moved swiftly into other areas. Some reps who were helping Eco-Me get into the big natural product stores, especially in California, suggested Robin consider other aspects of the business besides the do-it-yourselfers.

Eco-Me has been learning from its customers, adapting to their requests and needs. Although first starting with the home kits, they later moved into the body, baby, and dog and cat food areas.

Additionally, a business consultant told Robin that the best advice he could offer was to pay attention to everybody who says they don't like this, or who says this won't work, or who gives negative feedback. The positive feedback will feel good and be an ego boost, but such information won't get your company further. Those people buy what you offer already. If you want to grow your company, though, you'll need to listen to the negative feedback because those are all your lessons. He said not to think of it as a negative thing. Think of it as an opportunity, the inside track, changes that will grow you into an area you can't get into right now. Robin has paid heed to this advice and found it to be invaluable. She's grown her business accordingly.

STAYING PASSIONATE

The financial aspects of the business have been most challenging to Robin and she expects that to continue to be the case for another year or two. She and her husband had to mortgage their house and "beg, borrow, and steal just to try to launch the company" and give her the opportunity to step away from her job in animation.

Robin admits her family—husband, sister, parents and her background—gave her the "chutzpah" or courage to launch Eco-Me. Additionally, after returning from being with her sister for months through all her treatments, Robin found meetings in animation about trivial details insignificant when compared to her sister's life-and-death struggle.

For Eco-Me to launch, Robin had to sell the concept and the company and be out front. This was a challenging experience for her. She characterizes herself as someone who wants everybody to like her. Even though she has an aggressive edge, she also has an insecure, sensitive side. She had to put herself out there, stay focused, and move forward, and not wait for people to pat her on the back as she offered her products.

TAKING INCREMENTAL STEPS

Robin started small. She remembers mixing essential oil batches herself, a little bit of this, a little bit of that, testing combinations. Robin found making small-scale mistakes less costly than engaging a giant manufacturer or going overseas for product development. Her incremental approach minimized financial outlay and allowed greater creativity and nimbleness. Her only upfront monetary investments were establishing a corporate entity, building a Web site, and addressing legal issues. As a result, she was able to take the money she had and spread it out. And that helped.

Robin finds measuring her success difficult to assess because she likes to think really big and in different areas. She would like Eco-Me to be a household name so that people would become aware about the connection between the products we use and our health. Whether they choose to buy her products or not, she wants people to realize they can't expect the brand name companies such as Johnson & Johnson to look after them.

Success for Robin would be if her business, Eco-me, would lead people to start thinking for themselves about the quality of the products they regularly use. They need to be educated and empowered and not assume that government, manufacturers, advertising, and marketing are really what they appear to be.

Robin presents her products at many trade shows. She premixes everything so that people can see and smell and experience a full demonstration of the products. She realizes she has struck a chord with those watching her when people return to her area with their friends. These participants don't want *her* to talk about the products. Rather, the audience members are so excited, *they* want to share the story. They take over the demonstration! Such experiences give Robin much energy and a license to be different.

And also we get a ton of testimonials: My cousin is pregnant; she was just diagnosed with breast cancer. I'm buying a baby kit for her baby shower. Wow, being pregnant and being diagnosed with breast cancer, that's pretty crazy. And that's pretty common now too. Just by us sharing our story, other people are able to share their story. And they're happy to share their story and they're happy someone else is sharing their story and it just goes from there.

FINANCING SUPPORT AND PARTNERSHIP

Early on Robin had no money to pay consultants, so she looked for advice from people outside her field, gathering as much information as she could. She read every business book she could get her hands on and subscribed to numerous business and health magazines as well. In essence she was giving herself an MBA the entire time. Today, Robin has the resources to hire people. Her current business consultant gets paid on a per project basis. For instance, if Eco-Me does a round of investor financing, he'll assist, putting together a full business book with all the financial spreads and the language necessary for pursuing a company for a special partnership. The consultant will help Robin put together a plan and help her execute it.

Together they'll agree on his fee for the project, but Robin generally realizes she must remind him to invoice her. Often new ideas crop up, triggering more ideas and more action. The consultant will bring in somebody from overseas who wants to participate in yet another type of partnership. He's not necessarily asking for more money; he is interested in getting skin in the game. He just wants to be a part of the company because it's now inspired him in new ways.

ADVICE TO OTHER WOMEN WITH BUSINESS IDEAS

Robin advises women with a business idea to test their idea out with friends and family as well as strangers. She cautions women to be careful about giving out proprietary information, suggesting they have anyone who helps explore a concept sign a nondisclosure agreement. This precaution protects the business while providing opportunity for feedback.

Although it's sometimes difficult to hear or accept, Robin advises women to be open to people poking holes in the idea or sharing negative feedback. These comments can be as valuable as the positive feedback. Consider that if people have never heard of anything similar, it's probably a good idea for that very reason—it's unique.

Pay attention to those who claim it's a good idea, but give reasoning behind why it won't work. It's important to examine the reality expressed. And as Robin demonstrated in the way she incrementally started her business, she recommends such an approach for others:

So I would say start incrementally, really small stages so that you could basically walk away at any time and feel okay about it. So at every stage I feel like even today if I needed to turn around and walk away from this because something came up in my life, I would be okay financially, emotionally, and physically. So always make the decisions with your health and with your life, trying to separate it as much as possible.

ONE WOMAN'S ACTION INSPIRES MORE ACTION FOR OTHER WOMEN

Now that you have learned about Robin Levine's story and the actions she took to launch and succeed with Eco-Me, it's time to reflect on how this story can inspire you in your quest for your entrepreneurial adventure. Take some time to reflect on what you've just read and allow the following questions to guide you. Use your journal to take notes so that you can ground your understanding and learning for future reference.

1. What problem or issue have you encountered in your circle of family, friends, or colleagues that could lead naturally to something to share with the world?
2. How does the idea of incremental action help you think about getting started with a business idea?
3. What signs do you have that you are a doer?
4. What gets you into action?
5. How do you usually respond to negative feedback about your ideas? How could you put negative feedback to work for you?

WHAT CAN YOU LEARN FROM ROBIN LEVINE?

Robin offers an example of someone springing into action to rectify an issue causing harm to all of us. She did not let her lack of knowledge hold her back. She gained the equivalent of an MBA in the pursuit of her business. She has put what she learned to good use.

She has used the power of the Internet both as a research tool as well as a marketing opportunity. She took what she learned about details in the animation work she had done and applied that ability to her own business. She prods us to realize our previous work lives can offer useful foundations on which to build our business.

Robin's process in coming up with a business name is a good reminder of the power of brainstorming on one's own. She didn't need a fancy focus team or any particular branding procedure. What worked was asking herself what she wanted her business to stand for and challenging herself to keep her concept to a handful of words.

Through the advice she received from various consultants, Robin reminds us to take seemingly negative feedback and turn it into useful information to catapult the business further. Even though she is a recovering life-long pleaser, she has learned the value of hearing what is not working to provide her with actionable ideas.

Robin also reminds us to take reasonable actions. Her example is not of jumping off a cliff to make her business fly. She advocates taking incremental steps along the way and seeing what happens in the wake of these movements. She tells us she has gained satisfaction at each juncture because she can look back and recognize just what she has achieved.

YOUR TURN NOW—WHAT DID *YOU* LEARN FROM ROBIN'S STORY?

CHAPTER 13

ADESSO ALBUMS

A Conversation with Lesley Mattos, Founder of Adesso Albums, Inc. (www.adessoalbums.com)

Tell me, what is it you plan to do with your one wild and precious life?

—*Mary Oliver*

But I say do it [your business] at night, do it on the weekends, just start—do it; don't procrastinate.

—*Lesley Mattos*, founder of Adesso Albums, Inc.

Imagine traveling to a friend's wedding in Florence, Italy, your first time out of the country. You're at the end of a several-month hiatus from corporate America, where you have been working for nearly 30 years. A single mom for 15 years with the last of your four children off to college, this is your time to find yourself. And Lesley Mattos truly did.

Having moved up in her career from accountant to controller, to treasurer, to manager of investor relations, and, finally, to manager of executive communications for the CEO of Cisco, Lesley surprised everyone, especially her boss, when she walked into his office in 2002 and quit. She knew she had no idea what she was going to do next; she just knew it wasn't going to be that anymore.

So she took time off and did absolutely nothing for the first three months. Then in May of that year, Lesley departed for Italy and a friend's wedding.

She was asked by the bride to take Polaroid pictures of the guests at the wedding reception, scotch tape them into a beautiful Italian leather-bound scrapbook, and have guests write a message beside their picture to the couple. Not knowing many people at the wedding, Lesley found doing so to be the perfect reason to "mingle with a purpose" and, along with a fellow guest, took charge of creating this personal and unique memento for her friends.

THE SEEDS OF A BUSINESS

The next day, on a train to Rome, Lesley realized she might have stumbled upon something unique; returning home a month later, she busily explored her hunch. With the help of a friend, she turned the sketches of the album in her travel journal into a design. Then she identified someone to build her a prototype. By the end of the year, she had engaged a manufacturing source in China and had incorporated the company as Adesso Albums, Inc, *adesso* being the Italian word for "now."

Lesley hadn't planned on going into business, but she took one step after another and found that each time she did so, another door opened. As long as this happened, she kept on moving forward. At the same time, she was clear that she didn't want to return to the corporate world, having become disillusioned with big company politics.

Although she worked with a career counselor, nothing concrete emerged except the awareness that she needed to engage in something different. It was time for a big fat change.

Lesley didn't think much about where this small business she had started would take her. She just knew she liked what it was and that there was a big market to address. She realized she was not the only consumer who had a sense of what would be important to incorporate at a celebratory event.

NARROWING HER CONCEPT AND GETTING STARTED

The problem, however, was narrowing her focus to a manageable market. Her product, a unique album with slots for Poloraids and written messages could be used for birthdays, anniversaries, bar mitzvahs, weddings, funerals, and retirement parties. For the first six months, she found herself jumping around from one idea to another. Finally she said, "Enough, I have to focus on one market!"

Lesley chose to center on the wedding market, not only because it was where she had begun but also because it was the largest, most identifiable, and most accessible. Besides, she figured that everybody who gets married will have an anniversary, and most couples eventually will have babies.

She realized that her product was not one to put on a shelf at a stationery store; it wouldn't sell itself. It was something that had to be experienced and seen. She knew she needed to get a few people to use it, at a wedding for example, where it would be visible to 150 or so others. Her best means of presenting her product, she believed, would be through a viral marketing approach.

Immediately, Lesley launched a Web site and started a newsletter, which she sent to friends and family, asking them to forward it. From that collection of names she started building a database of contacts. Once a quarter she'd send her mailing out, announcing what was new at Adesso Albums. When she was interviewed by the local paper, for example, she'd let her newsletter readers know about her celebrity.

Mainly she marketed Adesso Albums through the Web site. Additionally, Lesley made a few phone calls to local stationery stores and tried to contact Polaroid; she figured they certainly would want to help support this product because it was going to sell film and cameras for them.

What she didn't know was that, even in 2001, sales of Polaroid instant cameras and film had been declining rapidly. The company eventually went through a bankruptcy and was bought out three years ago by Petters Group Worldwide. Through all this, Lesley never made any progress with Polaroid or Petters, even though partnering made perfect sense to *her*.

However, sales of Adesso Albums' Instant Photo Guest Books for Polaroids grew each year. Her primary market of 20 to 30 year olds who are getting married had not seen Polaroid cameras before and thought they were kitschy and retro. This became the bread and butter market for Adesso.

As the digital revolution raged on and printers became more compact and portable, Lesley decided it would be prudent to introduce an album that would accommodate a four-by-six digital print from compact photo printers. The size of a Kleenex box, such printers turn out images on the spot at an event. The benefit of this option for the albums is a marriage of the best of both worlds—an instant print as well as a lasting digital image.

HOW PEOPLE USE HER PRODUCT AND WHAT MAKES THE BUSINESS REAL

Adesso Albums keeps the process simple: they supply the patented album, packaged with the camera, film, and printer. Somebody at the event is assigned the task of seeing that the album gets filled with photos and remarks.

For example, at a 50th wedding anniversary, the children might mingle, taking pictures of all the guests and printing them either through the Polaroid or the digital technologies. They then slide the images into the pages of the book and have guests write messages to the celebrants, who now have an instant memento at the end of the party.

When Lesley started in 2002, she didn't concern herself about whether her business idea would fly. She didn't give that question much thought at all. To her this was just fun to do! If a door closed, as when Polaroid wouldn't call her back, another one would open. As long as doors kept opening, she just kept walking through them.

Yet what made the business real to her were the customers.

I'd get calls from customers after the events, and they'd tell me how they'd looked at their album on their honeymoon the next morning after the reception and stayed in bed, drank champagne and looked through all the pictures and saw what they'd missed the day before—because at an event like a wedding or any event where you are the guest of honor, it's a blur because all your friends and family are there. And to have this to look at the next day, it was just very rewarding to feel like you've given people a gift.

Most people who hire a photographer, recording their event in a more traditional way, wait weeks and even months to see their pictures. Yet with business being tight for professional photographers, Adesso Albums also happens to be finding professional photographers who will add this instant approach on as a part of their package as a differentiator. Lesley is happily making arrangements to work in tandem with this group as well.

TIMING AND MONEY

The right time to start a business, Lesley admits, is when you have the idea. Just go for it, she advises. Even if you've got a job, get started anyway. Some people are afraid to make that leap. "Don't let fear hold you back," she admonishes.

Lesley believes she was fortunate to be in the right place at the right time in the technology world, where she had done well and had accumulated some savings. She figured she had this money to fall back on, but it was also her retirement fund so she had to be wise about using it.

She knew full well she would be depleting her lifestyle as a consequence if she didn't have a plan. So Lesley mapped out a spending budget, with a two-year limit, and told herself when she went through that money she would stop or get a job to supplement it. But she was determined to continue pursuing Adesso Albums, no matter what. Although this approach worked for her, she admits some people aren't able to afford to give up their jobs while they pursue their idea.

But I say do it [your business] at night, do it on the weekends, just start— do it; don't procrastinate.

Two years into her business, Lesley could see the light at the end of the tunnel. But she didn't want to go any deeper into her savings. Coincidentally, she was having lunch one day with a former technology colleague, telling him about the evolution of Adesso Albums. During the lunch he said, "You know what? We should get a few people together and we should make an investment in your company." Lesley was surprised but delighted.

The man was true to his word and together they found two others to invest with him. Before anybody changed their minds, Lesley had the lawyers draw up a stock arrangement. These people became minority shareholders in Adesso Albums, to the tune of $150,000. She was flattered, found this process fun, and counted her investors among those whose company she enjoyed. To this day she's grateful to all of them for their faith in her and her business idea.

LEARNING HOW TO RUN THE BUSINESS

Having worked for as long as she had at levels in companies where she could see what was going on, Lesley always felt as if she had a strong sense of what made a business successful and what didn't. She had worked for CEOs or CFOs in a variety of different-sized companies, so she knew operations. From a business perspective, she had a minimal learning curve.

Her naiveté rested on never having built a Web-based business before, and that's what Adesso Albums has turned out to be. Ninety-nine percent of sales occur on the Internet. Consequently, Lesley's steepest understanding and greatest time commitment has come from discovering how to leverage her Internet presence.

She learned to optimize her Web site for the search engines: Google, Yahoo, MSN—all of them. Their technological spiders crawl the Web site, looking for key words. If someone is having a wedding and wants a unique "wedding guest book" at the wedding, she'll put that search term into a search engine. Adesso Albums has optimized its Web site for that term as well as related ones. As a result, Adesso Albums comes up on the first search page that's returned in Google, which results in increased traffic to the site, a portion of which converts to an actual sale.

Lesley has found that it takes much research and planning to decide how to word the copy that's on the Web site as well as determine how to lay out the page because Web sites are read in a certain way. Fortunately, four years ago she hired a woman who was an expert in Web site design and optimization. In a constantly changing Web world, Lesley's consultant stays on top of the technology.

I realized very early on that I couldn't learn everything. I needed to know enough to know if they were b.s-ing me, but after that I didn't have any trouble at all delegating that kind of stuff.

When Adesso Albums created its "instant photo guest book," the search engines at first wouldn't find it, even though these words constitute real search terms. Today her company ranks number one in many of the unique terms and appears on the first page of Google, thanks to the expertise of her SEO (search engine optimization) gal.

Lesley admits her biggest barrier to growing her business was sales. Because it was her idea, she felt as if she were selling herself each time she attempted to put the concept out there. She claims, "It just didn't feel right!"

I wasn't a very good salesperson. I'm pretty humble and taking the album into a store and saying, "Do you think you might want to carry this?" was really hard. I've gotten better.

She found she could overcome her reticence with practice and reliance on other people to sell for her. Lesley found the message was better received if it came from somebody not so closely attached to it.

Presently, she retains one dynamic employee who manages customer service and the office completely. Otherwise, Lesley relies on a constellation of consultants she found through networking to help her run her business. She has a business development person, a search engine optimization technician, a graphic designer, a PR person, lawyers, accountants, and Web developers. This group constitutes the anatomy of a Web-based business today, with its needed variety of satellite people.

Lesley marvels at how well this arrangement works, considering none are ever sitting together in the same room. Occasionally her graphic designer will spend several days in Lesley's office. She finds this fun because then the two can interact physically. There are some drawbacks to having the satellite-oriented business, such as feeling isolated at times, but clearly this approach has worked for Adesso Albums.

SUCCESSFUL MEASURES INCLUDE TENACITY

Lesley figures it took a total investment of $400,000 to launch her business. For the first few years she took no salary, paying herself out of her own savings for her living expenses (which she didn't cut back on!). Within three years, Adesso Albums turned a profit and was able to start operating as a real company.

In 2007 Adesso Albums brought in over $1 million in revenue and earned a significant profit. To Lesley, that level of business was quite a milestone.

Success to Lesley is hearing from the people who use her product about how it has made a difference in their lives. She also measures achievement in being able to support herself on an idea she had. It amazes her how she literally created something from scratch. She equally feels good about supporting other people who are a part of her team. Lesley gains a great deal of joy from knowing she has created some economic benefit for other people.

Lesley has created a product for a real niche market. Initially, friends warned her, "Oh God, somebody's going to copy your idea!" Rather than concern herself with this fear, she took appropriate steps to protect her product.

In 2001, even before she launched the company, Lesley filed a patent for her album with a patent attorney. She launched her business on the faith that she would be awarded the patent, and six and a half years and a bunch of examiners later, her patent indeed came through. It's an oddity in relation to most patents, because it's not a technology but a concept. Both the concept and the execution of the concept are patented. Lesley is very proud of this accomplishment; she displays her patent on the wall of her office.

Lesley counts her patent award as evidence of luck and also another example of doors swinging open for her. She offers a practical yet philosophical view of this process:

If there ever comes a day where for every disappointing thing something positive doesn't happen, then I'll know it's time to throw in the towel. But that day hasn't come yet.

Lesley sustains her passion with the feedback of her customers and the growth of the business. She also cites the continued ability to be creative every day as another path for her passion. As an example, the business departed from the trajectory it was on when the poor economic news emerged in September 2008. Leading up to the presidential election, business really slowed down. Rather than sit back and hope for a change to occur, Lesley became creative about marketing to her audience and making their experience with Adesso Albums a win-win.

Among other activities, Lesley quickly sent out an email to her database, as well as a press release, announcing "the Adesso Albums Economic Stimulus Program." She positioned this measure as a company just doing its part to help bolster the economy. Some might say Adesso Albums slashed prices, but she prefers to think about it as her stimulus program.

Her approach was tongue and cheek, but Lesley *did* reduce prices because the Web site traffic and conversion to sales were both down dramatically. Similar issues prevailed throughout the industry. The next thing she saw was that traffic increased on the site, but people weren't pulling the trigger on the purchase. Lesley then wondered what would happen if she lowered prices a bit further. Would that act cause people to make the leap and the purchase? Sure enough, the reduction worked.

Within a week she saw a marked improvement. Lesley believes that being a small business owner, rather than operating in a 40,000-person company, allows her to make such quick decisions and nimble moves. This enables her to be as creative as she wants to be. Sometimes her ideas result in belly flops, but much of the time, with a good attitude about it, she finds even those situations not to be the end of the world.

A WOMAN'S PERSPECTIVE IN BUSINESS

Lesley admits to having always been a "glass is half full" kind of person. Although she does have her tough days, she finds they don't last.

It's either the experience with creating this company or just getting older, or some combination of each, but the highs aren't as high and the lows aren't as low.

Lesley doesn't think she would have thought of creating a business such as Adesso Albums had she not been a woman because she would not have recognized the opportunity. Women are more in tune to keeping memories than men are, although men do understand the concept and have invested in her business. Being a woman has not hindered her in any way in running her business, probably especially because it's an Internet-based one.

Lesley believes women with an idea for a business should just go for it. She has many friends who have business ideas who don't take action. Lesley was fortunate to be in a position where she had the finances to support herself until she reached a point where the business became a profitable enterprise, but she thinks she would have found a way to launch anyway and encourages others to do the same. She sees friends who are in a similar situation who have ideas, but are afraid to take that first step.

Self-confidence, Lesley believes, is a major ingredient for a successful entrepreneur. She encourages women who were not born with self-confidence, or who did not have a family who encouraged it in them, to seek out experiences to build it.

Self-confidence was important to Lesley when she was getting her business off the ground. If people didn't like her concept, she didn't question what she was doing. She simply thought *they* just didn't get it. People would tell her, "Polaroid pictures, geez that's so old school!" But Lesley believed that for every one of those people there were 10 people who were lined up to buy her product, so the resistance didn't matter to her. Equally important, she didn't take the comments personally.

She doesn't know if her resolve came from being almost 50 years old at the time and having had a solid base of life experience behind her, or because she had come through a period in her life where she had transitioned from one world to another: having been the mom and the career woman and all that, and now taking a break and focusing more inwardly.

Leading up to the launch of her business, Lesley had spent a fair amount of time being introspective and reflective. She read spiritual books, such as *The Four Agreements* (by Don Miquel Ruiz) and *The Artist's* Way (by Julia Cameron) to expand her mind and provide a new structure to her life. She also listened to audio tapes on long hikes she took at the time of her transition from her corporate life. Her favorites include presenters such as Wayne Dyer and Deepak Chopra. She credits these authors with helping her build upon her spiritual and emotional foundation and open her mind to the possibilities in life.

HEALING THOSE SABOTEUR VOICES AND CREATING A SOLID FOUNDATION

Lesley confesses to having thought all along as she launched her business: *Who am I to do this and who do I think I am?* She often wonders, *How did this happen?*

She admitted as much to a room of 50 women in an organization called Ladies Who Launch. All had either started or were about to start a business of their own. She reminded women in the audience they are not alone, and it's not abnormal to wonder, "Who am I, who do I think I am?"

Lesley's answer is: You're somebody who has an idea, and if you can execute on your vision, then go for it. You're smart. You have a good idea, and you know the people with whom to surround yourself to help you execute your idea—otherwise you wouldn't participate in Ladies Who Launch.

Equally critical to her success, Lesley has found, is avoiding spreading herself too thin and trying to learn every aspect of every business herself. She was fortunate in her corporate life to be exposed at high levels to four or five different companies, some well run and some not so well run. Her takeaways were the pearls. She knew enough to recognize a manufacturer who could not deliver on his promises for an album. At the same time, she understood she never was going to learn every single part of her business in depth.

It's key to surround yourself with people A) who are qualified and B) that you trust. Lesley believes many people, even more women than men, have good instincts when it comes to these issues. She has verified this at times when she didn't trust her gut, where there was something just a little bit wrong and she went with a person anyway. Ultimately, she regretted the decision. She found her most costly mistakes were made in the face of not trusting her intuition.

You know that feeling when—somebody comes to you and says yeah, I can do marketing for you or PR for you and they talk a good game—and there's something, some nagging thought afterwards, but you go for it just because you don't have anybody else to do it at the time, and then a year later you find you spent a lot of money and got nowhere. And you can look back and say, "I knew it from the first day I met that person."

Lesley advises women not to rely on friends and family for decisions about their business, because they're going to be biased in one of two ways. They're either going to say the business is the best thing ever, because they don't want to hurt your feelings, or they're going to cast doubts.

The latter may result from their being envious or wondering to themselves why they didn't think of something like that. It may be sour grapes, "How come she gets to do that?" That's human nature. Alternatively, Lesley suggests reaching out to people who can be objective: a former business associate or your lawyer or somebody who's not your friend or a member of your family for good feedback. And then sit with the idea for awhile. Until you know what to do next—and you will!

For Lesley, sitting never took too long. Yet she would take time to weigh all the feedback she received, just to say to herself she had done it. Usually she decided to go do what she wanted to anyway, but in an informed manner.

NEW BUSINESS OPPORTUNITIES

Not long ago, Adesso Albums participated in a soft rollout for a new line of albums that accommodate a new printing technology. Petters Group Worldwide, the company that purchased Polaroid, spun off a division of Polaroid called ZINK Imaging. ZINK (standing for zero ink) developed a technology that essentially could be called the Polaroid of the digital age. Crystals are embedded within the paper, and when subjected to intense heat, they turn into colors and become a picture, eliminating the need for ink cartridges. ZINK is licensing their technology to companies such as Polaroid, Dell, and TOMY in Japan. This revolutionary printing process is green, portable, and presents yet another opportunity for Adesso Albums.

In addition to the bread-and-butter consumer market that it has served since inception, Adesso Albums is making inroads into other markets. Other channels of distribution are businesses that can use the albums, such as large-event planning companies. For example, Lesley is working with an association of luxury suite owners that hosts sporting events. The suites hold as many as 24 people at once. She proposed the idea of having an album and a tiny portable printer in every suite, so the company can document their guests and provide proof to the IRS that the space is being used for business purposes.

Dreaming up new ideas keeps the business fun. Adesso Albums now has distributers in the U.K., Canada, and Australia, who all became reps because they used the album at their own weddings. Three years ago, the night before her wedding, a woman named Helen in the U.K. phoned Lesley and remarked, "We just got our album. We love it. Can I be your exclusive distributor in the U.K.?" Lesley agreed. After a year, Helen was able to quit her full time job and focus exclusively on her very own company!

Three years later, after giving birth to her third baby, Helen had an idea for a green baby-related product, and was about to bring it to market in the U.K. She called Lesley and asked, "Would you like to be *my* U.S. distributor?"

I said, "Oh my God, yes," I said, "It would be great."

Helen's product, Cheeky Wipes, is a replacement for baby wipes, which are cold on a baby's bottom, chemical laden, and adding to the landfills. People are becoming more conscious of the environment, so new parents are returning to using cloth or biodegradable diapers. The distributor created terry wipes with natural ingredients that are kept immersed in water and lavender oil.

The new venture for Lesley is called Bottoms Up, and though it will be an entirely separate business, there is a lot of synergy between it and Adesso Albums. The next step in a bride's life, more often than not, is having a baby. Lesley figures she can link the two sites and the businesses. Besides, the women who are having babies are having baby showers, or their friends are. These people can use the album, so Lesley intends to cross-sell.

Lesley finds it fun partnering internationally with the young woman in the U.K.

I'm so excited for her because she's a really neat gal. She's in her early 30s, and she's got three young children under the age of six and doing these two businesses. So, yeah, it's kind of fun—it's fun to have partners like that. And all these people I work with are entrepreneurial, so I feel very fortunate.

With each of these new wrinkles to her business, Lesley Mattos demonstrates her willingness to move in directions that present themselves to her. She's a true woman of action who is ever ready for what's coming down the road.

ONE WOMAN'S ACTION INSPIRES MORE ACTION FOR OTHER WOMEN

Now that you have learned about Lesley Mattos's story and the actions she took to launch and succeed with Adesso Albums, it's time to reflect on how this story can inspire you in your quest for your entrepreneurial adventure. Take some time to reflect on what you've just read and allow the following questions to guide you. Use your journal to take notes so that you can ground your understanding and learning for future reference.

1. What idea(s) are you sitting on? If those business ideas were eggs, wouldn't they be ready to be hatched by now?
2. What do you make of Lesley's balance between taking time for herself and springing into action? How are these related?

3. What options does the Internet hold for reaching people for your business?
4. What do you know about obtaining patents? Trademarks? Copyrights?
5. Whom do you know who might be delighted to invest in your business idea?

WHAT CAN YOU LEARN FROM LESLEY MATTOS?

The very name of her business, Adesso, meaning *now* in Italian, reminds us of how action-oriented Lesley is. She sprang into motion after creating her prototype album. How many people would have dismissed the idea of creating a business based on an instant album as being cute, but untenable?

With a lifetime of experience behind her, as well as being a member of a generation on the earlier side of the digital divide, Lesley was nevertheless willing to learn how to run an Internet-only business. Early on, she realized that traditional retail stores would not be the right location from which she could market her product. Rather than getting discouraged by her interactions with stationery store proprietors who didn't know how to handle her product, Lesley moved forward, promoting her business on the Web.

She knew how to reach out to people who could increase her exposure effectively on the Internet, especially her Web designer. She sought and located the help that catapulted her to the top recognition spot for search engines.

Lesley also knew to reach out to the people she had known in her former life at Cisco. Without much fuss, she was able to gain investor support, which she smartly solidified by drawing up legal contracts to formalize the agreements. She knew to initiate proceedings for a patent on her concept, strengthening her position in relation to other companies that might eventually want to duplicate her idea.

Lesley sprang into action around her business, but also set a reasonable limit on herself as a checkpoint against depleting her life savings. She smartly secured boundaries around herself so that she could focus more on what she was doing, rather than spending time and energy second-guessing herself along the way. Once she determined her time-frame, she put any questions about her path aside and concentrated instead on her business.

Lesley Mattos is a nimble businesswoman who did not sit around wringing her hands when the economy started to slide in September of 2008. Using her sense of humor, she found a way to offer value to her existing customers as well as potential customers and used her capacity as a small business owner to make adjustments until she could see a positive outcome.

She is also a businesswoman who recognizes the difference between spreading herself too thin and diversifying her business when she was approached to do so by her rep in the U.K.

Rather than fearing change, Lesley readily embraces it. She is a woman who is ever ready to take advantage of the opportunities in front of her. Instead of waiting for new technology to run her out of business, she joined the bandwagon early on, gaining understanding of the emerging miniaturization of instant printing and how that could become a benefit to her business.

YOUR TURN NOW—WHAT DID *YOU* LEARN FROM LESLEY'S STORY?

— CHAPTER 14 —

PERSONAL LIFE MEDIA

A Conversation with Susan Bratton, Founder of Personal Life Media (personallifemedia.com)

Skill to do comes of doing.

—*Ralph Waldo Emerson*

So I still do the work, and that's what you do when you're an entrepreneur. You are an entrepreneur because you have a wide range of skills and the drive and ambition to bring your vision to fruition. And you're willing to do whatever it takes, even if you're 47 and cranky.

—*Susan Bratton*, founder of Personal Life Media

As often happens in a culture favoring work over just about every other area of life, Susan and Tim Bratton's marriage was languishing even as their professional lives were thriving. Had they ignored the warning signs, they might easily have headed for divorce. But instead, they took their know-how as serial entrepreneurs, launching successful startups for venture capitalists, into their own meaningful business venture they could engage in together and created new sparks in their marriage.

Personal Life Media, a podcast network of 39 shows, currently, emerged as an indirect result of Susan and Tim Bratton's marital troubles. After 11 years of marriage, they had truly grown apart. Whenever the couple faced a problem or didn't understand something, their first action would be to buy a book or attend a workshop, hoping for answers to their struggles. As a result, they decided to attend intimacy and relating workshops to meet their relationship challenge head on.

Now, more than six years later, the Brattons are truly grateful and thankful for the amazing talent of the people whose workshops they attended. Among the programs they valued were a seven-part series called Sex, Love and Intimacy from the Human Awareness Institute; Ecstatic Loving from the Insight Institute; OneTaste Institute classes; and Life Mastery and Date with Destiny from Tony Robbins. The couple dug into these programs with gusto, becoming veritable workshop junkies for several years. As you'll see, Susan found a way to repay her teachers by giving many of them their own podcast platform, sharing their brilliance with the world.

THE SEEDS FOR A PODCASTING NETWORK

Susan had been hosting a podcast since 2005 in the digital marketing and media space. She knew about podcasting, an Internet-based digital form of presenting audio information, because she had anchored her own show delivered through the podcasting medium. So the idea occurred to her to do a podcast on relationships and intimacy, inviting all these experts she had met to become guests on her show. She knew that many people had substantial information to share.

Besides, she knew many of her friends seemed unhappy in their own marriages, yet had done nothing about their challenges but complain. Susan and Tim realized they had the courage to take workshops, but they believed most of their friends did not. They'd say "my wife would never go," or "my husband would never go"— they would always have an excuse.

Susan wondered, "How can we package this stuff up?" How could she make it easy for her friends and the rest of the universe of 40-something, married, cranky people to have an opportunity to learn this material in the privacy of podcasting? What's great about podcasts is that the audio can be put on an iPhone, iPod, or mp3 player or listened to from a computer with a headset. With this in mind, Susan began seriously thinking about doing a show.

And then one day it just struck me. I thought to myself, wait a minute, I don't want to do a show. I want to start a whole media company! I want to do a whole bunch of podcasts. I don't want to have just a podcast where I interview Dr. Patty Taylor on one of my episodes. Dr. Patty Taylor needs a podcast, Chip August—he's like the new Dr. Phil—needs a podcast.

She realized that these people might not have technical experience and would never figure out how to do a podcast. Susan recognized that she had the technical chops and could get the programs done. She asked herself:

So why don't I just empower these people to do this—I call it the global microphone. I just give them this microphone and the whole world can now hear them.

All of a sudden these experts would be amplified to anyone in the world with an Internet connection. And yet, because it's podcasting, it's a private interaction between the listener and the host.

At the time, these people were in California helping couples learn to deepen their intimacy and connection. Susan wanted anyone in the world to have access to them—they work tirelessly in these workshops in their consulting and they accomplish amazing results. Giving them a podcast platform would enable these leaders to get better known.

TIME OFF GAVE PERSPECTIVE TO THEIR LIVES OF SERIAL ENTREPRENEURSHIP

At the time Susan had the idea to start a podcast network, she had taken a year off to play. She had left one of the companies that she and Tim had sold to Yahoo. Between them, she and her husband have undertaken eight startups. They live in the Silicon Valley and they launch companies; that's their life. However, they have always launched businesses for or with other people.

Now Susan was considering initiating a business on her own—with the help of her husband.

I was thinking about doing all this stuff. I thought first I was going to do a podcast, and then I thought, no, no, I'm going to do a publishing company.

Then I thought, okay, I'm going to do all these shows. Then I thought, oh my God, I can't have a sex show network, so what else am I going to do? What are the other things that are interesting?

As Susan was coming up with all these ideas, Tim was with her because they had taken the time off together. They had gone to live in Holland with their 11-year-old daughter and traveled the globe to decompress.

Tim listened to Susan consider her options while giving her more great ideas. He had been working on a startup of his own; and they were working at home together. One day she said to him, "You don't have a better idea than this. My idea's better than your idea." Susan proposed Tim come and work with her so they would work in tandem. They wanted to have a lifestyle company where they were doing something good for the world that took some courage to accomplish.

A PODCAST NETWORK IS BORN

Tim agreed to join Susan and they launched Personal Life Media with 16 shows in March of 2007. They had approached many of their workshop hosts, who gladly participated. As it happens, podcasting is a good medium for workshop leaders, who are naturally gifted speakers. The fact that the Brattons were going to handle all of the technical aspects made the prospect all the more appealing.

As it launched, Personal Life Media expanded beyond relationships and intimacy topics to cover all areas of mind, body, and spirit. Some of the programs were Living Green, Effortless Ecology for Every Day People, and Coaching by the Life Coach. Susan also launched Living Dialogues, which focuses on spiritual topics, and Beauty Now, which is all about plastic surgery, biomedical innovation, anti-aging, and longevity. Other shows Susan launched on the network include Evolutionary Sales and Modern Immortals, which are about health issues, and Conscious Business and Money Mission and Meaning, which are about finding purpose in work. A Purpose-Centered Life is about clearly understanding life purpose without being Christian focused.

TALENT BEHIND THE NETWORK

More than two years after starting the company, Susan and Tim have 39 shows on the Personal Life Media Network. This is not surprising to Susan because when she launched she was 100% convinced she could pull it off. What led to such confidence was her understanding of the world of media and her ability to monetize media through advertising. She understood the business model.

Susan had been selling advertising in the print and online worlds for 25 years. Her background had been advertising sales and content publishing. Previously, she had "always sold everybody else's stuff." She also has a talent for refining things.

I'm really good at co-creating a show with a host. Where they have ideas and then I can kind of get it really clear for them. They have the knowledge, but I know how to make the knowledge get through to people in a way they want to hear it.

She also knew that if her husband combined his technical expertise with her ability to do sales and marketing and finesse good content, together they would excel. Both Brattons, in fact, have an ability to improve upon whatever they have been handed.

We're really good at shucking and jiving and modifying our thought around the latest data that you have for whatever it might be that you need to do. And a lot of people don't have the ability to be super fluid about what they're doing. They have a plan and they want to execute it. And we don't need to have that. We can live in change and move through change together and both of us can do that. If one of us didn't and one of us did, it would be a disaster.

As an entrepreneurial startup, the couple gain when the two of them agree and are able to easily incorporate new ideas and change in real time. They are nimble and ready to tackle whatever they had set out to do differently as new information appears.

Susan believes whatever they had decided to do would have become a reality because she prides herself and Tim as being "manifestors." They both have much experience taking nothing and turning it into something. They had done that for many years for other people, especially for venture capital–based startups.

SUPPORT FROM OTHERS IN A TECHNOLOGICAL WORLD

Susan and Tim are fully self-funding this shoestring company. They work out of a studio in their home, and all of their employees, primarily contractors, work at home as well. In the Web 2.0 broadband-connected global world, the Brattons fully leverage all available technology. Additionally, they use workers in Malaysia to create transcripts.

To get started, the Brattons have received support from friends in the technology community who have let them use many of their platforms and technology solutions. Using all of the free technology that's available today, and through the gracious relationships of some of their technology providers, Susan and Tim have been able to keep their costs low enough to afford to launch and run this business.

One could say Susan launched Personal Life Media at a bad time. All of the people who had launched podcasting-oriented companies were starting to be shaky by the time she moved into the game. In the last two years, most of them have totally changed their models or gone out of business. Susan counts her company among the second generation of podcasting, with an ability to adjust for what didn't work for her early pioneering brethren.

You would have thought, "What, in 2007 you're launching a podcasting company? Don't you know nobody cares about that? [VC's] aren't backing it and the companies that are in it aren't doing well?" But we saw that it was really just that this was a new channel for consumers to get really good information that could be produced inexpensively and delivered easily.

Susan has found a growing audience of people who have discovered podcasts as time goes on. For the listeners of the world this is a wonderful medium. She expects more will flock to Personal Life Media as they hear about it.

LESSONS LEARNED FROM EARLIER PODCASTERS AND DOING THE DIRTY WORK

At the same time, lessons could be learned from the mistakes of the first time podcasters. Like the dot commers before them, they took piles of money from venture capitalists and ran their companies "really big and really fast." They also took an egocentric posture with their mantras: look how big we are, we're going to be huge, this is going to be so fabulous. None of this panned out for them. The advertising and sponsorship wasn't there. There wasn't enough scale early on. Unfortunately, the podcasts themselves were too unprofessional and unpolished.

As a result, Susan decided to act differently. The Brattons run their company in an extremely lean manner. They keep their costs down. They use global resources. They use many free tools and technologies. They have a green business that rests on telecommuting, but they also built out a platform that would allow them to scale, where they can add as many as 300 shows to their network fairly easily.

They have also spent time and funds where they need to, designing really good album art. Although attending to the visuals requires work, Susan believes it is worth the effort because people recognize quality with their eyes.

In spite of her background in advertising, Susan has found more difficulty than she expected in getting sponsors for her programs because podcasting is not even on their radar screens. A few marketers might listen to podcasts, but the medium does not yet command the attention of radio or television. She has found she needs to educate people about the merits of sponsoring the shows.

It's really been a gut wrenching experience, because I'm the one that does the ad sales. It's really, really hard. It takes it out of me. It's emotionally draining for me to work so hard calling so many people for so few orders. I'm 47 years old and I'm still doing cold calls. I wish I had a team of people and I could just tell them what to do and they could do it for me. It would be wonderful to not have to do this, what is truly incredible work. Getting on the phone and calling up anybody and trying to pitch them on it.

In spite of the challenges and doing the seemingly menial labor of selling, not knowing when popularity will hit, Susan keeps going. For one, she'd rather work for herself than anyone else in the world. And second, what she's doing is creating content that is life-changing for people. She revels in the emails she receives about how the podcasts have changed others' lives: they've figured out their purpose, they've reconnected with their spouses and never thought it was possible, or they've shot a beautiful picture because they listened to Camera Dojo or Digital Photography Life. People also send emails and just thank Personal Life Media for touching their lives in some way.

The Brattons model themselves after National Public Radio, without the pledge drive. And some listeners are actually reporting that they are switching from NPR to Personal Life Media, enjoying the quality of the programming of the latter. These people like raw, unedited, progressive thinking content.

COMPLEMENTARY PARTNERS OVERCOME CHALLENGES

Susan has surmounted some barriers to her business. One was the fear of being judged unfairly for the progressive content. She also wondered if working with her husband would be good or not. Would it work out? Would she be too demanding and authoritarian, and would that make him crazy?

Fortunately, these fears have not been realized. Tim is the behind-the-scenes guy, whereas Susan prides herself in being "the front facing" person. The couple is complementary in their roles and capabilities, and if they do have a disagreement, usually one of them has some insight the other hasn't gained.

And so once there's some explanation it's like, oh yeah right I get it, okay. You're right. And it's usually he's right and I'm wrong and that's fine too. He's a lot smarter than I am.

Susan teasingly concedes her position of comparison with her husband and admits to preferring to work with someone smarter because she's learning all the time. That's her perspective.

She thought long and hard about who should take various positions in the company, both from the perspective of whose idea the business was and what the implications of their genders might be on the business itself.

You'll notice that I'm the CEO and Tim is the COO. And a big part of that is because we were dealing with relationship and sensuality content, we wanted me to be the CEO, number one because I'm kind of the outbound person, and number two because it would be less questionable if a woman was the CEO of a company that had this kind of content.

It [the business] was my idea. I said to Tim, "Hey, since it was my idea and I'm the front person, how would you feel if I was the CEO and you were the COO." And he said, "I don't know, I need to think about that." He's always been the CEO. And then he said, "I think it's the right thing, I think you should be."

MEASURING SUCCESS

So far, Susan and Tim have been going without salaries, but they are bringing in enough money to build the business, do the engineering, and pay their technology team, production team, and audio editors, as well as all the people in Malaysia. The Brattons share all the revenue with the hosts, paying them first each time Susan makes a deal. She believes strongly in sharing the wealth with everybody. As a result, Susan and Tim are last in line for money. She believes that's how it should be, because it's ultimately their upside, creation, and company. Besides, at the two-year mark they have patience, knowing this situation is temporary. They've gotten the platform to a scale where they can add many new shows, which will give them the critical mass it takes to both gain a larger audience that's more attractive for advertisers as well as to package content in new ways.

Some of their current ideas include creating downloadable albums for sale on iTunes, such as an entire album on intimacy and visualization workshop exercises that contains varied experts on one thread of a concept. Another idea is transcribing content into downloadable eBooks because people still like to print and read information. Among other revenue streams they're working on, Susan sees this expansion as their future.

Being ever a woman who loves to create and then move on, Susan thinks her ultimate definition of success would be to be acquired for millions of dollars by a quality publisher who loves the content they've created and the audiences they've aggregated. Her "first stop on that trip" would be to make some good salaries for herself and Tim, followed by another company's successful acquisition of what they created.

ADVICE FOR OTHER WOMEN

Susan believes women with an idea for a business need to understand the competitive landscape. She sees many "need-to" businesses that don't have a unique point of differentiation and consequently are boring. Women must be careful about what they're trying to create for the customer, ensuring it's eminently differentiated.

Susan takes her own advice, recognizing her competitors and identifying what sets Personal Life Media apart from them. She admits Hay House and Sounds True produce a lot of content, but they're much more classic publishers who have a few artists and authors who are multiple creators with 10 books out on their own.

She sees her organization as more of a media company, producing episodic content, a hybrid of Hay House and NPR. Fortunately, nobody exists in particular in the podcast network world that's focused on the self-empowerment vertical space. Others are aggregating the kitchen sink, not acting as branded networks.

ACTIONABLE REQUESTING

People have been gracious and helpful to Susan and Tim in their business. Susan was at lunch recently in New York with an old advertising friend who quizzed her about what she was up to. She admitted she was looking for sponsors and wondered whom he might know who would be a good fit and would introduce to her.

And he said, "I can do that; who do you want to meet?" Susan admitted the perfect person for her number one show, Inside Out Weight Loss, would be a member of Weight Watchers. He said, "Oh my God, I went to Duke with all the people that run Weight Watchers."

And I said, "That's what I need because I can't get in there on my own." He says "Done."

Susan saw this as one of those perfect moments. It's an exquisite example of what every entrepreneur needs: a just-ask-for-anything-you-need attitude. But ask for it very specifically. It's not that what you want is not available to you. It's that you're asking the questions poorly or you're not asking for help at all or you're not asking for help in the right way. Women need to ask for actionable assistance.

ONE WOMAN'S ACTION INSPIRES MORE
ACTION FOR OTHER WOMEN

Now that you have learned about Susan Bratton's story and the actions she took to launch and succeed with Personal Life Media, it's time to reflect on how this story can inspire you in your quest for your entrepreneurial adventure. Take some time to reflect on what you've just read and allow the following questions to guide you. Use your journal to take notes so that you can ground your understanding and learning for future reference.

1. What's an area of breakdown in your life that could be "exploited" for bringing something of value to the world?
2. How have you been thinking "too small" about what you've wanted to do?
3. What "actionable assistance" do you need to ask for?

4. How could your life partner help you? Hurt you?
5. What would you be willing to do for your business that would be "beneath" you in a salaried job?

WHAT CAN YOU LEARN FROM SUSAN BRATTON?

How about—get into action and think big? Susan offers a shining example of thinking big. Instead of creating one podcast, she expanded her thought to many. She started her network with 16 programs, has since grown to 39, and has a vision of 300 programs. All along the way she has been cognizant of her need to create an entity that was truly scalable.

It should be remembered, however, that Susan's action came on the heels of time out to rest and recuperate—she was gaining some perspective on her life during her sabbatical time. Edgar Mitchell, moon astronaut and founder of the Institute of Noetic Sciences calls this "nonoperational time," government-speak for a period of nonaction and nonengagement, a space for doing nothing. Although Susan had the luxury of a year, the time-period is less important that allowing for an interlude.

By her own admission, Susan also knows that her strengths lie in maximizing others' abilities. She takes a hand in shaping the focus of her podcasters so it is sharp. She is bent on leveraging the content so that listeners can get the most out of it.

Susan is good at asking for help from others, but cautions women to be aware that they need to be careful how they ask for help. If their requests are not actionable, the help will not be forthcoming. She has honed the art of asking specifically for what she wants and needs and reaps the rewards accordingly.

Susan recognizes that even though her primary medium is audio, her public responds with their other senses as well. She is determined to produce quality visuals that draw people in.

She is also willing to do whatever is necessary to make her business a success. Nothing is beneath her. Even though Susan would prefer to turn the hard work of connecting with would-be advertisers over to a sales force, she knows she must do this foundational activity herself for now.

YOUR TURN NOW-WHAT DID *YOU* LEARN FROM SUSAN BRATTON?

—— CHAPTER 15 ——

ZHENA'S GYPSY TEA

A Conversation with Zhena Muzyka, Founder of Zhena's Gypsy Tea (www.gypsytea.com)

Creativity comes from trust. Trust your instincts. And never hope more than you work.

—*Rita Mae Brown*

I started with six dollars and an idea and a sick child. And that's how amazing the world is, that you can create something if you've got the guts.

—*Zhena Muzyka,* founder of Zhena's Gypsy Tea

If you were a single mother with a sickly newborn depending on you, what would your first order of business be to support yourself and your offspring? Would you be fearful? Would you give in to the larger culture and just settle for an ordinary job to pay the rent and put food on the table? Would you think of using your creative capacities to dream up your own business?

Imagine the forces surrounding Zhena Muzyka at the time she was confronting her dilemma of caring for herself and her child. Ironically enough, it was her tendency to get dreamy and rely more on her right-brain capacities than her logic that sent her off in the direction she pursued.

Instead of marching into an employment office, the young mother trekked up to a mountain top to pray, asking to be shown what to do. Dramatic as it may seem, she was given a vision of gypsy tea in response to her request, which is actually not surprising because Zhena is descended from a gypsy family. Her Ukrainian great-grandparents were trapeze artists in the Moscow circus and her grandparents had been pursued by the Nazis as undesirables. Besides, Zhena's love and comfort with medicinals arose in part from experiencing her grandmother's healing remedies.

Zhena Muzyka admits to having an enduring deep love of plants. As in love with flowers as she is with herbs and spices, she has always enjoyed formulating concoctions, and even studied herbal medicine. She turned to her hobby to help a friend suffering from multiple sclerosis deal with disease symptoms, creating special tea blends to respond to the woman's attacks.

So with the vision from the mountain top, Zhena's love of plants and of formulating potions came to her rescue when she needed to support her son, Sage, and herself. He was born with a severe kidney defect, requiring several major operations.

That's where it started. I had a vision; literally I saw the whole thing. Instead of thinking about what business books recommend, the creation of a mission statement, I created a vision statement and followed its path!

Prior to Sage's birth, Zhena had spent several years steeped in her gypsy heritage, researching it, hoping to write a book on the subject. Now in the midst of her vision, she saw her background and her passions for plants and herbs weaving together.

Gypsy is the only culture in the world that doesn't see any one country as their home; they see the whole world as their home, drawing from an exotic mixture of ideas. Such a perspective aligns perfectly with sourcing world-wide herbs and flowers and teas and spices.

Besides the gypsy culture, Zhena subscribes to a belief in a gypsy archetype, including more than those with gypsy blood. These are primarily women who love to care for their bodies and the earth; they love new experiences and need relaxing interludes. She sees these women as her target customers and counts herself among them.

THE IMPETUS FOR STARTING A VISION-DRIVEN BUSINESS

At the time Sage was born, Zhena had been living on a creative writing grant, supplemented by working in a clothing boutique. She thought of herself as a gypsy in her employment, being creative, earning small amounts of money, and treading lightly. In her early 20s, she hadn't had any major bills until her son arrived.

Even with the vision of gypsy tea, Zhena doubts she would have been as motivated to start a company if she hadn't been shouldering the responsibility of Sage and paying for his operations.

It was one of those things where I'm going to do this and I'm going to really have to make it happen. The cause was leading me to create a business, because I just didn't have the option not to. It was a survival mechanism to support me and my baby and then it became a cause driven company.

Like many businesses with meaningful underpinnings, Zhena's began with the necessity of supporting herself and her child, and she depended not only on her heritage and her vision but also on her values. She had been a fair-trade activist and proponent her whole life. When she started buying tea and selling it, she became curious about where it came from: Who plucked it? How was it processed? She wanted to ensure workers were taken care of.

She had always been an organic advocate, using only certified organic ingredients. But when she discovered fair trade, she took its mission to heart. Her business would rely on fair pricing and social and environmental standards to support the women in the tea fields plucking the tea. She wanted these women to afford health care and educate their children, just as she had dreams for her own son.

A dedication to ending poverty among women in the fields where the products were harvested became a compelling part of Zhena's vision. She believes every human being has a right to clean water, food, shelter, education, and health care. This concern drove her to think beyond the needs of herself and her son, calculating how much product she needed to sell to really make a difference in the world.

If I buy 50 kilograms of tea, 50 Euros will go back to the worker, on top of the price of the tea. So if I sell a million kilos of tea, a million Euros will go back to the worker.

Zhena has found, ironically, that what she relies on when she is scared or nervous is that she is cause-driven. As she did on the mountain top, she puts her faith not only in herself and her abilities but also in God and the Universe. She couldn't imagine that God would want her to fail because she is doing good work for so many others, wanting them to have the same opportunities people have in the United States.

Did she have doubts? She found herself moving through doubt every day. People wondered aloud, even as she had bared her heart and soul about her business: "Who needs another tea company?" "Oh there's way too many tea companies anyway," "Oh it's so competitive." Others questioned how she would compete with Lipton or other large tea companies. Her resolve and mantra became, "Because I'm not doing it for the money; I'm doing it for a greater good."

Is Lipton on a mission? Zhena doesn't know. But she is, and it is working. How do you argue with a mission to end poverty for the workers in the tea fields and to influence the industry?

Zhena sees that she has been successful influencing others to follow her. Competitors realize they need to adopt practices similar to hers to compete. In an ironic twist, she sees herself setting a higher standard for them to do what is right and just.

STARTING THE COMPANY

To start her company, Zhena had to learn about business. She sought out experienced people, asking them numerous questions. She engaged a tea master who taught her what he knew. One of her best friends, Mica, put up money for a computer, software, and a logo. This generosity and grace of others, as well as her own tenacity, become the basis on which she built her business.

Originally, Zhena had hoped to open a tea house, but she failed to gain enough investors. Rather than brooding about her missed opportunity, Zhena believed if she couldn't afford to buy a restaurant and open a huge tea room, she would need to adjust her sights and discover a means to start less ambitiously.

Her alternative solution was to sell tea from a small tea cart that she wheeled into her girlfriend's boutique shop. She had scraped together $3,000 from her family to purchase the cart. Miraculously, Zhena was able to pay her bills fairly quickly as she began making $50 to $100 dollars a day from her tea sales, which were popular with local hairdressers and teachers.

Zhena credits her success with taking the first step to empower herself to launch her business. She resolved not to back down, even in light of the drum beat that the world didn't need another tea company. Her response, as much to herself as to others, became "The world *does* need a fair trade tea company, and there isn't one out there yet." Basically she got it into her head that her business was something that was needed, and she enjoyed the sheer pleasure of creating it. To Zhena business and creativity are one.

As Zhena moved from selling tea from her cart to packaging it, she loved learning to work with graphic design. To her, joy was in the manifesting, taking that first step every morning. She plowed through the doubt to take her business to the next level. She enjoyed seeing her vision grow from a concept to reality, even as she started out small. She went online and found a business plan template that she drew upon to write her own. Zhena emphasizes how important that was for her because once she wrote her plan, her business manifested it.

BUILDING A FOUNDATION ON HER OWN WAY OF TAKING ACTION

Although Zhena did attend some college, focusing on herbal medicine, herbal therapy, and aromatherapy, she dropped out, to the absolute shock and horror of her family, choosing instead to travel to Peru to study herbal medicine with a group of ethno-botanists.

She found school difficult to handle, being there for the wrong reasons—she was just too independent and entrepreneurial. Today she continues to take classes as much as six months long on aromatherapy and herbal medicine, applying her understanding to her formulations. She also continues to take tea classes, recognizing how her education offers practical application to her work.

Zhena has demonstrated herself to be a "glass half full" (more appropriately, cup half full) person and sees this attitude as a necessity for an entrepreneur. She believes women can make the most out of the times within which they launch their businesses. She recognizes that "the economy is scaring the hell out of everybody right now," but she remembers that she attempted to raise seed capital for her tea company just as 9/11 hit. By all measures, that was a terrible time to start a business too.

As she saw it, she was providing "a cup of comfort for people." She wanted to be the tea for that mom who is really stressed out and scared by the global crisis. Zhena wanted to make something warm, cozy, nurturing, organic, and fair trade. She took advantage of timing by turning it into an opportunity.

Today, almost eight years later, Zhena's Gypsy Tea is a multi-million dollar company, selling the equivalent of 30 million cups of tea per year and enjoying 100% growth from 2007 to 2008.

One of Zhena's mentors, now her co-CEO, offered her wisdom she continues to abide by: Most entrepreneurs get hold of an idea and try to make money off of it. The most successful entrepreneurs have an idea that gets hold of them and then they live it. And that's a unique difference.

I didn't say I'm going to start a tea company and make lots of money. I said, I need to support myself and my son, I want to end poverty for these women and I've got to do something about it because I see something that needs to get done. I didn't say I'm going to go out and make lots of money. And honestly I'm not money-motivated at all, but the tenets of any business require that it turn a profit to stay in business. Staying in business offers the opportunity to progress and grow.

MOVING THROUGH HER BARRIERS AND GROWING THE BUSINESS

Money and lack of a business degree were Zhena's greatest outer barriers. Yet eventual investors have been impressed with her ability to write a business plan and amazed at her lack of formal credentials. She frankly admits possessing an intermittent lack of confidence. She also takes on too much herself and is often unwilling to delegate, but she also recognizes this tendency and realizes it can be detrimental to an entrepreneur.

Today Zhena's Gypsy Tea has 14 full-time employees and 16 part-time reps. There are five board members as well as a large advisory board. When the tea pluckers are counted, Zhena estimates her company affects an estimated 2,500 families.

Zhena started on a shoestring with low expenses. For her first products sold from her tea cart she created her own logo and stickers and improvised corsage bags for packaging to cut costs. With the positive feedback and sales from customers, she set out to sell her tea to local restaurants, delivering the products herself with her son, Sage, in tow.

She took some of her profits and invested in packaging with a goal of expanding. A buyer at Whole Foods markets took notice of her and liked her blend. Zhena found getting more visible fun and exciting and enjoyed the process of creating more products.

Investment began coming in small chunks and then slightly bigger chunks and then it just blossomed. Today, nearly eight years later, Zhena's Gypsy Tea is a profitable and healthy multi-million dollar company. It's still small by most standards because tea manufacturing is a multi-billion dollar industry, although most of its size rests on bottled tea. Zhena's goal is to be at $25 million in five years.

HER OWN DEFINITION OF SUCCESS

In spite of her monetary goals, Zhena defines success as having inner peace. She also equates success with having such confidence that if you come up against a challenge you don't think it's the end of the world. Being human, you might experience momentary doubts, but you roll up your sleeves and know that you can get through it. Having such inner strength and resources is far more important to her than the outer monetary rewards.

Zhena was raised in a very conservative Christian family, but today she focuses more on eastern spiritual traditions, practicing Buddhist and Hindu meditations. When she discovered yoga and meditation, she claims she began gaining a greater love for her life and the world. She teasingly admits the tea culture has gotten into her spirit. It's a religion of tea.

That's why we call ourselves the original spirit—we really live it!

Creativity motivates Zhena. She loves returning to the tea fields in Sri Lanka, India, China, and South Africa, working with the tea estate managers and the women who are in the field. These visits fuel her motivation to sustain her business. Typically she likes to go to the fields every three months. When she hasn't returned for six months, she feels the loss. She loves seeing progress in the women and children's lives. Nothing is more motivating to her.

Zhena stays balanced spending quiet time with her now healthy son and her new husband. She loves gardening and viewing butterflies and hummingbirds outside her window.

A WOMAN-OWNED BUSINESS

Zhena believes these days we're going beyond the male-dominated business era. With a populated world, women are not as motivated to procreate as they once were, so more women are putting the energy they would have put into procreation into creativity for "beautiful business endeavors." Being natural caretakers, women can show a compassionate side to their employees and thus be effective:

One of my employees was having a rough day yesterday and came into my office and just started crying. And I had to really fight to not cry because I just think women really are nurturing and we really care.

A nurturing spirit can be a plus as well as a negative when not warranted. Generally men lead much more from their heads, whereas women access their hearts, but sometimes women have difficulty being cold when needed. Sometimes business women have to make cold, hard, monetary decisions. Women tend to take so much into consideration, thought, that sometimes they overcomplicate their situation.

Zhena insists women who have an idea for a business must start now. She emphasizes: do it right now! They can think about it, write the business plan, but they must start now.

She encourages women to start telling people about their idea if it's not something that needs to be kept secret. Start talking to friends and asking for help, she admonishes. Sign up with S.C.O.R.E., a great resource of retired CEOs and executive level mentors. Nothing will happen if a woman just thinks about her idea.

You actually have to start—you have to take the idea, take the vision and put it through your hands and start making it happen. It's like clay when you're making a pot or tea pot. You sit there and you've just got this mound of potential and it doesn't do anything for you unless you start spinning the wheel and start shaping it.

Zhena gets adamant when asked what she tells women who wonder who they are to do their business:

Who are you not to do it? Dare to dare. The true secret to succeeding with your idea is in getting things done. Focus your energy and trust your instinct. Use your mind; don't let your mind use you. Nothing external, no adversity, difficulty or doubt can have any power over you unless you allow it to.

Zhena is a woman who insists every one of us owe it to ourselves to get into action and develop a business aligned to who we are, what we value, and what we can create based on our intrinsic gifts.

ONE WOMAN'S ACTION INSPIRES MORE ACTION FOR OTHER WOMEN

Now that you have learned about Zhena Muzyka's story and the actions she took to launch and succeed with Zhena's Gypsy Tea, it's time to reflect on how this story can inspire you in your quest for your entrepreneurial adventure. Take some time to reflect on what you've just read and allow the following questions to guide you. Use your journal to take notes so that you can ground your understanding and learning for future reference.

1. What traditions come from your family that are waiting to be tapped?
2. If you had a grand idea, how willing would you be to scale it back? How could scaling back help you move forward?
3. What mission in the world drives you?
4. Who could you turn to for bits of funding?
5. Who is your market? What does it most need?

WHAT CAN YOU LEARN FROM ZHENA MUZYKA?

It is clear that Zhena and her business are an outgrowth of her heritage. A gypsy in her soul, she embraces the whole world, hoping to see everyone thrive. She holds tenaciously to her vision, yet is able to adapt when she needs to, making corrections as she proceeds along.

Like so many other women we have featured in this book, Zhena continuously looks for how situations can work and turns them around to her advantage. Disappointed but undeterred, she started her business small with a cart rather than a restaurant. Improvisation worked for her when she used corsage bags for her tea, unable to afford anything else.

She stayed in action, in spite of the words around her that it would be difficult for her to compete with the established tea companies. Even so, she remained focused on her mission: to be the one tea company that operated as a fair trade organization. She realized that was a unique perspective for her and her company. It could separate her from the other companies out there as well as be a driving force for her to succeed. After all, she was engaged in commerce not only for the benefit of herself and her son, but for the many families in the field she was supporting.

Zhena sees it as a role of women to be out in the world creating businesses that are run differently than those that have been run traditionally by men. Having a vision as a mother of a world in which every family thrives is as important as offering the products themselves.

Zhena draws a connection between business and creativity. To her, they are one and the same. To be fully self expressed is to be in business and she champions this notion by setting herself as a prime example.

She is here to remind us of the efficacy in the dictum of Joseph Campbell to follow your bliss as well as the words of Marsha Sinetar to do what you love and the money will follow. In Zhena's case it's a matter of following your bliss, doing what you love, and above all being mindful of the wants and needs of your fellow human beings. She adheres to the compassionate words of all of the world's faith traditions: do what you would want others to do unto you. That's ultimately the kindest action we women entrepreneurs can take.

YOUR TURN NOW—WHAT DID *YOU* LEARN FROM ZHENA MUZYKA?

Moving into Action toward Your Scrappy Startup

Every one of the examples in this section of women who moved into action on their dream business is a testament to the possibility that you too can have success. They discovered that action begets more action, and before you know it, you've arrived at a successful enterprise.

Marissa McTasney started her venture by simply surveying sales people about what requests were being made about women's work clothing and boots. Robin Levine put her own simple concoction for cleaning together and paid attention to the positive comments from her friends. Zhena Muzyka made her tea blends and packaged them simply in affordable corsage bags.

There's a scene in the popular movie *The Secret*, where *Chicken Soup for the Soul* author Jack Canfield talks about driving from New York to California at night. If you were to do so, you could see only as far ahead as the headlight beams would illuminate. If you focused simply on what was immediately ahead of you and didn't worry much about what lay in the darkness, eventually you would reach your destination. It's a worthy metaphor for keeping focused on the destination.

SIMPLE ACTION TOOLS

Want a simple tool for getting yourself into action? Long before writing a business plan, you can create a mind map, laying out steps toward your dream. This is essentially a brainstorming tool that you

can create free-hand in your journal or with the aid of a piece of software, such as Mindjet. A good explanation of basic mind mapping
can be found at www.mindmapping.com.

If you use this process to decide what simple steps you can take to
launch into action with your business, you start by putting a name
for your business in the center of a page that you've laid in the landscape position. This gives you more space to create.

Let's suppose the name you've chosen is "Creative Space." You
draw a circle around this name that you've placed in the center of the
page. You then draw branches from the circle to designate various
steps you'd like to take to make your business real. One branch
could be for the products and services you will offer. Another could
be for your ideal customers. Another could be for the equipment or
materials you will need.

Off of each of these branches will be lots of other branches,
depending on the ideas you come up with. Mind mapping is essentially a tool that allows you to take the ideas that have been swim-
ming in your head and place them on paper or on a computer page
equivalent. The very act of drawing a mind map is an action. Taking
your idea from your head and placing it somewhere increases the
likelihood that something actually will happen with it.

If you'd like to get even simpler, utilize sticky notes and jot an idea
down on each individual page. Put these notes up on a wall, cork
board, or cardboard sheet. Challenge yourself to come up with many
ideas for getting started, and plaster them on this area, arranging
similar steps in specific areas of the space. Various colors of stickies
could designate certain activities.

Another trick is to draw a tic-tac-toe board on a page in your journal. In the center you place a word or a symbol designating your
business. Every other space on the board is a simple action you could
take, big or small. Play tic-tac-toe with yourself, engaging in the various actions and crossing them out as you accomplish them. It will
be satisfying to see what you have accomplished concretely, and
approaching this with game energy will keep the process of action
light hearted.

You could also have a "get into action party" for yourself, inviting supportive friends and asking them to brainstorm steps with you.
Hand everyone a sticky pad and have them write their ideas. Someone could be the orchestrator, whose job it is to put the ideas up on
the wall. This could be a lot of fun.

The point is to take the easiest ideas and start getting into motion with them. If you get stuck, just call up more people you know who are avid brainstormers—or get yourself a coach, someone trained for just such activity.

Make a commitment to yourself to take one single action toward your business each day.

You'll find more ideas for getting into action in the resources area of this book.

ALLIES AND STRATEGY

Getting back to our **Magic Approach,** the foundation of my coaching model, you'll remember that **Action** is surrounded in the Venn diagram by **Allies** on one side and **Strategy** on the other. As we can see from the scrappy startup stories we've read, every one of our entrepreneurs had people helping them succeed in their endeavors. Some assistance came from spouses, partners, and family members, other assistance came from former colleagues and friends who invested money in the business, and still more support came from volunteers half the globe away.

None of the women we've met turned away from the hands reaching out to them. These women were smart enough to realize that no one accomplishes anything alone. Just as our startup women have inspired us in so many different and unique ways, they also graciously demonstrate that leaders are ever ready to ask for and receive help.

My hope is that you'll recognize that having allies is as important to you as any other part of the equation. Even if you believe you don't have all the collaborators you'll need now or you don't know to whom you'll need to turn, recognize that allies can appear at any time and seemingly from out of nowhere. If you are not shy about asking for help, you'll find the right people showing up, often just in the nick of time. Social networking on the Internet makes connections more feasible than ever before.

Strategy is an equally important concept to understand in this model. Although many of the stories you've read demonstrate the improvisational nature of startup business, we have learned that each woman indeed had a strategy that conformed to who she was and what she was up to. Many have remarked that they discovered the importance of business planning, even if they found they needed to revise their process completely every three months.

Strategy includes listening to your intuition, setting goals, partnering with others, deciding to grow organically, using the power of the Internet, setting up a franchise, creating scalability, and many other approaches to operations and growth. The strategy you'll employ will conform to your nature, your business, and your meaningful contribution to the world.

IT'S TIME FOR YOU TO REALLY DO IT!

Now that you've gained a good dose of **Dream, Courage, Action** from all the inspiring stories of women like you who have put that mantra to use, I challenge you to do the same. Besides, I want to write about *your* story in my next scrappy startup book! The world desperately needs the meaningful, fun, unique business you have up your sleeve. (I want to hear about it!) Be sure to contact me at melanie@startingfreshcoaching.com and visit me at www.starting freshcoaching.com.

Use your unique mix of passions, values, strengths, and purpose; find beliefs that strengthen you; and open your heart and confidently get into action. Be sure to ask for help along the way, choosing great allies and adjusting your strategy as you move along. After all:

Knowing is not enough; we must apply. Willing is not enough; we must do.

—*Johann Wolfgang von Goethe*

SCRAPPY STARTUP RESOURCES

This section offers resources you can use to launch your own scrappy startup business. You'll find resources listed in accordance with the Magic Formula: Dream, Courage, Action! A separate section is included for Inspiration. Consider these resources allies you can confidently turn to for support.

DREAM

Books

Attwood, Janet and Chris Attwood	*The Passion Test*	Plume	2008
Buckingham, Marcus and Donald Clifton	*Now, Discover Your Strengths*	Free Press	2001
Edwards, Paul and Sarah Edwards	*Finding Your Perfect Work: The New Career Guide to Making a Living, Creating a Life*	Tarcher	2003

Ferriss, Timothy	*The 4-Hour Workweek: Escape 9-5, Live Anywhere, and Join the New Rich*	Crown	2007
Gladwell, Malcolm	*Outliers: The Story of Success*	Little, Brown and Company	2008
Leider, Richard	*The Power of Purpose: Creating Meaning in Your Life and Work*	Berrett-Koehler	2005
Levoy, Gregg	*Callings: Finding and Following an Authentic Life*	Three Rivers Press	1998
Lore, Nicholas	*The Pathfinder: How to Choose or Change Your Career for a Lifetime of Satisfaction and Success*	Fireside	1998
Palmer, Parker	*Let Your Life Speak: Listening for the Voice of Vocation*	Jossey-Bass	1999
Pink, Daniel	*A Whole New Mind: Why Right-Brainers Will Rule the Future*	Riverhead Trade	2006
Robinson, Ken, Ph.D.	*The Element: How Finding Your Passion Changes Everything*	Viking Adult	2009
Sher, Barbara	*Refuse to Choose: Use All of Your Interests, Passions, and Hobbies to Create the Life and Career of Your Dreams*	Rodale Books	2007

On the Web

Articles and Magazines

http://www.farsightgroup.com/publications_articles_futurepull
.cfm—article describes how having a vision can lead to making it real.
http://www.pinkmagazine.com/index.html—a magazine designed to
enable women to embrace their femininity and their strength—offers
ideas to dream into.

http://www.womenentrepreneur.com/—a magazine for and about women entrepreneurs.

Community

http://www.yourlifecompass.com—a community on the Web offering group coaching for women at affordable rates; a place to find women who will hold your dream with you.

http://www.freelancemom.com/—a support network for women working from home. Also offers ideas for freelancing.

http://ladieswholaunch.com—networking organization for women entrepreneurs found throughout the United States.

http://www.mominventors.com—site devoted to women inventor/entrepreneurs.

http://www.startupnation.com—site established by entrepreneurs for budding entrepreneurs.

http://startupweekend.com—create a business over a weekend with a group of other motivated people.

Expand Your Ideas

http://www.springwise.com—international Web site that tracks entrepreneurs throughout the world and provides numerous ideas for small business.

http://mywifequitherjob.com/how-to-open-an-online-store/—online tutorial for starting a Web based business inexpensively.

http://www.quickmba.com/entre/—offers short instruction capsules to help with issues related to business.

http://www.sba.gov—small business resource from the U.S. government offering many local and national features.

http://www.score.org/women/site.html—S.C.O.R.E. devoted entirely to women entrepreneurs.

http://www.score.org/business_toolbox.html—tools, podcasts and resources from S.C.O.R.E.—a group of retired business people dedicated to helping small businesses get started.

http://www.powerhomebiz.com/—site devoted to people starting home-based businesses.

http://www.socialent.org—The Institute for Social Entrepreneurs designed to offer training programs for people wanting to start businesses that are aligned with the social good.

http://www.barbarawinter.com/—the woman who pioneered working without having a job offers ideas for self employment

COURAGE
Books

Brach, Tara	*Radical Acceptance: Embracing Your Life With the Heart of a Buddha*	Bantam	2004
Chopra, Deepak	*The Seven Spiritual Laws of Success*	Amber-Allen Publishing	2007
Ford, Debbie	*The Secret of the Shadow: The Power of Owning Your Story*	HarperOne	2002
Ford, Debbie	*The Dark Side of the Light Chasers: Reclaiming Your Power, Creativity, Brilliance, and Dreams*	Riverhead Trade	1999
Frankel, Viktor	*Man's Search for Meaning*	Beacon Press	2006
Hay, Louise	*I Can Do It*	Hay House	2004
Hay, Louise	*You Can Heal Your Life*	Hay House	1999
Jeffers, Susan	*Feel the Fear and Do It Anyway*	Ballantine Books	2006
Kate, Byron	*Loving What Is: Four Questions that Can Change Your Life*	Three Rivers Press	2003
LeShan, Lawrence	*Cancer as a Turning Point*	Plume	1994
Ruiz, Don Miquel	*The Four Agreements*	Amber-Allen Publishing	2001
Sherwood, Ben	*The Survivor's Club*	Grand Central Publishing	2009

On the Web

Articles, Publications and Podcasts

http://mywifequitherjob.com/how-we-got-the-courage-to-start-our-own-business/—blog sharing true story of start-up courage.

http://www.mindtools.com/pages/main/newMN_TCS.htm—stress management articles and techniques.

http://philosophersnotes.com/—serial entrepreneur, Brian Johnson offers digests in written and mp3 format of content that includes materials to build courage and savvy.

http://www.darynkagan.com/index.html—former CNN reporter devoted to finding success stories of courage.

http://www.hayhouse.com—publishing company with numerous resources devoted to building courage.

Tara Brach podcast—go to iTunes (download software for free at www.apple.com/itunes) and search Tara Brach's name. Her weekly podcasts offer courage for living every aspect of life—and can only help.

http://speakingoffaith.publicradio.org/-Krista Tippitt's weekly public radio podcasts offer heavy helpings of insight into the human condition.

ACTION

Books

Allen, David	*Getting Things Done: The Art of Stress-Free Productivity*	Penguin	2002
Blanke, Gail	*In My Wildest Dreams: Simple Steps to a Fabulous Life*	Fireside	1999
Ditzler, Jinny	*Your Best Year Yet: Ten Questions for Making the Next Twelve Months Your Most Successful Ever*	Grand Central Publishing	2000
Gabor, Don	*Big Things Happen When You Do the Little Things Right: A 5-Step Program to Turn Your Dreams into Reality*	Prima Lifestyles	1997

Gerber, Michael	*The E-Myth Revisited: Why Most Small Businesses Don't Work and What to Do About It*	HarperCollins	1995
Horn, Sam	*POP!: Create the Perfect Pitch, Title, and Tagline for Anything*	Perigee Trade	2009
Horan, Jim	*The One Page Business Plan for the Creative Entrepreneur*	The One Page Business Plan Company	2004
Kingston, Karen	*Clear Your Clutter with Feng Shui*	Broadway	1999
Mcgee-Cooper, Anne	*Time Management for Unmanageable People: The Guilt-Free Way to Organize, Energize, and Maximize Your Life*	Bantam	1994
Morgenstern, Julie	*Organizing from the Inside Out: The Foolproof System for Organizing Your Home, Your Office and Your Life*	Holt Paperbacks	2004
Rottenberg, David and Jeffrey Shuman	*The Rhythm of Business: The Key to Building and Running Successful Companies*	Butterworth-Heinemann	1998
Winters, Barbara	*Making a Living Without a Job: Winning Ways for Creating Work that You Love*	Bantam	1993

On the Web

Investors

http://www.angelcapitalassociation.org/dir_directory/ directory.aspx—
    directory of angel investors by state.
http://www.goldenseeds.com/home/-angel investors devoted entirely
    to women—owned businesses.

http://www.makemineamillion.org/—organization devoted to helping women grow million dollar companies.

http://us.zopa.com—allows people to secure loans from ordinary individuals.

Organizations for Support

http://www.countmein.org—organization devoted to helping women entrepreneurs succeed through education and micro-loans.

http://luckynapkin.com—entrepreneurs in business to help budding entrepreneurs get into action with their ideas.

http://younoodle.com/—budding entrepreneurs join a community of start-ups and predict on others' success.

Productivity

http://www.toodledo.com/—free online tool allows you to organize your tasks.

http://www.writeboard.com/—allows you to write a draft for whatever reason and store it online for easy access.

http://www.zoho.com/—free suite of online productivity and business applications.

http://ping.fm—allows you to access and make changes to multiple social networking sites at once from one location.

INSPIRATION AND OTHER RESOURCES

Books

Zander, Rosamund Stone and Benjamin Zander	*The Art of Possibility: Transforming Professional and Personal Life*	Penguin	2002
Collins, Jim	*Good to Great: Why Some Companies Make the Leap . . . and Others Don't*	Collins Business	2001

| Keirsey, Cynthia | *Unstoppable Women: Achieve any Breakthrough Goal in 30 days* | Rodale Books | 2005 |

On the Web

Sites Featuring Entrepreneurs

http://www.evancarmichael.com/ Main.htm—site features famous and new entrepreneurs with tons of advice.

http://images.businessweek.com/ss/08/06/0627_fresh_entrepreneurs/index.htm - Businessweek's site featuring startup entrepreneurs.

Blogs

http://www.evancarmichael.com/Entrepreneur-Blog-Network/—features the best blogs on entrepreneurial topics.

http://blogs.personallifemedia.com/dishymix/—Susan Bratton's podcasts and blogs on business topics.

http://womensblog.score.org/—success stories of women who have utilized S.C.O.R.E.—volunteers helping new entrepreneurs.

Video and Podcasts

http://ecorner.stanford.edu/—listen to podcasts of lectures from Stanford University's series on entrepreneurship. (Also accessible through iTunesU if you use iTunes interface.)

http://www.robmcnealy.com/—Startup Story Radio with Rob McNealy—features inspiration and ideas for entrepreneurs.

http://www.ted.com—an annual conference devoted to technology, entertainment and design featuring bright, motivated and inspiring leaders whose video segments are posted online for easy viewing.

Organizations

http://www.kauffman.org/—world's largest foundation devoted to entrepreneurism.

http://www.score.org/small_biz_power_links.html—tons of entrepreneur resources from S.C.O.R.E.

INDEX

ABOUT THE AUTHOR

Melanie R. Keveles, MA, CPCC, MCC, and President of Starting Fresh Coaching LLC is a master certified coach, writer, and trainer who specializes in helping people achieve their career goals. Her clients are career changers, aspiring entrepreneurs, and creatives. In addition to managing a thriving international coaching practice, she is also a faculty member for one of the oldest and most prestigious coach training programs, The Coaches Training Institute of San Rafael, CA.

Prior to her coaching career, Melanie was a pioneer in the field of outplacement and co-authored with Judith A. Dubin, *Fired for Success: How To Turn Losing Your Job into the Opportunity of a Lifetime!* (Warner Books, 1990). She has more than 25 years of experience working with people from every walk of life and organizational level and helping them to reinvent themselves. In one of her incarnations with a career management company, she created one of the first Internet-based entrepreneurial and career-oriented Web sites.

Melanie has lived out many of her life dreams such as living in Europe for nearly five years and hosting a radio program. She has been known as a "mid-wife" for people who want to identify and live a work/life vision that has meaning and impact.

In addition to her coaching credentials, Ms. Keveles holds a master's degree in English/education. She lives in northern Wisconsin near Lake Superior with her college professor husband and miniature poodle. Her Web site is Startingfreshcoaching.com.